Best of British

Cinema and Society Series
General Editor: Jeffrey Richards

Published and forthcoming:

BEST OF BRITISH
Cinema and Society
from 1930 to the Present

New Edition

Anthony Aldgate and Jeffrey Richards

I.B.Tauris *Publishers*
LONDON · NEW YORK

Published in 1999 by I.B.Tauris & Co Ltd
Victoria Hiuse, Bloomsbury Square, London WC1B 4DZ
175 Fifth Avenue, New York NY 10010

In the United States and Canada distributed by St. Martin's Press
175 Fifth Avenue, New York NY 10010

ISBN 1 86064 288 8

A full CIP record for this book is available from the British Library
A full CIP record for this book is available from the Library of Congress

Library of Congress catalog card: available

Typeset in Garamond 11½ on 13½pt by The Midlands Book Typesetting Company, Loughborough
Printed and bound in Great Britain by WBC Ltd, Bridgend

Contents

For Jane Aldgate and Richard Taylor.

General Editor's Introduction

As British film-making experiences one of its periodic renaissances, with international success attending such homegrown productions as *The Full Monty, Brassed Off, Mrs. Brown* and *Sliding Doors,* there has been an upsurge of interest in the history of British cinema with new journals, new monographs and new series exploring the subject in all its aspects. In line with its policy of reprinting established texts in expanded and updated editions, the *Cinema and Society* series presents a new edition of *Best of British,* now subtitled *Cinema and Society from 1930 to the Present,* by Anthony Aldgate and Jeffrey Richards. Since its first appearance in 1983, it has been widely used by those interested in the utilization of film as evidence of British history during this century.

The basic text and structure of the book remain unchanged but there are three new chapters and a new resources section which surveys the literature and charts video availability. The twelve films selected for this study were chosen to represent subjects important to contemporary historians (politics, society, education, crime, industrial relations etc.) and to illustrate the preoccupations of the decades between 1929, when sound films were introduced to Britain, and the present. From the 1930s Aldgate and Richards chose *Sanders of the River* (1935) for its discussion of the British Empire and *South Riding* (1938) for its examination of Britain's domestic problems. The Second World War was a watershed in the history of the British film industry and presented special problems to film-makers. These are highlighted in the choice of a film about 'why we fight' (*A Canterbury Tale,* 1944) and a film about 'how we fight' (*The Life and Death of Colonel Blimp,* 1943). The immediate post-war period, which saw British society in the throes of far-reaching changes, is represented by *Fame is the Spur* (1947), a rare film about Labour Party politics, *The Guinea Pig* (1948) which looks at the role of the public schools in a changing society, and *The Blue Lamp* (1950), a groundbreaking police drama which testifies to the growing concern about crime in society.

British society in the 1950s is analysed through the classic Ealing comedy, *The Ladykillers* (1955), and industrial relations in that decade in the classic Boulting Brothers comedy, *I'm All Right, Jack* (1959). The contemporary mores and attitudes of the 1960s are explored through films from the beginning and end of the decade. A chapter on *The Loneliness of the Long Distance Runner* (1962) replaces one on *Saturday Night and Sunday Morning,* which was reworked in Anthony Aldgate, *Censorship and the Permissive Society* (Oxford, 1995). The out and out revolt of *If ...* (1968) contrasts strikingly with the moderate post-war reformism of *The Guinea Pig*. The book is brought up to date with *Scandal* (1989) which is examined in the context of 'retro movies', a *fin-de-siècle* preoccupation with revisiting and reinterpreting the *causes célèbres* of earlier decades. If nothing else, these films demonstrate the richness and breadth of the British cinema over the years and this examination of them will, it is hoped, inspire others to delve into this still under-explored mine of information about British culture and society.

Jeffrey Richards

Acknowledgments

Although this book was conceived as a unity and written according to a set of agreed principles, chapters 1, 2, 4, 7, 8, 9, and 12 were the work of Jeffrey Richards, and chapters 3, 5, 6, 10, 11, 13 and 14 were the work of Anthony Aldgate. The authors would like to thank the following for advice, assistance and information: Rowana Agajanian, Paul Berry, Roy Boulting, Elaine Burrows, Stephen Constantine, James Ferman, John MacKenzie, the late Tony Richardson, Michelle Snapes, and the late John Trevelyan. Thanks are also due to the ever-helpful Stills and Viewing Departments of the National Film and Television Archive, and the Library Services of the British Film Institute, to the British Board of Film Classification and to Pendennis Films Ltd. The stills reproduced in the book are from films originally distributed by the following companies to whom thanks are due: United Artists, GFD, Eagle-Lion, Pathé, Rank, British Lion, Woodfall Films, and Paramount.

1

Feature Films and the Historian

From the 1920s to the 1950s cinema-going was the principal leisure activity of a large proportion of the British people. The cinema attracted members of all classes, though in particular the working class. It appealed to both sexes and to all age groups, though least of all to the elderly. It occupied a place in people's lives which since the 1950s has been taken over by television, though some of the films that draw today's television audience are the ones that were seen and enjoyed by their parents and grandparents on their regular weekly visits to the cinema.

The cinema was an integral and important part of the mass media, closely associated with newspapers, wireless, pulp fiction and, latterly, television. Its influence was fully recognized in its heyday and was reflected in the regular parliamentary debates on matters cinematographic, in the creation of film propaganda organizations, particularly by the Conservative Party, and in the large number of local and national inquiries, conferences, commissions and investigative studies into the effect of cinema on its audience. The prevalent view was succinctly summarized by the 1936 Moyne Committee Report into the working of the Cinematograph Films Act:

The cinematograph film is today one of the most widely used means for the amusement of the public at large. It is also undoubtedly a most important factor in the education of all classes of the community, in the spread of national culture and in presenting national ideas and customs to the world. Its potentialities moreover in shaping the idea of the very large numbers to whom it appeals are almost unlimited. The propaganda value of the film cannot be overemphasized.[1]

Broadly speaking, the cinema operates in two ways – to reflect and highlight popular attitudes, ideas and preoccupations, and to generate and inculcate views and opinions deemed desirable by film-makers. Film-makers select in the first case material which they know will appeal to their audience and in the second material with which they can manipulate their audience and shape its perceptions. It may well be that a film will aim to do both things at once; perhaps the greatest problem with films is to distinguish deliberate propaganda from what Arthur Marwick has called ' "unwitting" testimony, the hidden assumptions and attitudes, rather than the conscious, and often biased, message'.[2] Marwick argues strongly for the particular value of this aspect of feature films for the historian:

> The more one makes a comparative study of films, the more one becomes aware that, however exceptional within the context of its own country, every film is in fact a product of its own culture. No film-maker, it becomes clear and clearer, can really go beyond certain assumptions accepted within his own country.... Over and over again, it has been pointed out to me at seminars and conferences that films are made by members of the upper and more prosperous segments of society. That I would never deny; but I am far more interested in the fact that ... films ... were seen by large audiences. There is a law of the market; the bigger its commercial success, the more a film is likely to tell us about the unvoiced assumptions of the people who watched it. It is the tedious documentary, or the film financed by political subscription, which tells us least.[3]

But the cinema can also act as a potent means of social control, transmitting the dominant ideology of society and creating for it a consensus of support.[4] First, films provide images of the lives, attitudes and values of various groups in society, created from recognizable but carefully selected facets of such groups. This is important because, as Hortense Powdermaker discovered, film audiences have a tendency to regard as accurate depictions of places, attitudes and lifestyles of which they themselves have no firsthand knowledge.[5] Thus, for instance, a working-class audience may well accept as authentic a cinematic depiction of upper-class life, however inaccurate, while it would reject an inaccurate depiction of its own circumstances.

Second, films provide images of society as a whole, again constructed of selected elements and aspects of everyday life, which are organized into a coherent pattern governed by a set of underlying presuppositions. The process of selection confers status on certain issues, institutions and individuals – say, for instance, the police or the monarchy – which regularly appear in a favourable light.

Third, what J. S. R. Goodlad says of popular drama is equally applicable to popular film: 'It may serve as the vehicle by which a community expresses its beliefs about what is right and wrong; indeed it may function instrumentally as a medium through which a community repeatedly instructs its members in correct behaviour.'[6] Popular films, and in particular *genre* films such as crime dramas, horror pictures or westerns, which regularly use the same elements, characters and situations, function as rituals, cementing the beliefs and ideals of society, enforcing social norms and exposing and isolating deviants.

Last, there is a tendency for the mass media to promote conformity not only of dress, hairstyle and vocabulary but also, and more subtly, of attitudes and world-view. It is therefore of central importance to discover who controls the production of films and what attitudes and ideas they are disseminating through them.

But the relationship between film and audience is reciprocal. An audience does not accept passively every message that is put across in a film. For one thing, it can choose which films to see and which to avoid. Even within films it can accept elements that it likes and reject unpalatable ones. In the last resort it is positive audience approval, expressed via the box office, that ensures whether a film succeeds or fails financially. So producers' calculations of what will appeal to their audiences inevitably influence what goes into a film. Direct propaganda rarely works, as the Nazis discovered in Germany. Their first three feature film exercises in promoting the Nazi Party, propaganda rarely works, as the Nazis discovered in Germany. Party, *SA Mann Brand, Hitlerjunge Quex* and *Hans Westmar,* were such disasters at the box office that Propaganda Minister Goebbels ordered that direct propaganda be confined in future to the newsreels, and he sought to work more covertly on audiences by inserting propaganda elements into 'straight' entertainment films.[7] Audiences the world over go to the cinema primarily to be entertained, not to be instructed. They go for relaxation, diversion and ready-made dreams. As Raymond Durgnat points out:

> For the masses, the cinema is dreams and nightmares, or it is nothing. It is an alternative life, experience freed from the tyranny of that 'old devil consequences', from the limitation of having only one life to live. One's favourite films are one's unlived lives, one's hopes, fears, libido. They constitute a magic mirror, their shadowy forms are woven from one's shadowy selves, one's limbo loves.[8]

The content of these dreams and nightmares and how they are arrived at are matters that historians cannot afford to neglect. Yet historians have been reluctant to quarry feature films for evidence of the social history of this century. As the eminent American historian Arthur M. Schlesinger Jr has written:

> Historians are professionally a conservative lot. Movies have had status problems ever since they emerged three-quarters of a century ago as a dubious entertainment purveyed by immigrant hustlers to a working-class clientele in storefront holes-in-the-wall scattered through the poorer sections of the individual city. Conventional history has recorded the motion picture as a phenomenon but ignored it as a source. Social and intellectual historians draw freely on fiction, drama, painting, hardly ever on movies. Yet the very nature of film as a supremely popular art guarantees that it is the carrier of deep if enigmatic truth.[9]

When in the 1960s historians began to admit the use of film to their deliberations, it was to newsreel and documentary that they turned. They were reassured by the presence of real people and real locations that they were somehow viewing 'reality'. But they were mistaken. Newsreels and documentaries no more presented 'reality' than did feature films, which told stories, used actors and were often made entirely in studios. In the case of the documentary and the newsreel what was seen on the screen was selected, shaped and placed there in pursuit of certain predetermined policies. Newsreel-makers and documentarists worked under the same constraints as feature film-makers, subject to interference from censors, sponsors and outside pressure groups. Admittedly, such films provide first-hand visual evidence of clothing, housing and transportation, just as photographs do. But beyond that surface 'reality', newsreels and documentaries were far from being objective. They were, in fact, highly selective and strictly controlled. As one newsreel chief put it in 1938: 'The newsreel companies were always ready to give, and in fact frequently gave, assistance to the government in portraying matters which were deemed to be in the public interest.'[10]

An extravagant mythology has grown up around the British documentary movement, which is often depicted, on the basis of a handful of genuinely moving films like *Housing Problems,* as the sole repository of realism and radicalism in a predominantly conservative industry. Raymond Durgnat, in a few deft and perceptive pages of analysis, has set the movement as a whole, particularly during 'the heroic age of Grierson', in its proper perspective. He concludes: 'Far from being progressive, these films are, in spirit, just what they were intended to be: literally speaking, commercials for the EMB or the GPO or any other part of the Establishment, and therefore for the *status quo* of – of all periods – the thirties.'[11]

More seriously, perhaps, documentaries were not on the whole seen by the mass cinema-going public. Gaumont British took a package of six, the so-called 'Imperial Six', and released them as supporting films. However, they were given new musical soundtracks and portentous commentaries and anyway dealt with such romantic subjects as lumberjacking and salmon fishing, topics far from the reality of the life of the urban masses. But the Gaumont British experiment was not repeated. For exhibitors were extremely reluctant to show documentaries, regarding them as box-office disasters. As Mr W. R. Fuller, General Secretary of the Cinematograph Exhibitors Association, speaking in 1936 of exhibitors' failure to interest the public in the EMB documentaries said acidly: 'No documentary . . . has ever set the Thames afire.'[12] Documentaries, then, can really tell us only about the aims and attitudes of their sponsors and their producers. The real value of the documentary movement of the 1930s was to act as a training ground for those directors who went into feature film-making during the war and brought a new patina of realism to fictional films. The idea that documentaries embodied a purer, higher truth is a dangerous fallacy.

It was feature films that were seen and enjoyed by the bulk of the cinema-goers, and it is feature films which have received least attention from historians. There are some signs that this is beginning to change. There have been several attempts in recent years to come to terms with the feature film as a source of historical evidence, and it is on these beginnings that we must build.[13] But among historians an attitude of Puritanical snobbery still prevails, inherited from the indigenous British film culture that emerged in the 1920s and 1930s. Its reaction to the popularity in Britain of Hollywood films has been acutely analysed by Peter Stead.[14] He defines this British film culture as consisting of 'a national film institute, a network of film societies, a number of intellectual film journals, a whole tradition of documentary film-making and close links between those interested in film and educationalists, especially those engaged in adult education'.[15] This resulted in a strong preference for art over entertainment, for Continental (particularly Russian, French and German) films over British and American, for documentary over feature film and for programmes to 'improve' and to 'educate' audiences. Although the film culture modified its approach, particularly after World War II, when journals like *Sequence* and, later, *Movie* came to appreciate the merits of Hollywood and British feature films, historians as a whole remained locked into the old perceptions. They have shied away from feature films because they were produced to entertain the masses and to make money.

Admittedly, film analysis poses a fundamental problem in that, unlike the painting or the novel, film is a collaborative rather than an individual art. Films are produced by a conveyor-belt, mass-production process. They are the end-product of collaboration between director, writer, cameraman, composer and actors and may often represent considered decisions made by men not actually involved in translating the script into visual images. These are the men with the final say, the producers and production supervisors, the men with logistic, financial and sometimes even overall artistic control. In acknowledgement of an understandable desire to confer artistic respectability on the cinema, the *auteur* theory of the 1960s argued for a single artistic vision in film-making and assigned this to the director. There can be no denying that the cinema has produced a high proportion of works of art and that a Hitchcock or a Hawks film, a Ford or a Sternberg, is as recognizable thematically and stylistically as a Dickens novel or a Velasquez painting. But the bulk of films are not so much personal works of art as, to use the term employed in the television industry, 'product'. They are not art but artefacts for instant consumption and discard. They cannot be understood in terms of artistic vision, but they can be seen as a direct response to the era which has produced them. For every Hawks and Hitchcock, for every Ford and Sternberg, there are a dozen Alfred E. Greens and Albert S. Rogells, directors who were merely proficient craftsmen, the servants of mass culture, taking their cue from current preoccupations rather than from timeless individual vision. For historians it is often the work of these journeymen rather than the work of the great artists that is interesting, just as popular novels, picture postcards and wall posters, designed for the moment and reflecting that moment, are interesting. Indeed, as they are collaborative, films are more likely to reflect, and respond to, the marketplace and thus the audience. The top box-office films have rarely been great works of art. A great work of art anyway usually tells us more about the artist than the society that produced him. So the films of Gracie Fields, for instance, are likely to be more valuable to the social historian than the poems of W. H. Auden or the novels of Virginia Woolf.

Nothing demonstrates the collaborative nature of film-making more clearly than the exemplary Wisconsin series of screenplays of key Warner Brothers films from the heyday of that company. Each script is accompanied by a meticulously documented essay, which traces the film's production, detailing its development stage by stage. To take just one example, Rudy Behlmer's essay on the classic swashbuckler *The Sea Hawk* (1940) begins in 1935, when Warner Brothers decided upon Rafael Sabatini's novel as a follow-up to its successful *Captain Blood*, which had launched Errol Flynn as a major star.[16] Behlmer shows how the book passed through the hands of four successive screenwriters, moving further and further from Sabatini's original novel until nothing but the title remained. The film was directed by Michael Curtiz, but it is clear that the Warner production chief, Hal B. Wallis, was deeply involved in every aspect of filming. We see him intervening constantly, ordering the testing of Dennis Morgan for the leading role in case the tempestuous Errol Flynn had to be replaced, seeking to curb Curtiz's desire to alter the script while on the set and insisting that it be shot exactly as written, restraining Curtiz from injecting too much brutality and violence in order to avoid the wrath of the censors, making constructive suggestions about the lighting and staging of individual sequences and tackling the problem of shooting the final duel raised by the total inability of the villain, Henry Daniell, to handle a sword. His mark remains on the finished film, though he actually made none of it himself. Apart from this, there were the contributions of the production designers, costumiers, composers and photographers who gave Warner Brothers films their distinctive look and feel. This kind of documentation is invaluable in assessing the true nature of film-making at the height of the great studio era, which coincided with the period of the cinema's greatest popularity.

There is a further factor which may have frightened off historians latterly, and that is the state of film criticism and film history in general. For much of the 1970s it was in serious disarray, wracked and scorched by controversy. Structuralism and semiology became the fashionable and dominant concepts in a new critical approach that involved the minute dissection of films according to strict, almost mathematical, formulae. Because of the convoluted and jargon-ridden texts which this school of criticism produced, its general accessibility was minimal and its application limited to the elect, the initiates of an intellectual mystery, whose cult words – 'syntagma', 'phoneme', 'signifying construct' – identified members readily to each other and just as readily excluded the outsider. The high priests of this new critical religion, drawn largely from the avant-garde of Eng. Lit., looked to France for their inspiration, to Marxism for their ideology and to linguistics and psychoanalysis for their conceptual models.

But this critical approach has come under increasing attack for its narrowness and intolerance, its intellectual arrogance and its deliberate obscurantism, and it is now losing ground. Our intention is not to enter into a debate about the pros and cons of this approach but to draw attention to a new development which seems to us to offer a challenging, productive and accessible way forward. This development comes not from France but from the United States of America, finding its inspiration and methodology in history. It deals not in pure speculation but in solid research, the assembling, evaluation and interpretation of facts, the relating of films to the world, the search for an understanding through the medium of popular films of the changing social and sexual roles of men and women, the concepts of work and leisure, class and race, peace and war, the real determinants of change and continuity in the real world.

This approach can best be called 'contextual cinematic history', for it places particular emphasis on the exploration of the context within which a film was produced. It has already resulted in two authoritative and stimulating general social histories of the American cinema: Robert Sklar's *Movie-Made America* and Garth Jowett's *Film: the Democratic Art.*[17] It has produced also Lary May's *Screening Out the Past,* subtitled *The Birth of Mass Culture and the Motion Picture Industry.*[18] This bold, absorbing, infectiously readable book takes as its subject the American cinema's formative period, 1890–1929, and, by examining its development in the context of the age, produces what the French would call *une histoire de mentalité.* May sees the cinema as a key element in the development of a new urban culture, concentrating on the issues at the heart of change and contributing to the transition in America from what, for simplicity's sake, he calls the 'Victorian Age' to the 'Modern Age'. He demonstrates quite convincingly that in the first decades of the twentieth century the film industry was the focal point of a revolution in morals, expectations and attitudes in American society and that the films themselves reflected, highlighted and advanced the change in the relationship between work and leisure, men and women, and in the promotion of a new success ethic and dominant lifestyle.

His method – and the value of his book lies almost as much in this as in its conclusions – is to analyse the content and structure of groups of films, box-office trends, star personalities and their appeal, contemporary reviews and reactions, staging, lighting and action styles, the role of fan magazines, censorship and picture palaces, and to locate all these elements firmly in the political, social and cultural context. In relation to the products of a mass popular culture, this is surely the right way forward, for it extends our understanding and appreciation of films and their world and, above all, illuminates their place in culture and society.

Another recent and admirable book, *American History/American Film,* subtitled *Interpreting the Hollywood Image,* edited by John E. O'Connor and Martin A. Jackson, takes the contextual approach a stage further and applies it to individual films.[19] It contains fourteen essays with such titles as 'The Great War viewed from the Twenties: *The Big Parade* (1925)', 'Our Awkward Ally: *Mission to Moscow* (1943)' and 'An American Cold Warrior: *Viva Zapata* (1952)'. The essays are bound together by two threads: they all attempt to explain both the way in which the film in question documents American social history and captures the state of mind of the American people at the time it was released, and the way in which it illustrates the development of the American film industry.

What we would like to see is the application of this technique to the British cinema. Although there are highly competent general surveys of British film history, useful biographies and autobiographies of producers and directors and pretty well exhaustive studies of the documentary movement, the British feature film industry remains virtually virgin territory as far as contextual history is concerned. An honourable exception is Charles Barr's indispensable book *Ealing Studios.*[20] He has revealed the multi-layered richness of Ealing's films by relating them to their background. He demonstrates their key role in the dramatization of World War II as the 'People's War', the struggle to maintain consensus and at the same time to highlight and defuse social discontents during the period of the post-war Labour Government and, finally, the drift to conservatism and the complacency which followed the return to power of the Tories in 1951. He relates the films to the structure and nature of the studio itself, to the character and attitudes of the personnel involved and to the rise of a middle-class radicalism among the generation that voted Labour for the first time in 1945 and then retreated towards Conservatism in the 1950s. He uncovers the debates and dichotomies between age and youth, tradition and change, subversion and conformity. This study gives an entirely new range of meaning to films like *Passport to Pimlico, Kind Hearts and Coronets* and *The Titfield Thunderbolt,* a depth of interpretation which can be understood only in context. But his book remains a solitary beacon in the darkness. What of other British film companies – Rank, Gainsborough, Associated British, Hammer, for instance? What of the social history of censorship and the social role of cinema-going? What part did reviewing play in the film culture? The materials exist for such studies, but, except for a few pioneering articles, they lie unused.[21]

What of British film stars? How did Gracie Fields, Googie Withers and Anna Neagle, for instance, relate to the roles and aspirations of women in British society? What of male stars like Robert Donat, Jack Warner and Jack Hawkins? What did they embody? What audience needs did they fulfil? What too of the changing style in film heroes from, say, Kenneth More to Albert Finney? What does this tell us of the changing nature of the film industry, of British society, of popular fashions and mores?

For the American cinema in its first decades Lary May has asked these questions and has provided answers. It remains for scholars in this country to start asking similar questions. We hope to help the process along by applying the technique of contextual history to twelve British films. They are not (repeat *not*) the twelve best British films of all time, but they would probably figure somewhere in the top hundred. They are certainly representative of the subjects and eras which can be illuminated by the use of film.

In examining each of them in turn we have borne in mind three main concerns. The first is the need to analyse what the film is saying, and that involves looking at the structure and meaning of the film, as conveyed by script, visuals, acting, direction, photography and music. Second, we attempt to put it in context with respect to both the film industry itself and the political and social situation which produced it. Third, we try to find out how the films were received and what audience reaction to them was. To some extent all three strands are interwoven, for popular cinema has an organic relationship with the rest of popular culture, and popular culture as a whole plays a part in the social and political history of its time. Many films were based on books, for instance, and were not so much original cinematic creations as 'cinematizations' (as the industry called them) of literary properties, whose success with the public in their original form led producers to assume a guaranteed audience. Also many films were based on plays, and the stage provided (much more in Britain than in America) not only material but also performers – music-hall artists, musical comedy stars and dramatic actors – who became film stars.

We try to elucidate the production histories of the films and the intentions of the film-makers to see who was responsible for what is actually on the screen. Occasionally such information can be gleaned from interviews conducted either at the time and recorded in magazines and newspapers or in later years. But the oral history method presents grave problems, for quite apart from faulty memories, some directors may seek to mislead or may revamp facts to fit their legends. Ford and Von Sternberg, for example, took pleasure in mystifying, confusing and sending up interviewers, while others, like Douglas Sirk on his period in Nazi Germany, could be understandably evasive.

We have already noted that it may not be the director who is ultimately responsible for what is on the screen. The guiding intelligence behind the productions of London Films, whoever may have been directing officially, was usually that of producer Alexander Korda, while Michael Balcon, as production chief at Gaumont British in the 1930s, has the final say on almost every aspect of production. He left people in no doubt as to who was the dominant creative force at GB when he defined the role of the producer in 1933:

> The work of the film producer is to determine the choice of subjects, of directors and of artistes for every picture and to decide the cost to be borne. Under his supervision director, scenario editor and unit executives prepare the script, the plans of sets and the time schedule for each production. When the film is in the making its daily progress is reported to him. He is the sponsor. and the guide, and the ultimate court of appeal ... the kind of energy which the producer must stimulate and direct is based upon the creative and artistic impulses of directors, writers, cameramen and artistes. Such impulses are so personal that they constantly require the close attention of one directing mind to blend them into the harmonious unity which is essential for any successful achievement in a form of entertainment which depends upon the specialized work of many different hands.[22]

Another element which must not be overlooked is the role and iconography of the stars. It was the stars, after all, whom the public went to see: successive surveys revealed that the stars and the story were what attracted the mass audience to the cinema. Fan magazines and fan clubs charted their doings and their lifestyles. The stars set the fashions in clothes, hairstyles, speech, deportment, even lovemaking. As Andrew Tudor observes: 'The basic psychological machinery through which most people relate to films involves some combination of identification and projection'[23] and what audiences identified with and projected themselves on to was the stars. This inevitably had an influence on films and on the roles that were chosen and shaped to highlight the qualities and characteristics of a particular star. As Raymond Durgnat notes: 'The star is a reflection in which the public studies and adjusts its own image of itself ... the social history of a nation can be written in terms of its film stars.'[24]

Beyond the immediate production context there are further constraints to be considered. In wartime propaganda objectives had to be met, and the Ministry of Information provided detailed guidelines for the content of feature films. But in peacetime there was a continuing framework within which film-makers operated the censorship system. It is impossible to understand the development and nature of the British cinema without a full appreciation of the work and influence of the censors. Unlike that of other countries, censorship in Britain was not state-controlled. The British Board of Film Censors was set up by the industry itself as an act of self-preservation in 1912. The 1909 Cinematograph Act had given local authorities the right to license build-ings used as cinemas. The intention was for them to concern themselves with fire precautions, but the wording of the Act was loose enough to be interpreted as conferring powers of censorship. The possibility that the licensing authorities, estimated at 700 in 1932, might give different verdicts on the suitability of films obviously constituted a threat to the industry's commercial viability, so central self-censorship by the industry was deemed necessary. Its stated aim was 'to create a purely independent and impartial body whose duty it will be to induce confidence in the minds of the licensing authorities and of those who will have in their charge the moral welfare of the community generally'.[25] The basic censorship rules were drawn up by the Board's second President, T. P. O'Connor, and known as 'O'Connor's 43'. The censors were, he said, 'guided by the main principle that nothing should be passed which is calculated to demoralize an audience, that can teach methods of or extenuate crime, that can undermine the teachings of morality, that tends to bring the institution of marriage into contempt or lower the sacredness of family ties'.[26] In fact, their aim was to maintain the moral, political, social and economic status quo and to avoid anything that smacked of controversy. The censors' favourite term of approval was 'harmless', which indicated the negative way in which they viewed the cinema. Their hold on the industry grew during the 1930s as the scope of their activities extended from the vetting of completed films to the inspection of scripts prior to shooting. The rules were relaxed over the years, though always in response to perceived changes in public toler-ance of matters like sex and violence. This was particularly true in the 1960s, but by then the cinema was ceasing to be a mass entertainment medium and becoming a sectional and minority one.[27]

The great imponderable in all this is always how the audience reacted. The old hypodermic idea that the audience as a whole was directly injected with the message of a film has long since been discredited. The idea that the entire film output of a country directly reflects the collective psyche of that country has also been seriously questioned. These approaches, seen now as too mechanistic, underlay the pioneering work of Siegfried Kracauer, who saw the whole of German cinema as foreshadowing the rise of Hitler in his classic but now controversial work *From Caligari to Hitler*.[28] The relationship between film-maker, film and audience is now seen to be more sophisticated, a two-way process operating in areas of shared experience and shared perception.[29]

It is reasonable to assume that an audience's reaction depends ultimately on the age, sex, class, health, intelligence and preoccupations of that audience, both as individuals and as a group. Some general evidence exists in the form of box-office returns, where available, and in the record of reissues, which usually signalled a film's success at the box office. The popularity of stars can be gleaned from the polls taken, particularly the influential annual poll in the *Motion Picture Herald* which lists stars according to their box-office draw. But one little-used source of contemporary evidence is newspaper reviews. Allowance has to be made for the attitude and readership of the various newspapers, but the critics were writing with the tastes and interests of their readers in mind. What they wrote was heeded. As Winifred Holmes testified in a contemporary study of film-going in an unnamed Southern town in the 1930s: 'Newspaper reviews of films are read with interest and play a large part in influencing people of all classes in an appreciation of the films shown'.[30]

When all this evidence has been taken into account, we hope to show how feature films can be used to illuminate the history of this century at various key points. It is our hope that it will encourage both those who teach and those who research our recent history to make greater use of feature film evidence. The Open University already does so, and the growth of video equipment and video tape puts feature film evidence within the range of everyone who is interested.

Notes

1. *Cinematograph Act 1927: Report of a Committee appointed by the Board of Trade,* Cmd 5320, London, 1936, p. 4.

2. Arthur Marwick, *Class: Image and Reality,* London, 1980, p. 22.

3. ibid.

4. See Stuart Hall, 'Culture, the media and the "Ideological Effect"', in James Curran, Michael Gurevitch and Janet Woollacott (eds.), *Mass Communication and Society,* London, 1979, pp. 315–48, for a good outline of the means of social control.

5. Hortense Powdermaker, *Hollywood the Dream Factory,* London, 1951, p. 13.

6. J. S. R. Goodlad, *A Sociology of Popular Drama,* London, 1971, p. 7.

7. Richard Taylor, *Film Propaganda: Soviet Russia and Nazi Germany,* London, 1979, pp. 161–3.

8. Raymond Durgnat, *Films and Feelings,* London, 1967, p. 135.

9. John R O'Connor and Martin A. Jackson (eds.), *American History/American Film,* New York, 1979, p. ix.

10. Anthony Aldgate, *Cinema and History,* London, 1979, p. 193.

11. Raymond Durgnat, *A Mirror for England,* London, 1970, p. 119; cf. pp. 117–29.

12. Board of Trade: Minutes of Evidence taken before the Departmental Committee on Cinematograph Films, 1936, p. 89.

13. See in particular Paul Smith (ed.), *The Historian and Film,* Cambridge, 1976; K. R. M. Short (ed.), *Feature Films as History,* London, 1981; Pierre Sorlin, *The Film in History,* Oxford, 1980. Feature films are also used to elucidate the subjects of war, empire and class in Leif Furhammar and Folke Isaksson, *Politics and Film,* London, 1971; Jeffrey Richards, *Visions of Yesterday,* London, 1973, and Arthur Marwick, *Class: Image and Reality,* London, 1980. The *Historical Journal of Film, Radio and Television* has since 1981 provided a continuing forum for such research.

14. Peter Stead, 'Hollywood's Message to the World', *Historical Journal of Film, Radio and Television,* 1, 1981, pp. 19–32.

15. ibid, p. 27.

16. Rudy Behlmer (ed.) *The Sea Hawk,* Wisconsin/Warner Bros. Screenplay series, Madison and London, 1982. Seventeen other screenplays are currently in print, and more are planned.

17. Robert Sklar, *Movie-Made America,* London, 1978; Garth Jowett, *Film: the Democratic Art,* Boston, 1976.

18. Lary May, *Screening Out the Past,* Oxford and New York, 1980.

19. John E. O'Connor Martin A. Jackson (eds.), *American History/American Film,* New York, 1979.

20. Charles Barr, *Ealing Studios,* London, 1977.

21. The first steps towards an analysis of the social role of Gainsborough films have been taken in Sue Aspinall and Robert Murphy (eds.), *Gainsborough Melodrama,* BFI Dossier 18, London, 1983. On the role of cinema-going in working-class life in the 1930s, see Peter Stead, 'The People and the Pictures', in Nicholas Pronay and D. W. Spring (eds.), *Propaganda, Politics and Film 1918–45,* pp. 77–97. On the ethos and standards of film reviewers in the 1940s, see John Ellis, 'Art, Culture and Quality', *Screen,* Autumn 1978, pp. 9–49. For the British cinema between 1945 and 1958 Durgnat, *A Mirror for England,* idiosyncratic, sometimes inaccurate, often impenetrable, remains indispensable. Since this paragraph was first written a number of major studies on key aspects of British cinema have been published. They are discussed in Chapter 14.

22. Michael Balcon, 'The Function of the Producer', *Cinema Quarterly,* 2, Autumn 1933, pp. 5–7.

23. Andrew Tudor, *Image and Influence,* London, 1974, p. 76.

24. Durgnat, *Films and Feelings,* p. 138. On the phenomenon of stars, see Richard Dyer, *Stars,* London, 1979; Edgar Morin, *The Stars,* London, 1960; and Alexander Walker, *Stardom,* Harmondsworth, 1974.

25. *Bioscope,* 21 November 1912.

26. *BBFC Annual Report, 1919,* p. 3.

27. On censorship and its role, see in particular Neville March Hunnings, *Film Censors and the Law,* London, 1967; Nicholas Pronay, 'The First Reality: Film Censorship in Liberal England', in Short, *Feature Films as History,* pp. 113–37; Dorothy Knowles, *The Censor, the Drama and the Film,* London, 1934; John Trevelyan, *What the Censor Saw,* London, 1973; Guy Phelps, *Film Censorship,* London, 1975; Jeffrey Richards, 'The British Board of Film Censors and Content Control in the 1930s', *Historical Journal of Film, Radio and Television,* 1, 1981, pp. 95–116; 2, 1982, pp. 39–48. Now see also James C. Robertson, *The British Board of Film Censors,* 1985, and *The Hidden Cinema,* 1989; and Anthony Aldgate, *Censorship and the Permissive Society,* 1995.

28. Siegfried Kracauer, *From Caligari to Hitler,* Princeton, 1947.

29. Tudor, *Image and Influence,* p. 28.

30. *World Film News,* December 1936, p. 4.

Sanders of the River (1935)

2

The Sun Never Sets
Sanders of the River

I t is often said that the masses were indifferent to the British Empire during the inter-war years. But this is an oversimplification. To begin with, it, mistakenly, equates Empire with expansion, militarism and jingoism, which are only phases of the imperial experience. Admittedly, there was no 'mafficking' and no public demonstrations over *causes célèbres* like the plight of Gordon in Khartoum. Emigration to the colonies was declining. Dreams of military glory, so prominent in pre-war literature and thought, had faded in the cold light of the bloody slaughter in the trenches and noman's-land. Pacifism had gained in strength and standing; in 1933 the Oxford University Union passed the celebrated motion that 'This house will in no circumstances fight for its King and Country', and an anti-war candidate won the East Fulham by-election. But the Empire, which had passed from its aggressive, expansive phase to a period of administration and consolidation that was bound to be quieter, was seen and depicted now as a force for peace, stability and democracy. As Professor Reginald Coupland wrote in 1935: 'Surely this is a time when a world society such as ours, dedicated to freedom, yet knowing it can only be preserved or rightly used in unity, should stand firm for the defence of civilization as we understand it.'[1] 'Civilization as we understand it' was generally seen to comprise parliamentary democracy, the rule of law and the enlightened and equitable administration of colonies and protectorates. If the Empire is seen in this light, then James Morris is surely right when he notes: 'Most Britons still considered it, all in all, as a force for good in the world, and only a minority could conceive of its actually coming to an end.'[2] The fact that none of the major political parties even contemplated its dissolution suggests that such a policy would have commanded little electoral support.

There were prominent and vocal critics of the Empire, but they were on the whole drawn from the left-wing intelligentsia, which is almost always unrepresentative of national opinion as a whole. Just as 'serious literature' in the inter-war years was almost uniformly hostile to the public schools, so too was it critical of the imperial mentality. But for most people – those for whom literature meant Edgar Wallace, Warwick Deeping and P. C. Wren – the public schools were not represented by those tormented, repressed public school boys who figure in the works of Graham Greene and E. M. Forster. They looked instead to the idealized Greyfriars of Frank Richards or James Hilton's Brookfield, to the world of Harry Wharton, Billy Bunter and Mr Chips. Similarly, the Empire was not the arrogant, hollow, hypocritical sham of George Orwell. It was the mythic landscape of romance and adventure; it was that quarter of the globe that was coloured red and included 'darkest Africa' and 'the mysterious East'; it was 'ours'. It may have been true, as H. G. Wells claimed, that nineteen Englishmen out of twenty knew as much about the British Empire as they did about the Italian Renaissance,[3] but most people were not bothered about actual conditions in the Empire. It was the imagery that they absorbed and endorsed, and that imagery was romantic, adventurous and exotic. It was the rich variety of produce and artefacts on show at the Empire Exhibitions and at the Imperial Institute. It was the Prince of Wales's tours of the Empire, so widely publicized in the newspapers and the newsreels. It was the popular novels about derring-do on the North-West Frontier of India or in the jungles of Africa. It was the colourful scenes depicted on picture postcards and cigarette cards. It was an image inculcated at school via lessons about the history and geography of the Empire, via the annual celebration of Empire Day, with its religious services and imperial displays, and via the popular boys' books like those of G. A. Henty and F. S. Brereton, which continued to fill school library shelves, to be awarded as prizes and to be much sought after as Christmas and birthday presents. This image stayed with schoolchildren as they grew into adulthood and was confirmed by all the popular media, including films.[4]

If we take the evidence of popularity at the box-office as 'unwitting testimony' of popular attitudes and preconceptions, then the flourishing cycle of imperial films in the 1930s in both Britain and the USA speaks volumes for the continued attachment of audiences to the concept of Empire,[5] for all these films depicted it as beneficent and necessary. It is on the face of it rather curious that the United States, which still retained strong traditions of both isolationism and anglophobia, should have celebrated the Empire from which it had successfully seceded in 1776, but from *Lives of a Bengal Lancer* (1935) through to *Sundown* (1941) such films were popular with audiences on both sides of the Atlantic. The reason for their popularity was given by Margaret Farrand Thorp in her study of the American film industry, published in 1939:

> The immediate explanation of this burst of British propaganda is a very simple one. As continental audiences dwindled, Britain, which had always stood high, became an even more important section of the American movies' foreign public. It was highly desirable to please Great Britain if possible, and it could be done without sacrifice, for the American public, too, seemed to be stirred with admiration for British Empire ideals. Loyalty as the supreme virtue no matter to what you are loyal, courage, hard work, a creed in which *noblesse oblige* is the most intellectual conception; those ideas are easier to dramatize on the screen than social responsibility, the relation of the individual to the state, the necessity for a pacifist to fight tyranny, the nature of democracy, and the similar problems with which the intellectuals want the movies to deal.[6]

What the Empire stood for was distilled by Hollywood screenwriters from the works of Kipling and his imitators, either directly or indirectly. The extent of the pro-British propaganda that they therefore contained is evidenced by the banning in Mussolini's Italy of the Hollywood films *Lives of a Bengal Lancer, Charge of the Light Brigade, Clive of India* and *Lloyds of London,* specifically because of their pro-British slant.[7]

In Britain Alexander Korda, the producer who had singlehandedly put British films on the world map with the phenomenal success of his *Private Life of Henry VIII* (1933), produced a trilogy of imperial epics.[8]

He spared no expense, seeking always to make films which would equal Hollywood's in their polish and appeal. Two weeks after the opening of *Henry VIII* in August 1933 the director Zoltan Korda, brother of producer Alexander, left London for Africa with two film units, one to shoot location footage in East Africa and the other in West Africa. They seem to have had no script but to have been aware that the intention was to produce a film based on Edgar Wallace's popular *Sanders of the River* stories. They returned with many reels of African flora and fauna and of tribal ceremonies and dances. Thereupon Alexander Korda, in script conferences with the writer Jeffrey Dell and Lajos Biro, his regular script editor, worked out a narrative involving the characters, locale and situations from the Wallace stories to fit the location material. An African village was built at Sound City Studios under the direction of Major Claude Wallace (no relation of Edgar), an old Africa hand, and peopled with black dockers imported from Cardiff, Liverpool, Glasgow and London. The script was completed and shooting began in the autumn of 1934, with Leslie Banks playing Sanders and the popular black American singing stars Paul Robeson and Nina Mae McKinney in the roles of Bosambo and Lilongo. None of the stars actually went to Africa. The finished film was released on 5 April 1935.[9]

The film fulfils a distinct ideological purpose, presenting a selectively constructed but positive view of British colonial administration in Africa and of the nature and capabilities of the African. The plot is straightforward. The film opens with Commissioner Sanders firmly in control of the River Territories of West Africa. We see him laying down the law to King Mofalaba and appointing Bosambo as chief of the Ochori. For five years the natives enjoy peace and order under the just and watchful eye of Sanders. But then he goes on leave, and Commissioner Ferguson takes his place. The gun runners Farini and Smith spread the rumour that Sanders is dead, and the tribes rise in revolt. Ferguson goes alone to the Old King's country and is murdered. Bosambo stays loyal to Sanders, but his wife Lilongo is kidnapped by the Old King's men. When he goes after her Bosambo too is captured. Sanders returns hurriedly from leave, sails upriver in his steamer, the *Zaire,* and arrives in time to rescue the captives. The Old King is killed and Bosambo is installed in his place. Peace and order are restored.

The tone and theme of *Sanders of the River* are set by the prologue: 'Sailors, soldiers and merchant adventurers were the pioneers who laid the foundations of the British Empire. Today their work is carried on by the civil servants – the Keepers of the King's Peace.' Peace is a recurrent theme. War is repeatedly denounced, and King Mofalaba himself confirms the Empire's commitment to peace when he declares cynically: 'It is easy to lie to the English. They want peace. If you say you want peace, they will believe you.' Then over a map of Africa is superimposed the legend: 'Africa – tens of millions of natives, each tribe under its own chieftain, guarded and protected by a handful of white men, whose work is an unsung saga of courage and efficiency.'

The film's central figure, Commissioner Sanders, is seen as the ideal colonial administrator, and the film is constructed to demonstrate his attributes. Quiet, pipe-smoking, good-humoured and authoritative, Sanders has virtually single-handedly brought law and order to the River Territories over the previous ten years. He has banned slavery and the running of gin and guns, 'the most dangerous gifts of civilization to the natives'. Having brought peace and order, he now seeks to maintain it, a direct reflection of the situation in the contemporary British Empire.

Backed as he is by only a handful of white officers and a single regiment of native troops, he rules by force of personality. The key sequences in the film are predicated on Sanders's charismatic strength. When he summons the troublesome King Mofalaba to palaver, Mofalaba comes with his warriors, who outnumber British forces by ten to one. Yet Sanders curtly reads the riot act to the king, warning him to behave, and then dismisses him with an abrupt: 'The palaver is finished.' Mofalaba and his men could easily have fallen on to the British and slaughtered them. Instead they go home obediently. The rapid crumbling of the situation when Sanders goes on leave and war and revolt flare up indicates just how essential the personal charisma of Sanders is to the government. The missionary priest Father O'Leary cables the Colonial Office: 'Send four batallions or Sanders.' Sanders returns from leave, descending godlike from a plane, and puts down the unrest. But he expects no thanks. He does the job out of a sense of duty, telling Lieutenant Tibbetts at the start that he is in for 'tramping through swamps and jungles, your only decoration – mosquito bites'. It should, however, be noted. that although it is never mentioned, this moral authority is underpinned by Western technology in the form of an airplane, a paddle steamer and machine guns.

The characteristics that Sanders embodies are entirely in line with the criteria actually employed to select colonial administrators. The selection was virtually controlled from 1910 to 1948 (with the exception of the World War I period) by one man – Sir Ralph Furse. Furse selected his men specifically on the basis of character and recruited them mainly from the public schools. He wrote: 'We could not have run the show without them. In England, universities train the mind; the public schools train character and teach leadership.'[10] The public schools taught duty and responsibility, a sense of fair play, qualities of leadership, above all a benevolent paternalism. Experience as a public school prefect and thus an exemplar of these virtues Furse regarded as an ideal training for colonial government. After a prefectship the next best qualification was a university rugger blue, preferably a captaincy. Indeed, the Sudan was described as 'a country of blacks run by blues'. Lord Plumer put it well, if cryptically, when he said in 1916: 'We are often told that they taught us nothing at Eton. It may well be so, but I think they taught it well.'[11] In other words they supplied training rather than an education. Robert Heussler, in his book on the Colonial Service, gathered together some of the testimonial letters used to make selections, which include such statements as: 'He would be capable of dealing with men. His mind is well-balanced, his manner agreeable and in every respect he is a perfect gentleman' and 'He would maintain the best traditions of English government over subject races. . . . He is a gentleman, a man of character.'[12] These could well be descriptions of Sanders. For Wallace had indeed created his hero as 'a mixture of Harry Johnston and the other West African Commissioners of whom he had heard such romantic and bloodcurdling tales'.[13] It is worth noting that not only did the film distil the essence of the ideal District Officer but it also influenced others to follow it. As a former District Officer told Charles Allen: 'Most of us had seen a film called *Sanders of the River* before we went out, and suddenly here was this thing, and it was real; one was walking behind a long line of porters – and it was just like the film.' Another talks of the '*Sanders of the River* touch' in describing his conduct of affairs.[14] Thus nature imitates art.

The film is a celebration of that 'character and spirit' which, according to his biographer Karol Kulik, Alexander Korda so much admired in the British and which Sanders embodies. His character is the justification of British rule. There is no complex ideology, no constitutional justification for Empire. The man is the message. Korda's films offer no concrete political, economic or constitutional justification for the Empire's existence; nor is there any indication of the state of flux in which the empire actually found itself during the inter-war years, when it seemed to be evolving into something rather different – the Commonwealth. The Empire is justified by the apparent moral superiority of the British, as demonstrated by their adherence to the code of gentlemanly conduct and the maintenance of a disinterested system of law, order and justice. As Lord Curzon put it in 1923:

> We have endeavoured to exercise a steadying and moderating influence on the politics of the world, and I think and hope that we have conveyed not merely the impression but the conviction that whatever other countries or governments may do, the British government is never untrue to its word and is never disloyal to its colleagues or its allies, never does anything underhand or mean; and if this conviction is widespread, as I believe it to be – that is the real basis of the moral authority which the British Empire has long exerted and I believe will continue to exert in the affairs of mankind.[15]

As long as this lofty view of Britain's world role persisted, as long as Britain regarded it as her God-given duty to ensure fair play for all the world, the maintenance of the Empire was inescapable. It was this lofty view that the Korda films projected, seeing British rule as timeless and eternal. The inevitable result was to foster what Francis Hutchins called 'the illusion of permanence' – the idea that whatever they might say about progress towards ultimate independence, the British in fact expected and believed that their Empire would last for a thousand years.[16]

The message of *Sanders* is reinforced by the other two main characters, the archetypes of the 'Good African' and the 'Bad African', their responses to British rule determining their relative goodness and badness. The British govern the River Territories through nominated chieftains, an accurate dramatization of the policy of 'indirect rule', operated in West Africa. Sanders's particular favourite is Bosambo, chief of the Ochori. Their relationship is established from the outset when Bosambo, in reality a Liberian convict, passes himself off as the legitimate chief of the tribe. Sanders confronts him with the truth; Bosambo shamefacedly admits to it and is rewarded with the chieftainship. Appropriately enough, they meet over Sanders's desk, Sanders seated and Bosambo standing. Reprimanding a naughty child and then rewarding it with responsibility is a classic technique for winning loyalty, and in Bosambo's case it works. The headmaster-pupil nature of the relationship is thus clearly established. It is confirmed in the song that Bosambo sings in praise of his master:

> Sandi the strong, Sandi the wise,
> Righter of wrong, hater of lies,
> Laughed as he fought, worked as he played,
> As he has taught, let it be made.

Bosambo is conceived entirely in Western terms as an archetype well established in imperial fiction: a combination of doglike devotion, boastful sexuality and childish naughtiness. Similarly, his relationship with his wife Lilongo is seen in strictly European terms. They love each other. She bosses him about. He risks his life to rescue her. Yet, as Boris Gussman has written: 'The main difference between African and European marriage is that the idea of romantic love does not occur among Africans.'[17] There is equally little appreciation of the African character judged in African terms. Gussman also writes: 'To these Europeans, because they failed to understand the motives that prompted him or the bonds that held him in check, he was seen as superstitious, irrational, lazy, immoral and of a childish or at least adolescent mentality.'[18] The father-child relationship between Sanders and the natives is repeatedly commented upon by characters in the film – the missionary, the gun runners, Captain Hamilton.

The 'Bad African' of the film is King Mofalaba, who is sly, cruel and overbearing. He murders Commissioner Ferguson, kidnaps Lilongo and conducts slaving raids against neighbouring tribes. Where Bosambo loyally serves the British, Mofalaba plots against them. But he does so not in the interests of the Africans, of freedom or principle: he seeks to get rid of the British because they prevent him from tyrannizing the people. They stand between him and the despotic exercise of power that he seeks. At the end of the film he is killed and replaced by Bosambo, who will rule under the British in peace and justice and will not seek to destroy his people with war or tyranny.

The film gives every indication that the tribes will carry on as they always have under British protection – 'at peace in their primitive paradise', as the film puts it. The consent of the governed is implied by the scene in which Sanders, about to go on leave, asks Bosambo if he will still be a popular chieftain when Sanders returns. Bosambo replies: 'I have learned the secret of good government from your lordship. It is this, that a king should not be feared but loved by his people.' 'That,' replies Sanders with a knowing smile 'is the secret of the British.' The inescapable conclusion is that British rule is changeless and unchanging.

There is an implicit subtext in the apparent fragility of British rule, given that it collapses the moment Sanders leaves the scene. One of the great paradoxes of British imperial history was the simultaneous dominance of twin emotions, confidence and fear – confidence in the rightness of the British presence in far-off lands and fear that British rule would be violently overthrown. There was ample justification for such fear. Imperial rule in Africa had been established only in the face of a succession of revolts (the Matabele War, the Ashanti War, the Zulu Revolt, the Mad Mullah's Revolt in Somaliland). The British in India never quite got over the shock of the Mutiny and always secretly dreaded the possibility of another. The plots of all three films in the Korda trilogy are strikingly similar in outline and almost give the impression of having been constructed to exorcise this fear. Just as in *Sanders of the River* Commissioner Sanders puts down a native uprising in Africa and rescues his ally, Chief Bosambo, from the evil King Mofalaba, so in *The Drum* Captain Carruthers joins forces with the Indian boy prince Azim to put down an uprising on the North-West Frontier led by his uncle, the wicked Ghul Khan, and in *The Four Feathers* a disgraced British officer Captain Harry Faversham redeems his honour, assisted by the pro-British chieftain Karaga Pasha, by helping to put down the Khalifa's Revolt in the Sudan. In each film the exercise of power by the British is supported by the consent of the governed and defined by the opposition of self-seeking despots who, if left alone, would prey unmercifully on their own people.

On the surface *Sanders* would seem to be a rather uneasy blend of travelogue, with its sequences of animals and native dances, and drama, with the narrative sequences filmed in Britain. But the mixture is sweetened by the four songs written for Robeson and based on native melodies recorded on location. They are superbly sung and bind the film together, serving to reinforce the central message by supplementing the imagery and the ideology. The African flora and fauna and dancing natives support the contemporary view of the 'Dark Continent' as a place of exotic mystery and beauty, while the songs both hymn the virtues of Sanders and confirm the primitive savagery of the natives, in the words of the 'Killing Song':

On, on into battle, make the wardrums rattle,
Mow them down like cattle,
On and on, on into battle, stamp them into the dust, into the dust,
Charge, kill, shoot, spill, and smash, smite, slash, fight and slay!

The sequences of bare-breasted native girls were a positive attraction, drawing a horde of appreciative adolescents. But they too embodied a racist attitude, for no white woman would ever have been permitted to appear bare-breasted on the screen. The natives, however, being considered inferior, counted as ethnic curiosities.

Leslie Banks, who was offered the role of Sanders after Raymond Massey and Ralph Richardson had turned it down, effectively projects the authority and dependability of the District Commissioner. As Bosambo Paul Robeson gives a performance that is virile, charismatic and enormously engaging. He shows no sign of the embarrassment that he claims to have suffered over the part. There is also a memorably malignant performance from Tony Wane as King Mofalaba.

Zoltan Korda directs efficiently, using the conventional narrative form of long shots for action, punctuated by close-ups for emphasis. It is a style dictated by the need to blend the documentary location sequences with the studio scenes. At one point his meshing of the film's two elements creates a memorable piece of montage, as he dissolves from a shot of two vultures feeding on a corpse to scenes of the tribal uprising following Sanders's departure, thus wordlessly making the point. But, more important, he renders the narrative as a series of vivid and memorable images which remain in the mind long after the detail of the story has faded, and this is the enduring strength of popular film. These images are Sanders with a handful of Houssas defying the numerically superior might of the Old King and dismissing him with a curt 'The palaver is finished'; Sanders, riddled with malaria, ordering his ancient steamer upriver on a journey never before undertaken; Sanders and his men racing ashore amidst bursts of machine-gun fire to rescue Bosambo and his wife in the nick of time; and the finale with Sanders, pipe in mouth, leaning on the rail of the boat, the Union Jack fluttering over his head and Bosambo with his warriors hymning his virtues from their canoes. In these images is contained the essence of the message.

Who was responsible for this message, and what motivated him? The film was produced by Alexander Korda, the dynamic head of London Films, and it is clear that his was the decisive voice in the film's creation. He chose the subject, sat in on the script conferences and, when it came to disagreements, imposed his view on the director, his brother Zoltan.

Why did Alexander Korda settle on a film of Empire and, in particular, *Sanders*? First, to remain in business he obviously needed to make financially successful films. He had a policy of acquiring the rights to best-selling books. Edgar Wallace was a phenomenon, a massively popular, astonishingly prolific and consistently best-selling writer. His 'Sanders' stories had first appeared in a weekly magazine in 1909, and since then he had written 102 of them, which had appeared in eight successive hardback collections. They had been continuously in print since their first appearance, and Wallace himself was the most filmed British author of the 1930s. Thirty-three of this plays and stories had been made into films in Britain and America by 1940. There was obviously a ready-made audience.

Second, Korda wanted to capture a larger share of the Empire market and believed that films set and partly filmed in the Empire would contribute to that. In January 1935, three months before the release of *Sanders,* a reporter who had discussed Korda's plans with him noted: 'Korda, having become horizon-conscious; is going out for Empire markets in a big way. He intends to make pictures with specific appeal to different parts of the Empire.'[19]

Third, there was a personal and political reason for Korda's choice. Korda wanted to stress the virtues of the British imperial system, the doctrines of fair play and moral authority at a time when the rise of Fascism was threatening these ideas and offering a different soft of world. Karol Kulik has written: 'He was a confirmed Anglophile who saw the Empire-builders as the embodiment of all the most noble traits in the English character and spirit.'[20] His predilection for imperial settings is demonstrated by the fact that he produced not only the imperial trilogy *(Sanders of the River, The Drum* and *The Four Feathers)* but also films of two of Kipling's classic children's stories of India 'Toomai of the Elephants' (filmed as *Elephant Boy)* and *The Jungle Book.*

But there may have been more than just a personal motive at work. Korda had close links with the Conservative Party, which he advised on film propaganda throughout the 1930s.[21] There was considerable

pressure both inside and outside the Government for the production of feature films promoting the imperial idea. There were calls
at successive imperial conferences for such films. Sir Philip Cunliffe-
Lister, President of the Board of Trade, called in the Commons in
1927 for more use of the cinema to promote imperial unity, saying,
'The cinema is today the most universal means through which national
ideas and national atmosphere can be spread.'[22] This statement was
quoted as summarizing current British Government thinking on the
subject in 1936.[23] Sir Stephen Tallents, Secretary of the Empire
Marketing Board, called for the positive projection of Britain:

> In the discharge of our great responsibilities to the other countries
> of the Commonwealth, we must master the art of national projec-
> tion and must set ourselves to throw a fitting projection of England
> upon the world's screens. The English people must be seen for
> what it is − a great nation still anxious to serve the world and
> secure the world's peace.[24]

Winifred Holmes wrote in *Sight and Sound* in 1936:

> It is essential for the continued unity and good will of the Empire
> that more and better British films should be distributed everywhere
> and that these films should add to England's prestige and show
> more of her ideals and epic qualities than before.[25]

But the government was reluctant to spend its own money and preferred
to work indirectly by encouraging friendly producers. In a memorandum
of notes and suggestions about propaganda sent in April 1934 to Neville
Chamberlain by Joseph Ball, Deputy Director of the National Publicity
Bureau, he suggested:

> The cinema trade as a whole parades the fact that it is opposed to
> political propaganda in cinema theatres, but much has neverthe-
> less been done without protest from the public by means of the
> 'newsreels'. Here again, as in the case of the press, an obvious line
> of approach is to bring influence to bear on the proprietors of
> the various cinema news organizations.... It should also be
> possible to ensure the adoption by some of the more enlightened
> producers of scenarios dealing with e.g. historical or imperial
> subjects in such a way as to enlist the sympathies of audiences on
> the side of the present government.[26]

There can be little doubt that Korda was one of these 'enlightened producers'. For in 1938 Ball was reporting to Chamberlain: 'I have cultivated close links with the "leaders" of the British film industry and I am satisfied that I can count upon most of them for their full support to any reasonable degree.'[27] He specifically mentions Korda in this context. It could well be, then, that a hint was dropped to Korda that the Government would not be averse to an imperial epic, something that coincided with his own film-making aims. Certainly, Korda's film units received full co-operation from the colonial authorities in Africa, and he acknowledged in particular Sir Bernard Bourdillon, Governor of Uganda, in a foreword to the film.

Whether or not he was directly inspired by sources close to the Government, Korda was determined to make a film that would glorify British colonial administration, and this brought him into conflict with his brother, the director Zoltan. Karol Kulik records that they disagreed about the emphasis of the film.[28] Zoltan wanted to make maximum use of his location footage to depict African tribal life and customs; Alexander wanted to stress the imperial administration aspect. 'My father loved Africa; he loved the black man,' Zoltan's son David told Karol Kulik. This love was movingly and sincerely expressed in Zoltan's film of Alan Paton's classic novel *Cry the Beloved Country* (1952), but it did not mean that he was hostile to a favourable depiction of the District Commissioner. For, returning from Africa, he had written in a magazine article:

> The white government of Africa is one of the wonders of the world. No doubt there are some commissioners who are inefficient, but I did not meet any. Those with whom I came into contact combined the patience of Job with the wisdom of Solomon, and were completely representative of the great traditions that has made us regard them as quite unequal to their work unless they perform miracles. It is to these men that my film is dedicated.[29]

Zoltan did manage to get several of his location sequences highlighted in the film, and he did win a dispute with Alexander about whether or not Sanders and Bosambo should shake hands when Sanders went on leave. (Alexander seems to have felt that the implication of equality might offend white audiences.) On the whole, however, the conception and message must be seen to be Alexander's. That conclusion is confirmed by the reaction to the film of its star, Paul Robeson. Robeson, a communist and tireless campaigner for negro rights, had come to live in London, where he found less discrimination than in America. Having seen the African location footage, he had signed to play Bosambo, believing that the film would accurately depict African culture. But when he saw the complete film at the premiere, he walked out, claiming that he had been tricked and swore never to work for Korda again.[30] He insisted thereafter on inserting in his contracts a clause giving him approval of the final cut of the films in which he appeared. Interviewed by a black American journalist in 1936, Robeson was told:

> This picture ... was a slanderous attack on African natives who were pictured as being satisfied with the 'benevolent' oppression of English imperialism. You yourself played the role of selling the natives out to the imperialists. Such a role is inconsistent with your professed love for the Soviet Union and what that country represents. ... You became the tool of British imperialism and must be attacked and exposed whenever you act in such pictures or plays.

Robeson replied: 'You're right, and I think all the attacks against me and the film were correct.'[31] Ironically, it is Robeson's robust and attractive performance that is one of the film's enduring strengths.

The final question we must ask is how was the film received. The critics took the message of the film clearly enough. The right-wing critics exulted. Sydney Carroll in the *Sunday Times* declared delightedly:

> The films are always providing surprises. The latest cause for astonishment is that they have given us the felicity and success with which foreigners, folk who can have no claims, by birth, origin or association with our Empire, can yet evolve moving pictures which voice far more eloquently than we can ourselves the better purposes of our imperial aspiration. These aliens have shown a truer, sounder British nationalism that we ourselves appear capable of displaying. We have lately seen Americans, with the aid of Hollywood's international resources, producing a *Cavalcade* completely in tune with Noel Coward's conception, a *Clive of India* stirringly patriotic and British. Now comes Alexander Korda and his brother Zoltan, two Hungarians, revealing in *Sanders of the River* a sympathy with our ideals of colonial administration, giving us a grand insight into our special English difficulties in the governing

of savage races, and providing us with a documentary film of East African nature in its raw state, a picture which could not be improved upon for the respect it displays to British sensibilities and ambitions. *Sanders of the River* owes a tremendous lot to Zoltan Korda. He has directed it brilliantly. He has made it part travelogue, part romance, part thriller. It is crowded with the excitements of life on the Congo. He has displayed the native ceremonials, the delirious and ecstatic dances, the tribal rhythms of African negroes, the apprehension of giraffe, hippo, crocodile and bird shot from an aeroplane, the terrors and delights of contact and conjunction between civilization and savagery, the white man's burden and the Englishman's rule.[32]

The *Sunday Express* was less fulsome but none the less approving:

There's marvellous stuff in this picture but it is a film of brilliant fragments rather than good entertainment all along the line. It is big in scale and thrilling in theme – the theme of the white man fighting a lonely battle in the African jungle and trying to establish law among the tribes. Much more might have been made of that. One cannot be modest about an Empire.[33]

The left-wing critic and film-maker Paul Rotha, writing in *Cinema Quarterly*, poured scorn on the film:

So this is Africa, ladies and gentlemen, wild, untamed Africa before your very eyes, where the White Man rules by kindness and the Union Jack means peace! . . . You may, like me, feel embarrassed for Robeson. To portray on the public screen one of your own people . . . as toady to the White Man is no small feat. For the others, they do not matter. Just one moment in this film lives. Those aeroplane scenes of galloping herds across the Attic Plains. It is important to remember that the multitudes of *this* country who see Africa in this film are being encouraged to believe this fudge is real. It is a disturbing thought.[34]

It was a view shared by the Nigerian scholar Dr Nnamdi Azikwe, who wrote in 1937:

Whoever sees this picture will be shocked at the exaggeration of African mentality, so far as superstitious beliefs are concerned, not to speak of the knavery and chicanery of some African chiefs.

I feel that what is being paraded in the world today as art or literature is nothing short of propaganda.[35]

As to how the British public reacted, there is less clear-cut evidence. But it all points to their approving of both the film and its message. It was so successful when shown in 1935 that it was reissued in 1938, 1943 and 1947. It inspired a stage version, *The Sun Never Sets,* which also starred Leslie Banks and featured songs by Cole Porter. Paul Robeson's recording of the 'Canoe Song' became a hit. *Kinematograph Weekly,* the usually perceptive trade paper whose business it was to assess a film's potential selling points, described it as 'a fine tribute to British rule in Africa' and said:

Not only is the film a glorious piece of clean, engrossing entertainment, but it has in its title, cast and ready-made public, represented by the popularity of the author's work, unprecedented box-office credentials.[36]

The box-office success of *Sanders* was such as to inspire Korda to produce *The Drum* (1938), set in India, and *The Four Feathers* (1939), set in the Sudan, both in the then comparatively rare Technicolor. As Paul Holt wrote in the *Daily Express* in 1938:

Mr Korda plans to make a lot of films about the Empire in future. That is good news for this newspaper. It is also good business for Mr Korda. He knows that films about the Empire make money. He knows that films of his like *Sanders of the River* and *Elephant Boy* and *The Drum* have been far more successful at the box offices of this country than any equal amount of sophisticated sex nonsense. . . . Patriotism goes with profit.[37]

It might be argued that the public went to the film not because it was about the Empire but because they wanted to hear Robeson singing or to see African wildlife or bare-breasted native dancers. But they would not be able to avoid the adventure story anchored within a framework of beliefs in which the chief characters embodied clearly defined ideals and attitudes to life. Given the election and re-election of a predominantly Conservative National Government, the fervent national celebrations of King George V's Silver Jubilee, the immense popularity of the 'Sanders' stories with the reading public, the evidence of 'unwitting testimony' would be that the film genuinely reflected widely held beliefs about the role and function of the British Empire.

There is an interesting footnote to the story, which shows that the life of a film far exceeds its decade. In 1957 *Sanders* was shown for the first time on television, by ATV, as part of the season of Korda classics. *The Times* reported that the Nigerian High Commissioner, Mr M. T. Mbu, had protested to the television company about the showing, saying that it was 'damaging to Nigeria and brought disgrace and disrepute to Nigerians'.[38] The Commissioner regretted that ATV should show a film 'portraying Nigeria as a country of half-naked barbarians still living in caves without any contact with the outside world'. He thought that it would create ill-feeling against Nigerians living in Britain. The *Guardian* carried the same story, with an additional note from its Lagos correspondent observing that the film was very popular in Nigeria and had been showing to packed houses at three Lagos cinemas during that very week.[39]

Notes

1. Reginald Coupland, *The Empire in These Days,* London, 1935, p. 5.
2. James Morris, *Farewell the Trumpets,* London and Boston, 1978, pp. 315–16.
3. ibid., p. 299.
4. This argument is developed at length in John MacKenzie, *Propaganda and Empire,* Manchester, 1984.
5. On the cinema of Empire, see Jeffrey Richards, *Visions of Yesterday,* London, 1973.
6. Margaret Farrand Thorp, *America at the Movies,* New Haven, 1939, pp. 294–5.
7. Colin Shindler, *Hollywood Goes to War,* London, 1979, p. 2.
8. On the Korda imperial trilogy, see Jeffrey Richards, 'Korda's Empire', *Australian Journal of Screen Theory,* 5–6, 1979, pp. 122–37; Jeffrey Richards, 'Patriotism with Profit: British Imperial Cinema in the 1930s', in V. Porter and J. Curran (eds.), *British Cinema History,* London, 1983.
9. Production details of *Sanders* can be found in Karol Kulik, *Alexander Korda,* London, 1975, pp. 135–7.
10. Robert Heussler, *Yesterday's Rulers,* Oxford, 1963, p. 82.
11. Jonathan Gathorne-Hardy, *The Public School Phenomenon,* Harmondsworth, 1979, p. 151.
12. Heussler, *Yesterday's Rulers,* pp. 19–20.
13. Margaret Lane, *Edgar Wallace,* London, 1939, p. 225.
14. Charles Allen, *Tales from the Dark Continent,* London, 1979, pp. 79–80.
15. Correlli Barnett, *The Collapse of British Power,* London, 1972, p. 241.
16. Francis Hutchins, *The Illusion of Permanence,* Princeton, 1967.
17. Boris Gussman, *Out in the Midday Sun,* London, 1962, p. 82.
18. ibid., p. 64.
19. Unidentified newspaper clipping, BFI *Alexander Korda* microfiche.
20. Kulik, *Alexander Korda,* p. 135.
21. T. J. Hollins, 'The Conservative Party and Film Propaganda between the Wars', *English Historical Review,* 96, April 1981, pp. 359–69.

22. *House of Commons Debates,* vol. 23, col. 2039.

23. Board of Trade, Minutes of evidence taken before the Departmental Committee on Cinematograph Films, 1936, p. 14.

24. S. G. Tallents, *The Projection of England, London,* 1932, pp. 39–40.

25. *Sight and Sound,* 5, Autumn 1936, p 74.

26. Neville Chamberlain Papers, NC 8/21/9, 14 April 1934. I am indebted to Dr Stephen Constantine for this reference.

27. ibid., NC 8/21/9 June 1938.

28. Kulik, *Alexander Korda,* p. 136.

29. Unidentified clipping, BFI *Sanders of the River* microfiche.

30. Marie Seton, *Paul Robeson,* London, 1958, pp. 77–9, 96.

31. P. Foner (ed.), *Paul Robeson Speaks,* London, 1979, pp. 107–8.

32. *Sunday Times,* 7 April 1935.

33. *Sunday Express,* 7 April 1935. .

34. Paul Rotha, *Rotha on Film,* London, 1958, pp. 139–40.

35. Dr Nnamdi Azikwe, *Renascent Africa,* Lagos, 1968 (reprint), pp. 153–5.

36. *Kinematograph Weekly,* 4 April 1935.

37. *Daily Express,* 9 July 1938.

38. *The Times,* 22 November 1957.

39. *Guardian,* 22 November 1957.

South Riding (1938)

3

The Age of Consensus
South Riding

The mainstream British cinema of the 1930s has invariably been characterized in simple terms. It was a 'dream factory', and for the many millions who frequented the cinemas week after week it offered 'an escape from reality into a fantasy world'.[1] Thereafter, we are told, British films were traditionally, in Dilys Powell's words, 'an inferior substitute for the American-made film'. The Americans 'colonized' the British cinema during this period; there was no tradition of British films and scant evidence of a 'national' cinema, and in consequence British films had no important part to play in the 'national life' until the advent of World War II.[2]

The film producer Michael Balcon endorsed many of these arguments in his autobiography, which was published in 1969. There he lamented the absence of any 'social reality' in the mainstream British films of the 1930s. Not one of his own films, he readily admitted, 'in any way reflected the despair of the times in which we were living'. Indeed, 'Hardly a single film of the period reflects the urgency of these times', he commented and added, 'On my bookshelves to this day I find *The Town that was Murdered* by Ellen Wilkinson, and all the other Left Book Club publications, but little of their influence is reflected in the films we were making.'[3]

This passing reference by Balcon to the Left Book Club started by

Victor Gollancz in 1936, to its publications and to Ellen Wilkinson's 1939 account of the plight of Jarrow is particularly interesting, for it bears witness to the enduring impression which such 'dole literature' made and to the vision which it projected of the 1930s. Similarly, Balcon's references to the 'despair' and 'urgency' of the times testify to the image which has been set for the 1930s in general. For Balcon, as for many other commentators, the vision of the cinema as a 'dream factory' was predicated upon this image of the period.

For many people then, as now, the 1930s were the 'devil's decade'. They symbolized economic disaster, social deprivation and political discontent; it was an era of mass unemployment, hunger marches, Fascist demonstrations and appeasement. The country was beset by innumerable crises both at home and abroad, and inevitably, so the argument goes, both the crises and the solutions which were adopted to tackle them simply conspired to produce a Britain so divided along social and political lines that the very stability of the country was threatened.

Despite the gravity of Britain's situation during that period, however, some historians have argued that its actual effects upon the country remain open to question, and recently more emphasis has been placed upon the idea of an inherently stable country. One historian commented in 1975, for example, that 'for all the divisions in its social structure', on the eve of World War II Britain remained 'a small and closely knit community, insular, and bound together by strong patriotic or perhaps nationalistic feelings which no historian has yet fully documented'.[4]

In 1977 John Stevenson and Chris Cook set out to document those feelings in part, while at the same time addressing the larger question of the 'myths and realities' of Britain in the 1930s. With regard to unemployment, for instance, they argue that while one must not underestimate its disastrous effects – with rarely less than 1.5 million out of work and at one stage as many as 2.75 million, and with great hardship and personal suffering alleviated only occasionally by the existence of the dole – none the less 'There were never less than three-quarters of the population in work during the 1930s and for most of the period considerably more.' By the middle and late 1930s unemployment had become a regional problem once again, and 'alongside the pictures of the dole queues and hunger marches must also be placed those of another Britain, of new industries, prosperous suburbs and a rising standard of living.' 'For those in work,' the authors believe, 'the 1930s were a period of rising living standards and new levels of consumption, upon which a considerable degree of industrial growth was based.'[5]

On a wider front they argue that 'the economic and social climate for political extremism during the inter-war period was much less favourable than has often been depicted.'[6] The Communist Party and the Fascists never enjoyed widespread support. 'Crucially,' Stevenson and Cook continue, 'the existing political parties do not appear to have been discredited by the depression for more than a minority',[7] and consequently there was no major swing either to the left or to the right. The leadership of the Labour Party and the Trades Union Congress was, for its part, committed to a moderate line and there again 'Violence . . . like political extremism, was a minority response in the thirties to the impact of mass unemployment.'[8]

Their research leads them far and wide, but throughout they talk of factors such as the 'conservatism' and the 'more fundamental unifying aspects of British society'. They quote, approvingly, George Orwell's references to the 'emotional unity' that he felt was evident in the country and, more significant, 'the considerable agreement that does unfortunately exist between the leaders and the led'. All of which prompts them to conclude that 'Even in the face of the slump, Britain remained a relatively cohesive and insular society in which there were still a large number of shared assumptions.'[9]

But what of the British cinema in the midst of this historical revision of British society during the 1930s? Is there any reason to believe that it too is in need of some revision? Certainly, one commentator at least would seem to think that the notion of the mainstream cinema as a mere provider of escapist entertainment merits closer scrutiny. In his *Critical History of British Cinema* Roy Armes makes the following comments:

> The characteristic works of 1930s cinema do not therefore lay bare social contradictions. . . . They are rather films which organize the audience's experiences in the sense of fostering social integration and the acceptance of social constraints. Emotional problems are shown to find an easy solution in matrimony, and potentially explosive political or legal issues are defused by being turned into mere clashes of character. It is simplistic to treat such a form of

cinema as merely harmless – or even harmful – escapist entertainment. The Odeons of the late 1930s did not offer oblivion on the lines of the gin palaces of Victorian times. Instead they consistently gave their audiences a deeper reassurance through a facsimile world where existing values were invariably validated by events in the film and where all discord could be turned to harmony by an acceptance of the status quo.[10]

Clearly, Armes credits the British cinema with having played a far greater role than Balcon and other commentators have suggested. It fulfilled an ideological role, he is arguing, and projected a vision of the world which underpinned the social and political structures of British society at the time.

Indeed, one could go further to argue that the British cinema had both a 'reflective' function, in that it reflected the cohesive society which some historians tell us was in fact prevalent at the time, and a 'generative' function, in that it sought to encourage the assumption that society should continue to cohere and unite as it passed through the changing circumstances of the 1930s. To that extent it may be said that the British cinema had a positive and purposeful part to play in shaping the 'national life' because it helped (along with many other factors, of course) to achieve that high degree of consensus which seemingly characterized British society during the 1930s.

There are several ways in which one might set about exploring this revised picture of the British cinema. One might examine the reasons for Government intervention in the affairs of the British film industry in order to point out the cultural objectives which lay at the heart of the 1927 and 1938 Films Acts.[11] One might consider the purpose and process of the censorship imposed by the British Board of Film Censors in order to look at the subjects that were precluded by that body and to highlight the values that it sought to inculcate.[12] Alternatively, one might utilize the evidence that is available regarding the relative 'popularity' of British films with British audiences to suggest that they were far more popular, in many senses, than they are often given credit for being and to argue that the 'Americanization' thesis must be greatly qualified, at least for the 1930s.[13]

All of these avenues could and should be followed up by any comprehensive survey of the British cinema during the period of the 1930s. Here, though, the intention is to look at the characteristic forms rather than the institutions of British cinema and, in particular, to single out *South Riding* for scrutiny in order to outline the projection of Britain that it depicted and the consensus that it sought to evoke.

Such a course of action is clearly open to the criticism that one film is hardly representative of the mainstream British cinema of the day, which is usually divided into the large 'prestigious' productions (Korda's epics and the like, into which category *South Riding* falls) and the so-called 'provincial' comedies (from George Formby, Gracie Fields, Will Hay and others). The former strain generally receives attention; the latter rarely does and is often dismissed in the same curt tone that was employed by critical commentators on first viewing the films. However, the division is arbitrary. The comedies merit equal attention, certainly, and they can be a rich historical source, as I have sought to show elsewhere.[14] Ultimately they differ little, if at all, in intent from their supposedly 'prestigious' counterparts, and the intent of a film such as *South Riding* can be taken as symptomatic of the mainstream British cinema generally.

The film of *South Riding* was based upon Winifred Holtby's novel, which was published in February 1936. Within a month the book had sold 25,000 copies and was acclaimed Book of the Month. By the end of 1936 it had gone through eight impressions. It was obviously a success and, like all literary successes, was therefore likely to attract the attention of many a film producer. Victor Saville was quick to snap it up. On 25 March 1936 he bought the film rights and paid £3,000 for them to Holtby's estate (she died in September 1935) through the person of Vera Brittain, the literary executor of Holtby's will and her close friend over many years.

Saville determined to make a 'film of quality' out of the novel, a film with literary pretensions and aspirations to do more than simply entertain.[15] There was to be extensive exterior shooting; an international cinematographer of repute, Harry Stradling, was engaged, along with a noted scriptwriter, Ian Dalrymple, and art director, Lazare Meerson; and a large cast was headed by some accomplished British actors. Robert Donat was sought for the leading role, but he fell ill, and it was subsequently offered to Ralph Richardson.

The film was released early in 1938. It turned out, Saville thought, to be his best film. 'They're real people,' he commented later, in interview, of the characters whom he had created on the screen.[16] Vera Brittain recorded in her autobiography that she had reservations about the film, though she conceded, 'According to the standards then expected by film-goers, Victor Saville had made a memorable picture.'[17] In fact, the film found favour with the cinema-going public (it was re-released, though in edited form, in 1943 and 1946) and the critics alike. And in general the critics greeted the film on its release in much the same terms that Saville later used.

'Here is an English picture which is really English,' commented the *Daily Telegraph*. The *Daily Mirror* believed the film provided a 'scrupulous, authentic picture of English life for the first time on any screen', and the *Sunday Pictorial* praised its 'wonderfully authentic settings'. Even the more 'informed' sources of criticism considered that the film was for the most part 'realistic'. 'Well worth seeing as a well acted, well produced story of the realities of English life', commented the *Monthly Film Bulletin* of the British Film Institute, and the *New Statesman* added on 8 January 1938: 'For a time we sit ecstatic upon our plush, unable to believe our eyes and ears – something positively real is unrolling before us', though both these latter sources also subscribed to the opinion that the climax of the film was a 'major blunder', ending 'regrettably, in sheer bathos'.[18]

The plot of the film is simple enough. Squire Carne (Ralph Richardson), the MFH, is increasingly burdened by financial problems. His wife Madge (Ann Todd) is in an expensive mental home, and he lives alone at Maythorpe Hall with his daughter Midge (Glynis Johns). He is the only member of the South Riding County Council who objects to a new housing scheme which would abolish a ramshackle shanty village known as 'The Shacks'. Carne, however, is suspicious of the motives behind the scheme. His suspicions turn out to be well founded. Astell (John Clements), a 'genuine social reformer' as the synopsis describes him,[19] unwittingly accepts the help of two fellow council-lors, Snaith (Milton Rosmer) and Huggins (Edmund Gwenn), who promote the scheme but intend to turn it to their own financial advantage.

Carne's finances go from bad to worse, and on the advice of his good friend Alderman Mrs Beddows (Marie Lohr) he decides to send his daughter to the local school. He discusses the matter with its new headmistress Sarah Burton (Edna Best). They begin to meet often and finally fall in love.

Sarah overhears Huggins in a conversation which reveals his duplicity, and she goes straight to Carne. He has been to the mental home where his wife has lapsed into a coma. And when Sarah arrives at Maythorpe Hall, she finds he has gone alone into the woods with a gun. She follows him and stops him from committing suicide. At the Council meeting later that afternoon Snaith and Huggins are exposed, and Carne thereafter decides to back the housing scheme. The new housing estate is opened amid the joyous celebrations of Coronation Day.

But what kind of 'reality' is constructed in the film of *South Riding*? What sort of 'English landscape' does it project, and what 'pictorial impression' does it give of England in the 1930s?

The introductory sequences to the film, which comprise the credits and a prologue, seemingly encapsulate the way in which the drama will unfold. They serve also ostensibly to highlight the issues and to spotlight the protagonists who will dominate the fictional representation that is to follow.

Opening captions pay brief homage to Winifred Holtby and state that she 'realized that local government is not a dry affair of meetings and memoranda, but "the front-line defence thrown up by humanity against its common enemies of sickness, poverty and ignorance"'. Then each of the leading characters makes a brief speech to camera, as follows:

Beddows: Mr Chairman, I stand for the fair administration of the limited funds at our disposal. if we give too much here, another will have to go without there.

Snaith: I take the practical view. I ask myself, is it good business? If it's good business, well, it's right.

Huggins: What I say is, public affairs is a trust from above. We 'ave dedicated ourselves to the service of the people.

Astell: I started life as a socialist. I'm sorry. I'm unrepentant. My ambition is to see the lives of the working masses improved.

Carne: Cheap houses, free education, hospitals and so on, all very excellent. But aren't we teaching people to rely on others, instead of themselves? In which case there's no future for England.

Burton: England's future is in the hands of her children. Give them what they need.[20]

The issues raised in those six statements are socially pertinent and appear to confirm the film's indebtedness to Holtby's novel, in which the chapters are headed 'Education', 'Public Health', 'Housing and Town Planning' and the like. Together the characters making the statements constitute a cross-section of interested informed opinion.

There is the liberally inspired, fair-minded Alderman Mrs Beddows, full of common sense; the practical, down-to-earth businessman Alderman Snaith; Councillor Huggins, the religious zealot, it appears, who believes in a God-given mission; the Labour Councillor Astell, consumptive (he coughs during his speech and continues to cough at appropriate and telling moments elsewhere in the film), yet dedicated to improving the lot of the workers in this world rather than the next; Councillor Carne who trots out the traditional conservative platitudes about self-improvement and the state of the nation; and the visionary Sarah Burton, a schoolteacher, imbued with confidence, optimism and a belief that the youth of today provide hope for the future, given the right sort of start in life. These characters form 'a part of the changing England that is typical of the whole', as another opening caption puts it. Yet it is a society fraught with problems and contradictions, as their statements reveal. The matters that are addressed are of public concern, but the philosophies, as expounded, seem irreconcilable; there is conflict and a difference of opinion.

How, then, does the film effect a resolution of these problems and the conflicting sets of interests?

It does so, to begin with, by personalizing the problems and turning them into clashes of character (an opening caption readily admits that: 'Our story tells how a public life affects the private life, and how a man's personal sufferings make him what he is in public'). Thereafter, the film marginalizes those elements of social commentary which occupied the centre stage in Holtby's original literary narrative and doubtless provided a major source of inspiration for her work, and it moves to the foreground, in their stead, other elements which are determined more by the classic dictates of mainstream narrative cinema than by anything else. Finally, the film achieves its purpose by extirpating the 'evil' and disruptive forces in the society that it creates on screen while negotiating a series of compromise solutions to bring about a consensus of opinion within the remaining 'productive' forces.

Compromise and consensus, in the best interests of society and the nation as a whole, are largely what the film of *South Riding* is about. And the 'moral' of the film, if one chooses to use such terms, is that nobody is above learning how to compromise if important issues are at stake. In this the film is greatly at odds with the novel, which is permeated by an acute sense of loss and unfulfilled promise, though it also concludes with a good deal of sustained emphasis upon the compensations of 'belonging to a community', of being 'one with the people' and of 'national unity'.

Those characters, like Snaith and Huggins, who are not willing to compromise at all but seek rather to secure their own selfish ends by whatever devious means at their disposal, must be weeded out. Again, this is somewhat different from the novel, in which Snaith is construed as 'subtle as a serpent, yet serving his generation', and Huggins is described simply as having a 'passion for righteousness at war with his appetites'. Neither one is there meted out the retribution that is dispensed in the film. Carne, intransigent and narrow-minded because of his heritage and the personal problems which beset him, must learn to compromise in the face of the changing society around him if he is to survive at all – in the novel he does not do so and he dies. Sarah too must learn to compromise if she is to achieve her goals; but force of circumstance has already taught her, as it has Astell and to some extent Mrs Beddows, something about the need to compromise. (The characters of Sarah and Mrs Beddows are nearest to the novel's original conception of them, though in the novel Sarah does not marry Carne, of course, as she does in the film. Astell's screen persona is ostensibly the complete antithesis of that in the novel. In the latter he finally leaves the South Riding and declares: 'I'm a militant again, thank God, quit of the shame of compromise.')

There are several key sequences that make clear the film's insistence upon the need for compromise in all its forms. In the first one, early in the film, Sarah Burton is interviewed for the post of headmistress at Kiplington High School:

Astell:	Why do you want to come here when you've been teaching in London?
Burton:	I wanted to come back to Yorkshire.
Beddows:	We had a much better vacancy in Flintonbridge last year. Why didn't you apply for that?
Burton:	Because I didn't think I would get it.

Beddows:	Why not?
Burton:	Well, you see, I'm not by birth a lady.
Carne:	What do you mean, you're not by birth a lady?
Burton:	My father was a blacksmith.
Carne:	Well, what part of the Riding do you come from?
Burton:	Liptonhunter. My mother was the district nurse.
Carne:	Oh, yes, I remember. . . .
Burton:	Go on, say it. My father was a drunkard. He drank himself to death. And my mother went to the West Riding and worked herself to the bone to educate me. I'm proud of my mother.

Despite Carne's obvious reservations, Sarah does get the post and, once appointed, she tries to enlist Astell's support for the school:

Burton:	The young are important. Oh, you're just yellow.
Astell:	Oh no, I'm not. I'm not even pale pink. I'm red. Scarlet. But one thing at a time. It's uphill work. And I'm tired *(coughs)*. You don't know the opposition. I'm worn out with it. And much of it's reasonable, that's the rub. You start by demanding world revolution and end up being satisfied with a sewage farm
Burton:	That reminds me. You haven't seen our cockroaches.
Astell:	Oh no, not that. I'm a snob about cockroaches, an absolute Carne.

Subsequently, Sarah catches Midge Carne, newly arrived at the local school because her father cannot afford to send her to a private school, fighting with Lydia Holly, a naturally intelligent girl but born into the poverty and degradation of 'The Shacks'. She takes Lydia aside and counsels her:

Burton:	Now then, Lydia, you've got to be kind to Midge Carne.
Lydia:	Yes, Miss Burton.
Burton:	You don't seem very keen.
Lydia:	Miss Burton, I do try, but. . . .
Burton:	No, you don't, Lydia.
Lydia:	No, Miss Burton.
Burton:	You think because she's better off than you, you'll get your own back and take it out of her, don't you?

Lydia: Yes, Miss Burton.

Burton: Well, you're wrong, Lydia. She isn't better off than you. She's unhappy. She's lonely. She's got no brothers and sisters and no mother. You're the lucky one, Lydia, and you're happy. You've got health and strength and brains and everything's fun for you.

Lydia: Yes, Miss Burton, it is. I begin to see what you mean.

Burton: Life's got such lots in store for you, Lydia, if you'll only work hard. For a start I want you to work for a scholarship. Because of all the girls in this school, you're the one who ought to go to college.

Lydia: Oh, Miss Burton, college, if only I could. It's what I've dreamed about. If you'll help me, I'll mother Midge Carne. I'll, I'll do anything for you. I'll be your slave, I'll. . . . Oh I'm so happy.

But Lydia's mother dies, and there is a threat that Lydia will have to leave school in order to look after the family. So Sarah attempts to secure a boarding scholarship for the girl, with Mrs Beddows's help:

Burton: Mrs Beddows, if the school governors would make a special grant for Lydia to board at school, I'll pay a woman to look after the Hollys.

Beddows: My dear, that's wonderfully generous of you, but it can't be done. You can't afford that sort of thing, and we haven't the power or the means to create a boarding scholarship.

Burton: You're going to allow this to happen?

Beddows: We're hardly to blame for people having families they can't support.

Burton: It's a stupid waste of such an intelligent child.

Beddows: It will make a fine woman of her.

Burton: A fine woman. A drudge.

Beddows: If you consider hard work drudgery, then we're most of us drudges. We do what we can with limited resources. We need patience.

Carne does not so much compromise throughout most of the film as relents, and usually in a reluctant fashion at that. He relents over the appointment of Sarah as headmistress; he relents over sending Midge to the local school; he relents finally about pushing through a scholarship for Lydia to keep her at school. And it is because of his stubbornness that he is driven to desperation and attempted suicide. Yet he does begin at last to learn how to compromise, thanks largely to his blossoming relationship with Sarah. The first signs are evident when he allows Sarah to help him with the delivery of a calf, though initially his response is cold and hostile:

Carne:	What the . . .! How did you get here?
Burton:	I heard that awful sound.
Carne:	But you can't come here. This is no place for a woman.
Burton:	Well, the cow and I are both females.
Carne:	Now go away, please.
Burton:	I'm going to help.
Carne:	What on earth help do you think you'll be?
Burton:	Oh, you forget I was brought up to this sort of thing.
Carne:	All right. Well, do exactly what I tell you.
Burton:	Naturally.
Carne:	Yes, well, you won't want that. There's a bucket of water there. Hey, take it easy, take it easy. The beastman's drunk. Now quickly. . . . (*Later*) . . . Mother and son doing well. I'm awfully grateful. I wouldn't have done it without you.
Burton:	Nonsense, I only seemed to get in the way. No vet could teach you anything.

Where though does all this compromise get everybody? What sort of consensus is brought about as a result of it?

The narrative thrust of the screenplay reaches its inevitable conclusion during a confrontation in the council chambers. A council debate reinstates in the foreground the proposal for a housing scheme, always in danger of being lost in the course of the film. Snaith and Huggins are exposed as corrupt and self-interested. Astell is shown to have acted stupidly though with the best intentions. Carne, of course, emerges triumphant. His change of heart and new-found sense of compromise solves all the problems over the housing scheme – he donates his estate to the council for houses and a new school. His wife has died; his private anguish is over; and he has formed a romantic alliance with Sarah, a former antagonist.

Furthermore, the gentleman farmer carries with him another former antagonist, the now repentant socialist Astell, in an alliance that suggests a meeting of the classes for which they stand. The people of the South Riding can only benefit from this symbolic overthrow of social conflicts. Together the paternalistic gentry and the progressive forces in society will forge a new England.

The final scenes show 'the people' gathering together on the Coronation Day of King George and Queen Elizabeth, when the housing estate and high school are to be opened. The camera scans the assembled ranks of firemen and nurses in uniforms, children and rows of people from the community – a representative sample of British society – singling out in the process a small band made up of Astell, Sarah and Carne, happy and smiling. Everybody sings 'Land of Hope and Glory', and the chairman of the council makes a patriotic speech:[21]

> People of the South Riding, today millions of our people line the streets of London and all over the country our townsmen and villagers come together to celebrate the crowning of our new King and Queen. Without boasting and vainglory, we can be proud of our country. Let us remember those who work for the common good, follow their lead and work in our turn for the happiness and the betterment of our people. In this spirit, let us undertake our model coronation housing estate which I now have the honour to inaugurate.

Thus a fitting climax is provided for a film which celebrates essentially a vision of England as one happy, close-knit community, a vision of domestic harmony and national integration to be found most often in British films of the 1930s. And since such films and sentiments were much in evidence, it is little wonder that the British cinema contributed towards the remarkable stability of British society during the period.

Notes

1. George Perry, *The Great British Picture Show,* London, 1975, p. 85. Other standard popular accounts that put forward that argument include, for example, Charles Oakley, *Where We Came In,* London, 1964, and Ernest Betts, *The Film Business,* London, 1978. My own reactions to the argument, and to the arguments for American 'colonization' of the British cinema and against the 'popularity' of British films with British audiences, are charted at greater length *in British Cinema of the 1930s,* Unit 7 of the Open University course *Popular Culture,* Milton Keynes, 1982. My thanks to the OU for allowing me to use in this chapter some of the material I wrote for that course.

2. Dilys Powell, *Films since 1939*, London, 1947, pp. 64–5. See also A. J. P. Taylor, *English History 1914–1945,* Oxford, 1965, p. 315, where he states that, apart from Korda and Hitchcock, 'the Americans had it all their own way'. The Americanization thesis still holds good in some quarters, as Peter Stead demonstrates in 'The People and the Pictures', in Nicholas Pronay and D. W. Spring (eds.), *Propaganda, Politics and Film, 1918–1945,* London, 1982.

3. Michael Balcon, *Michael Balcon Presents . . . A Lifetime of Films,* London, 1969, pp. 41–2, 90.

4. Paul Addison, *The Road to 1945,* London, 1975, p. 276.

5. John Stevenson and Chris Cook, *The Slump: Society and Politics during the Depression,* London, 1977, pp. 4–5.

6. ibid., p. 30.

7. ibid., p. 142.

8. ibid., p. 193.

9. ibid., p. 276.

10. Roy Armes, *A Critical History of British Cinema,* London, 1978, pp. 113–14. For a more recent assessment, see James Curran and Vincent Porter (eds.), *British Cinema History,* London, 1983.

11. 'Should we be content', the President of the Board of Trade asked on the second reading of the Films Bill in 1927, 'if we depended upon foreign literature or upon a foreign press in this country?' The film exhibitors, who did not welcome the Government's interventionist policies, were well aware of that Bill's intentions. One of their organizations commented: 'The object of the Cinematograph Films Bill now before your honourable House has been stated by supporters of the Government to be to promote the making of British films for the purposes of propaganda – commercial, religious, social and political. . . .' In 1936 the Moyne Committee, paving the way for the 1938 Films Act, also asserted that 'The propaganda value of the film cannot be overemphasized' and clearly indicated an acute awareness of film's propaganda potential on the cultural front 'in the spread of national culture and in presenting national ideas and customs to the world'. By contrast, for an interpretation that plays down those cultural objectives, see Peter Stead, 'Hollywood's Message for the World: the British Response in the 1930s', *Historical Journal of Film, Radio and Television,* 1, March 1981.

12. See Jeffrey Richards's two articles, 'The British Board of Film Censors and Content Control in the 1930s', in *Historical Journal of Film, Radio and Television,* 1, October 1981, and 2, March 1982. See also two articles by Nicholas Pronay, 'The First Reality: Film Censorship in Liberal England', in K. R. M. Short (ed.), *Feature Films as History,* London, 1981, and 'The Political Censorship of Films in Britain between the Wars', in Pronay and Spring, *Propaganda, Politics and Film, 1918–1945,* though my own article, 'Comedy, Class and Containment: the Domestic British Cinema of the 1930s', in Curran and Porter, *British Cinema History,* raises some questions regarding the practical effectiveness of the BBFC during the 1930s.

13. See, for example, Simon Rowson's evidence to the Moyne Committee (*Minutes of the evidence taken before the Departmental Committee on Cinematograph Films, 1936*), where he stated that though there were more American than British films in circulation in Britain between 1933 and 1936, none the less his statistics showed that each British film had been screened on average 6 per cent more frequently than its American counterpart. For the second half of the decade, see the First Report of the Cinematograph Films Council which concluded, in 1939, that 'there was an insistent

demand by exhibitors for British films which was not limited by the extent of their statutory quotas and as a result any satisfactory British picture had an eager market in this country.' The slump in British film production in 1938, furthermore, bore little or no relation to the 'popularity' of British films. The plain fact was that no matter how 'popular' a British film might be with British audiences, it could rarely hope to recoup its outlay and make a profit, thereby sustaining film production in this country, simply because of the inadequate system of financing and floating a production and because of the delay in getting films ready for release and subsequently released. Such deficiencies meant, according to Rowson, that making a film in Britain involved the employment of from 70 to 80 per cent more capital than it cost to make a film in America. It was, he concluded, 'a dangerous spiral'.

14. See, for example, the two television programmes made to accompany Unit 7, *British Cinema of the 1930s,* of the Open University course *Popular Culture,* viz., TV 3, *Comedy,* and TV 4 *South Riding.* Both were presented by myself and produced by Susan Boyd-Bowman, and both are broadcast on BBC TV each year throughout the life of the course.

15. Interview conducted with Ian Dalrymple, 12 May 1980.

16. In Cyril B. Rollins and Robert J. Wareing (eds.), *Victor Saville,* London, 1972, p. 12, where Saville also announced, 'I never attacked the establishment in any way.'

17. Vera Brittain, *Testament of Experience,* London, 1979 (reprint), p. 188, where she describes her reaction after attending the first night of the film at the London Pavilion in 1938: 'According to the standards then expected by filmgoers, Victor Saville had made a memorable picture, renewing Winifred's spirit through the candid Yorkshire scenes rather than by an over-romantic treatment of her moving but astringent story. A more realistic film could be made today, showing Sarah Burton and Robert Carne as the star-crossed middle-aged semi-lovers whom Winifred created and depicting Alderman Mrs Beddows as a patriarchal 74 instead of the glamorous 66 presented by the young-looking Marie Lohr.'

Holtby's book was successfully dramatized for a 1974 Yorkshire Television series with Dorothy Tutin, Hermione Baddeley and Nigel Davenport, which won a BAFTA award as best series of the year. And her career and writings have lately been the subject of further scrutiny, which has provided the occasion for a modest revival. See, for example, Stuart Hall *et al., Culture, Media, Language,* London, 1980, pp. 249–56; Mary Stott, 'Winifred Holtby: Cause and Effect', *Guardian,* 18 November 1981; and Joy Holland, 'Rediscovering a Feminist Novelist', *Spare Rib,* 117, April 1982, pp. 17–18. *South Riding* was last reprinted in 1981 by Fontana, and in that same year the Virago Press reprinted Holtby's *Anderby Wold* and *The Crowded Street.*

18. See the microfiche on the film compiled and held by the British Film Institute Library, London.

19. ibid.

20. The BFI Library holds an accurate dialogue continuity script of *South Riding* (6 November 1937). My thanks to Paul Berry, literary executor of the Winifred Holtby Estate, and to Pendennis Films Ltd for allowing me to quote extracts from the script here and elsewhere.

21. The 16 mm print of *South Riding* currently in distribution runs for ninety minutes. The 35 mm print of the film, on its initial release in 1938, ran for ninety-one minutes. An analysis of the film and the dialogue continuity script reveals that the Coronation Day scenes at the climax of the film have been cut slightly. It is clear that originally this sequence began with a short rendering of a few lines from 'Land of Hope and

Glory' and was followed by the chairman of the council's speech, and that the whole proceedings were rounded off with everybody launching into the first verse of 'God Save the King'. This is confirmed by the *New Statesman* review of the film, in which the critic notes that 'there is a macabre fascination in the spectacle of the entire cast singing first "Land of H. and G." and then "God Save the King". "Send him victorious," warbles Miss Best; "Happy and Glorious," counters Mr Richardson; "Long to reign o'er us," adds Mr Clements, sheepishly however, because, you see, he is really a horrid Red.'

We are obviously spared such delights, though if one looks carefully at the three shots of Best, Richardson and Clements in the closing scenes of the film as it presently stands, one can spot a definite lack of synchronization between what they are singing and the sound of 'Land of H. and G.' coming over the soundtrack. This is obviously the point where they should be singing 'God Save the King'. Why, when and where these changes were made is difficult to ascertain. The print of the film in the National Film Archive, London, is of little help on this score, since it is obviously a copy of the re-released, re-edited version of 1943 or 1946. This is shorn of the opening sequences in 'The Shacks' and the closing Coronation Day scenes, an unwitting comment in itself perhaps of the relevance which these particular scenes were felt to have for the 1930s, though not the 1940s.

A Canterbury Tale (1944)

4

Why We Fight
A Canterbury Tale

A t the outbreak of World War II all cinemas in Britain were closed.
But their value to the maintenance of morale was soon appreciated, and they were reopened to become one of the principal sources
of recreation for the nation at war. Feature films were seen as providing
not just escapist entertainment but also instruction and information. So
for the duration of the war they operated under the watchful eye of
both the British Board of Film Censors and the Ministry of Information. Lord Macmillan, the first wartime Minister of Information, issued
a memorandum in 1940 suggesting three themes for propagandist
feature films: what Britain was fighting for, how Britain was fighting
and the need for sacrifice.[1] The industry responded to these suggestions and, in so doing, experienced perhaps its finest hour. It enjoyed a
surge of creativity, an explosion of native talent such as it had not
before witnessed. The nature and demands of the situation focused the
mind of the film world squarely and continuously on the projection of
Britain and the British people, something that had on the whole not
occurred in the 1930s.[2]

The earliest British war film, *The Lion Has Wings,* rapidly put together
by producer Alexander Korda and on view by November 1939,
embodied many of the themes which were to be reworked by later and
better films. It established the images of the two sides for the duration
by contrasting the goodnatured, decent, hardworking, democratic British,

with their sense of humour and their love of sport, and the regimented, fanatical, jackbooted Nazis, marching in faceless formation.

The film looked both to the future and to the past – to the future in the documentary-style reconstruction of wartime operations, and to the past in the staged sequences of the response to the war of a 'typical British couple', the very upper-middle-class Ralph Richardson and Merle Oberon, scenes which evoked the rigidly stratified class system enshrined in the films of the 1930s. Initially the cinema continued to reflect this class-bound 1930s tradition, resolutely middle-class in tone and values and with little realistic evocation of the lives of working-class people. In films like Carol Reed's *Night Train to Munich* (1940) the war was treated as a gentlemanly jape, in which an upper-class hero (Rex Harrison) ran rings around the humourless, ranting, dunderheaded Hun. The apotheosis of the romanticized, class-bound and hopelessly out-of-touch war film was Ealing's *Ships With Wings* (1941), a *Boy's Own Paper* yarn in which a disgraced Fleet Air Arm Officer (John Clements) redeems his honour by undertaking a suicide mission. It received such a hostile press that Michael Balcon, head of Ealing, took the decision to produce essentially realistic stories of Britain at war. He turned therefore to the only group in Britain that was familiar with the evocation of real life – the documentarists. This group, nurtured in the 1930s by John Grierson, was committed to the concept of realism in setting, mood and content and to the dramatization of the everyday experience of ordinary people. Several of them, notably Harry Watt and Alberto Cavalcanti, went to work for Ealing Studios, and from that time on the documentary influence permeated the whole field of feature film production.

The image of a nation divided by class barriers and epitomized by the notorious slogan of the early war years – '*Your* courage, *your* cheerfulness, *your* resolution will bring *us* victory' – was replaced by the concept of the 'People's War', the idea of ordinary people pulling together to defeat a common foe. Ealing's war films exemplify the new image. Typical of them is *San Demetrio-London* (1943), recounting the true story of the salvaging of a Merchant Navy tanker by part of its crew, a cross-section of ordinary chaps, and *The Bells Go Down* (1943), dramatizing the work of the Auxiliary Fire Service in London. Significantly, neither of these films had an officer-and-gentleman hero. Indeed, the lifestyle and rationale of the old-style officer and gentleman was comprehensively demolished in Michael Powell's and Emeric Pressburger's controversial *The Life and Death of Colonel Blimp* (1943).

Comradeship and co-operation, dedication to duty and self-sacrifice, a self-deprecating good humour and unselfconscious modesty character-ized the films about the fighting services. The war produced a masterpiece for each. For the Navy there was *In Which We Serve* (1942), written, produced, co-directed and scored by Noel Coward, who also played the leading role. It was based on the true story of the sinking of HMS *Kelly,* the ship commanded by Coward's friend Lord Louis Mountbatten. Carol Reed's *The Way Ahead* (1944), scripted by Peter Ustinov and Eric Ambler, was a semidocumentary account of how a group of conscripts from all walks of life were welded into a disciplined army unit. Anthony Asquith's *The Way to the Stars* (1945), scripted by Terence Rattigan, recalled life on a single RAF station between 1940 and 1944, its joys and losses, its tragedies and camaraderie.

The contribution of women to the war effort was vital, and the cinema's tribute to them reflected the dramatic change in their social role and expectations. Leslie Howard's *The Gentle Sex* (1943) was a female version of *The Way Ahead,* a realistic account of the training of a group of women from all classes and backgrounds in the ATS. Frank Launder's and Sidney Gilliat's moving and memorable *Millions Like Us* (1943) dramatized the experiences of another mixed group of girls drafted to work in an aircraft factory. All these films contained characters and situ-ations that were sympathetically and realistically depicted. They both reflected the shared experience of the audience and promoted that spirit of co-operation and self-sacrifice which was needed to win the war.

Films about *why* Britain was fighting were rarer than films about *how* she was fighting, perhaps because of the difficulty of constructing acceptably entertaining stories around sophisticated ideological and philosophical concepts. Probably the best programmatic account was provided by Michael Powell's and Emeric Pressburger's *49th Parallel* (1941). Financed by the Ministry of Information, it told the gripping story of a stranded crew of a Nazi submarine making their way across Canada towards the neutral United States and encountering en route various representatives of democracy. An uncommitted French Canadian trapper (Laurence Olivier) turns against the Nazis when they maltreat the 'racially inferior' Eskimoes. A democratic Christian community of Hutterite exiles, led by Anton Walbrook, demonstrate the workability of a system of equality, co-operation and Christian love. A donnish aesthete (Leslie Howard) beats one of the Nazis to pulp when they burn his books and pictures. Finally, an ordinary Canadian soldier (Raymond Massey) takes on and defeats the Nazi 'superman' commanding the fugitives (Eric Portman). The Nazis are thus effectively depicted as standing for cruelty, tyranny, arrogance and philistinism.

It was clear what we were fighting against. But what sort of England were we fighting for? The war brought into sharp focus the meaning of England and Englishness. The result was a spate of books analysing and investigating England and the English, books with titles like *The English People* and *The Character of England.*. Anthologies of poetry and prose also sought to project an image of England. One such was Collie Knox's *Forever England* (1943). It contains poetry by Shakespeare, Wordsworth, Kipling and Browning apostrophizing England, speeches by Churchill, Asquith and Disraeli eulogizing England, essays on the armed forces, the church, cricket and the public schools, and comments by sympathetic foreigners on what they see as the essence of Englishness. Over and over again, in these and similar works, one finds the ideas that together represent the concept 'England' – a love of tradition, balance and order; a belief in tolerance and humanity; a sense of humour. But also highlighted is that visionary aspect of Englishness, that fey, mystical quality, that striving after the secrets of the eternal that crops up periodically in English history and English thought. It is there in the music of Elgar and Vaughan Williams, in the writings of Kipling and Haggard, in the poetry of Newbolt and Rupert Brooke. It is associated inextricably with war and can be seen in the lifestyles and ideas of a remarkable succession of soldier-mystics who sought out deserts and high places in order to commune with the Almighty – Lawrence of Arabia, Gordon of Khartoum, Younghusband of Tibet and Orde Wingate of the Chindits.[3]

It is deeply Romantic and deeply emotional. But then there is in wartime a heightening of the emotions, a quickening of the pulse. It is a time for poetry and brave words, for sentiments can be uttered and felt and believed that in prosaic peacetime seem inflated, exaggerated, unreal. Feelings come bubbling to the surface in people who face every day the prospect of death, feelings that in ordinary times are buried so deep that their existence may not even be consciously acknowledged.

That is why C. A. Lejeune, the influential film critic of the *Observer,* was wrong when, reviewing *The Gentle Sex* in 1943, she wrote:

> It seems tolerably clear by now that the best thing the war is likely to draw out of the cinema is not poetry but prose; no masterpiece but a number of small, candid snapshots of the soul of the people. . . . To create or to savour the larger forms of art requires leisure of mind, and that is a thing we have not.[4]

She had reckoned without the mystical vision summoned up by the war in the Romantic Right (Michael Powell and Emeric Pressburger) and the Romantic Left (Humphrey Jennings), whose meditations on England were to produce celluloid poetry of the highest order.

Few film-makers have been as controversial, as innovative, as adventurous or as deeply Romantic as Michael Powell and Emeric Pressburger.[5] Working within mainstream commercial cinema, they produced a succession of films that were both popular entertainment and high art, that were distinctively and recognizably personal, yet said something profound about England and the English. They were without question the most remarkable of several film-making teams that occupied an influential place in British cinema. The others include the Korda Brothers (Alexander, Zoltan and Vincent), the Boulting Brothers (Roy and John), Frank Launder and Sidney Gilliat, Basil Dearden and Michael Relph, and Herbert Wilcox and Anna Neagle. It was Alexander Korda who first teamed Powell and Pressburger to make *The Spy in Black* in 1939. Pressburger, a Hungarian writer and refugee from Nazi Germany, and Powell, the Kentish director who had gained a critical reputation after making *Edge of the World* (1937) on the island of Foula, worked so well together that in 1942 they formed The Archers, one of a number of independent production units working under the overall umbrella of Rank. They signed their films jointly – Produced, directed and written by Michael Powell and Emeric Pressburger – though it was generally recognized that Pressburger provided the script and Powell directed. They were anxious to contribute to the cinema's war effort and made two films on the subject of 'how we fight' *(One of Our Aircraft is Missing* and *The Life and Death of Colonel Blimp)* before turning back to the subject of 'why we fight', first explored in *49th Parallel.* Powell subsequently described *A Canterbury Tale* (1944) as his version of 'why we fight'; it was an exploration of the spiritual values for which England stands, testimony to the belief that the roots of the nation lie in the pastoral and to the idea of England as synonymous with freedom. He also called it a 'crusade against materialism'.[6]

The England evoked by *A Canterbury Tale* is the England of Chaucer and Shakespeare, a rural England of half-timbered cottages and stately country houses, quiet, leafy churchyards and rich hopfields, an England whose spirit resides in Thomas Colpeper, gentleman farmer, magistrate, historian and archaeologist, a man who understands England's nature and seeks to communicate her values. It is a film, on the one hand, of astonishing tranquillity and entrancing visual beauty and, on the other, of riveting power and mystical suggestiveness. Superbly photographed at genuine Kentish locations, it hymns the beauties of the countryside, which are seen as timeless and unchanging. The film recreates the Canterbury pilgrimage for a trio of latter-day visitors in search of spiritual peace. The timelessness is encapsulated at the outset, as Esmond Knight reads the introduction to Chaucer's *Canterbury Tales* in Old English and the camera moves in on a map of medieval England to rest on the road to Canterbury. Then, amid laughter and the jingle of accoutrements, Chaucer and the pilgrims are seen riding along the Pilgrim's Way, the camera picking out individual faces. A falconer unhoods his bird, which flies away; it dissolves into a plane sweeping over the same countryside; the director cuts back to the falconer's face, but it is now the face of a man wearing modern army uniform. The narrator merely underlines what the camera has shown us – the land is still the same and the people are still the same. But there are new pilgrims now – and armoured troop carriers lurch suddenly into view. For all this, the spiritual values are eternal; a return to them will bring peace of mind. It is why we fight.

Much of the action of the film is set in and around a Kentish village, which appears at the outset almost as a spirit village like Brigadoon, emerging from the enveloping mist and from a distant past. It is called Chillingbourne, and with its stationmaster called Duckett, its squire Colpeper, its innkeeper Woodcock and its inn, where Queen Elizabeth I herself is reputed to have slept, the 'Hand of Glory', its image and ambience is purest Elizabethan. It even has a village idiot.

Colpeper (Eric Portman) is first discovered working at his desk in a sixteenth-century panelled office in the town hall. He is shot from a reverential low angle across a wooden beam inscribed with the words 'Honour the Truth'. Later he is seen scything his grass like some stout

Tudor yeoman, eliciting from Alison, one of the modern pilgrims, the admiring comment: 'He looks so right.' Colpeper talks of miracles, appears and disappears mysteriously, is seen haloed with light during his lecture in the village hall. Like the village, he seems magical, causing events to happen, manipulating lives like a latter-day Prospero. Magic is an integral part of Powell's vision, evident both in his world-view and in the technical realization of his films, which often amounts to visual wizardry. It is no coincidence that a film of Shakespeare's *The Tempest* was a long-cherished but unfulfilled project of Powell. Spells, prophecies, sorcery and mysticism bind together such apparently disparate films as *The Thief of Bagdad, The Red Shoes, The Elusive Pimpernel, Black Narcissus, Gone to Earth, I Know Where I'm Going* and especially *A Matter of Life and Death,* which Powell himself described as 'a most wonderful conjuring trick'.[7]

The three modern pilgrims on their way to Canterbury are the American Sergeant Bob Johnson (Sergeant John Sweet), the Englishman Sergeant Peter Gibbs (Dennis Price) and the English Land Army girl Alison Smith (Sheila Sim). At the outset they are in the dark — literally — and as the film progresses they find their way towards the light and the truth. They arrive at Chillingbourne in the middle of the night, their faces unseen initially by us or by each other. They set out to walk to the village and are beset by a mysterious attacker in a military overcoat, who pours glue on Alison's hair and flees. They chase him into the fog and lose him, but learn that this is the eleventh such attack by a figure known locally as the 'Glue Man'. They decide to find out who he is. Although there are elements of detective work in the plot, as the three visitors question previous victims, establish the time scale of the attacks and search for evidence of glue purchases, it is obvious from the outset who the 'Glue Man' is, for Colpeper chides himself for not closing the black-out curtains properly, and the camera moves into a bold close-up of his hastily abandoned Home Guard jacket in a cupboard. The question with which the film is really concerned is his motive for making the attacks, and that leads to an exposition of the message of spiritual peace, which changes the lives of the three 'detectives'.

All three are troubled souls. Bob Johnson is worried because he has not heard from his girl and thinks that she has left him. But Bob also serves two other symbolic functions. First and most obviously, he underlines the need for Anglo-American solidarity.[8] The film carefully exposes the locals' patronizing attitude towards this 'Yank': the station master rejects his claim to be a sergeant because his stripes are the wrong way up; the police sergeant retorts, 'This is Chillingbourne, not Chicago' when Bob asks if he is armed; and the fluttering, giggling maid at the inn insists he have early-morning tea rather than his usual coffee. But he is sceptical about the weight of British tradition and cannot understand the telephones, the driving on the wrong side of the road and especially the incessant tea-drinking. But, as Peter points out to him, it is the tea-drinkers of the world – the Soviet Union, China and Britain – who have successfully resisted the onslaught of the Axis powers. Bob is to find that he has much more in common with the English than he had supposed; in particular, his co-operation with the English pilgrims, Alison and Peter, successfully unmasks the 'Glue Man'.

But, more centrally, Bob is spiritually and aesthetically asleep. He has spent all his leaves in the cinema and has not sought out the beauties of the countryside. Even when in Salisbury he noted only its fine cinemas. Colpeper, hearing of this, laments the fact that all Bob has seen of England has been its movie houses and expresses his concern lest people become used to seeing England from their cinema seats. He urges Bob to visit Canterbury Cathedral ('You can't miss it; it is just behind the movie theatre').

The first step towards Bob's spiritual awakening and his appreciation of the English is taken when with Alison he visits the rural wheelwrights, the Hortons, and discusses their craft with them. He wins their admiration through his knowledge of the techniques of wood seasoning and reveals that he comes from an Oregon family of lumberjacks. 'We speak the same language,' says Bob of his encounter with Jim Horton, an encounter which celebrates both the innate virtues of rural craftsmanship and the common bonds of England and America. Alison, baffled by the discussion, replies sadly: 'I'm English, and we don't speak the same language.' This is one of the film's most important themes, reinforced by the character of Peter, that the city dweller, the product of urban culture, has lost touch with his rural roots and the values that they embody. Bob's experiences in Chillingbourne lead him to tell Peter on the Pilgrim's Way that his mind is truly at peace for the first time.

Alison too finds peace. She was a shop assistant in a garden furniture department before the war. She loved the countryside but as a visitor.

She never understood it. Now she is mourning the loss of her fiancé, a geologist with the RAF who has been shot down. His father had disapproved of his son's relationship with a shopgirl. 'It would need an earthquake to change his mind,' she says. 'We're having one,' replies Colpeper. But what the film sees as important is that while there may be social change, and the reconciliation of her fiancé's father with Alison acknowledges this, there must be cultural continuity. Alison falls under Colpeper's spell completely. At a lecture in the village hall, attended by soldiers from the local camp, Colpeper talks, with the aid of slides, of the beauties of the countryside and of Old England. His talk is beautifully delivered by Eric Portman in silhouette, with only his eyes visible, until his face is suddenly and dramatically lit up at the climax of the speech. Alison is so entranced that in her mind she hears the clatter of horses' hooves and the merry chatter of the medieval pilgrims. She does so again when she goes walking on the Pilgrim's Way and Colpeper suddenly appears from the long grass to talk to her of miracles.

The third pilgrim, Peter Gibbs, holds out longest. A cynical materialist, he calls on and denounces Colpeper as just another missionary ('The trouble with this country is that every other man has got a bee in his bonnet about something'). He explains to Colpeper that although trained as a church organist, he now plays a cinema organ in the West End for a good wage. He is indifferent to the countryside and admits to spending his Sundays playing cards and waiting for the pubs to open.

The climax of the film comes after they have identified Colpeper as the 'Glue Man', and Gibbs insists that they report him to the police in Canterbury. All three travel to Canterbury with Colpeper, who seeks to explain his motive for the attacks. He had sought for years to spread a knowledge of the country and a love of its beauty, but before the war no one would listen. When the war came an army camp was established at Chillingbourne, and he tried again. But the soldiers were interested only in girls and in going with them to the cinema and dances. So in order to save the village girls from the consequences of these casual liaisons, to protect the wives and sweethearts of the soldiers left behind, and to drum up audiences for his lectures, he launched the 'Glue Man' attacks.

There is a distinct element of misogyny in Colpeper's stance, and the film makes no apology for it. He is a bachelor, living with his mother. He rejects the services of Alison as a land girl on his farm, preferring a male farm worker. At almost his first appearance he demonstrates with approval the use of the ducking stool, for dealing with gossiping women, to Sergeant Johnson. Although he admits later that he has been wrong about Alison, who has come to share his mystic vision, he firmly answers 'No' when she asks if it has ever occurred to him to invite girls to his lectures. He seems to see girls as essentially silly, frivolous and second-rate, weaker vessels who serve only to lead men on and to distract them from their duties to their families and their opportunity to learn about the true meaning of England.

Alison and Bob accept Colpeper's explanation of his behaviour, but Peter is adamant that he must be reported. Colpeper is prepared for whatever may happen, observing serenely: 'There are higher courts than the local bench of magistrates' and gazing out at the Cathedral. They alight from the train and converge, with foreordained inevitability, on the Cathedral. Gibbs learns that the police inspector whom he wishes to see is there. Entering, he picks up a sheet of music that the cathedral organist has providentially dropped and is invited to play. He strikes up with Bach's *Toccata and Fugue,* loses himself in the music and rediscovers his real vocation. Bob, his face transfigured as he recalls that his grandfather built the first Baptist church in Cedar County, Oregon, meets a fellow soldier bearing a sheaf of letters from his girl. She has not forgotten him but is in Australia with the WAACS.

Alison searches for the garage where she has left the caravan that she and her geologist fiancé shared on their holiday there in 1940. The camera tracks her along the bomb-damaged streets, but above the ruins towers the Cathedral, eternal and indestructible. When she eventually finds the caravan it is cobwebbed and moth-eaten and, faced by this symbol of her lost happiness, she bursts into tears. Colpeper appears and talks cryptically of the transitoriness of caravan life and the inevitability of moving on. Suddenly the garage owner arrives with a message from the father of her fiancé, Jeffrey. He has been looking for her to tell her that Jeffrey is alive and at Gibraltar. She turns to tell Colpeper, but he has gone as mysteriously as he appeared. Joyously, she throws open the windows of the caravan.

The film ends with a regiment of soldiers, about to leave for action overseas, processing through the Canterbury streets to the Cathedral, where Peter plays the organ triumphantly. Bob, Alison and Jeffrey's father join the congregation, and Colpeper, unseen, slips in too. All sing

'Onward, Christian Soldiers'; the bells ring; and the last shot is of the Cathedral as seen from the Pilgrim's Way. This final sequence prefigures the inevitable victory for which we fight on behalf of our country, freedom, beauty, tolerance and spirituality.

A Canterbury Tale rejoices in a sense of the living past, in country crafts, rural beauty, the intimacy of man and nature, and this joy is conveyed in passages of pure camera poetry, with much use of point-of-view shots to lead the audience into the countryside and the Cathedral. These sequences do not advance the plot but celebrate the mood and message. There is the soaring evocation of Canterbury Cathedral around which the camera tracks, pans and cranes as the organ music surges. There is the loving depiction of country crafts, which picks out local faces, felled timber and age-old instruments. There is, in particular, the wonderfully shot sequence of a battle between two sets of village boys; one army, on a boat, is tracked along the river bank by the camera and attacked by its rivals in a sequence of staccato cutting and bold close-ups. The leaders of the armies are recruited by Bob to help search for evidence on the 'Glue Man', but the sequence as it stands exists to celebrate boyish high spirits in the pristine heart of the countryside.[9] The cumulative effect of such sequences wholly justifies the decision of Prudence Honeywood, who tells Alison that the only man who ever asked her to marry him wanted to take her away from this to live in the town and she refused him.

The film is constructed like a symphony, orchestrating the themes of the three pilgrims, which merge and mingle with a central and dominant theme (Colpeper and his message) until all blend triumphantly at the climax, with the converging of the characters on the Cathedral, cut to the music. Powell later observed:

> At the time nobody thought that *A Canterbury Tale* worked, but I must say that it contained some of my favourite sequences . . . you take the last three reels of the film when all three pilgrims converge on Canterbury. I thought that had a most wonderful movement.[10]

Powell is, of course, powerfully assisted by Pressburger's script, by Erwin Hillier's camerawork, which was universally praised, and by a strong cast. There was considerable critical praise for Sergeant John Sweet, an American soldier who had previously acted on stage in the all-soldier cast of a production of Maxwell Anderson's *The Eve of St*

Mark, put on in London by the Special Service Division of the US War Department. He was not a professional actor and was chosen, according to the film's press book, because he had 'all the attributes of the ordinary young man'.[11] But the film is dominated and held together by the soft-spoken, enigmatic Eric Portman, whose performance as the Nazi submarine commander in Powell's and Pressburger's *49th Parallel* had made him a major star and who was to carve out a career unique in British films by playing a succession of haunted murderers, quirky maniacs and demented millionaires. There was something cold, sinister but compelling about his personality, something out of the ordinary, and Powell utilized that quality here to imbue Colpeper, the self-confessed missionary, with an unearthly yet serene omniscience.

In celebrating the countryside as the source of national strength, Powell was in the mainstream British tradition, which has been so brilliantly expounded (indeed, indicted) by Martin Wiener and which is encapsulated in the words of the popular song of World War II:

> There'll always be an England while there's a country lane
> Wherever there's a cottage small beside a field of grain.

Wiener sees in the glorification of the countryside and all things rural a deliberate rejection of the urban and industrial reality of Britain by a non-industrial, non-innovative and anti-materialist patrician culture. Endorsed by a gentrified bourgeoisie, this attitude led to what Wiener calls 'the cultural containment of industrial capitalism', a process which contributed powerfully to Britain's industrial decline.[12]

The cultural conservatism of the dominant elite determined the prevalent image of England and Englishness. Donald Horne, seeking to understand what made England tick, proposed two rival metaphors for Englishness – the Northern, which was pragmatic, empirical, calculating, Puritan, bourgeois, enterprising, adventurous, scientific, serious and struggle-oriented, and the Southern, romantic, illogical, muddled, lucky, Anglican, aristocratic, traditional and frivolous.[13] Whereas the Northern was urban and industrial, the Southern prevailed because it was rural, because it was able to accommodate the apparently irreconcilable ideals of the Romantic Right (country house, country church, squire, parson and deferential society) and the Romantic Left (folk society, the village, rural crafts and the honest peasantry). *A Canterbury Tale,* deliberately designed as a 'crusade against materialism', provides a perfect visual expression of all these elements.

The myth of England as essentially rural and essentially unchanging appealed across party lines to both conservatives and socialists. Rudyard Kipling turned in later life from celebrating the robust spirit of Empire to hymning the beauties of rural life in Sussex *(Puck of Pook's Hill,* 'Our England is a Garden', etc.), and Sir Henry Newbolt wrote of the magical qualities of the English landscape in *The Old Country*.[14] The distaste for modern industrial society that lay behind such Arcadian exercises was summed up by another right-wing writer, Sir Arthur Bryant, who in a series of talks entitled *The National Character,* first delivered on the wireless and later published in book form, declared:

> The most important thing about our English civilization is that it grew in the country and has only comparatively lately been transported to the town. Half our present troubles can, I believe, be traced to this. Our industrial discontent, the restless, dissatisfied state of our family life, the discomfort, ugliness and overcrowding of our towns, in part spring from the fact that every Englishman is so certain that the only lasting Utopia for him is a rose garden and a cottage in the country that he can never settle down seriously to make himself comfortable in a town. . . . Most of us today are town dwellers, yet there are very few of us whose great-great-great-grandparents were not country folk, and, even if we have no idea who they were or from what shire they hailed, our subconscious selves hark back to their instincts and ways of life. We are shut off from them as it were by a tunnel of two or three generations – lost in the darkness of the Industrial Revolution – but beyond is the sunlight of the green fields from which we came.[15]

The same feeling animated socialists like William Morris and Robert Blatchford, who propounded the potent myth of a timeless and idealized medieval village and agricultural society. Blatchford's *Merrie England* (1894) was described by G. D. H. Cole as 'the most effective piece of popular socialist propaganda ever written'.[16]

After World War I, perhaps as a result of it, this rural nostalgia intensified. There were novels about the countryside, books about the English heritage and the English character stressing the rural myth. As Sir Denis Brogan wrote in 1943, in a book seeking to explain England to the Americans:

Most people in England live in large industrial towns; but they are not written about. Millions live in the great urban aggregate that is called London without seeing Piccadilly Circus or St Paul's once a month. Mr Priestley has done a good deal to restore the balance, but no one has done what Arnold Bennett did – given a view of English life outside London and the country that was accepted as a natural literary phenomenon. We have gloomy stories of the depressed area; we have innumerable detective stories. But *Love on the Dole* and *Murder in the Home Counties* do not cover all or nearly all of English life. The English people show that they know this by reading American fiction with avidity, just as American people show their good judgement in preferring their own more lively, human and truthful fiction to the English standard brands. And the great sin of English fiction, English movies, English plays, English public relations in general, is the refusal to admit that the Englishman is a townsman.[17]

This 'sin' was apparent even in a comic novel like A. G. MacDonell's *England, their England,* which had Scot Donald Cameron searching for the meaning of England. He discovers at the end, when he has a mystical vision of a sort of pilgrimage of poets, all wreathed in good humour, as he lies on a perfect summer day in the grass near Winchester Cathedral, that it is to be found in the mingling of the pastoral and the poetic. The vision fades:

And there was no longer any trace of the passing of that absurd host of kindly, laughter-loving warrior poets but only what they have left behind them – the muted voices of grazing sheep, and the merry click of bat upon ball, and the peaceful green fields of England, and the water meads and the bells of the cathedral.[18]

It is hard to believe that we are not looking here at the seeds of the idea that gave rise to *A Canterbury Tale.*

This vision was shared by the man who epitomized England, if anyone did, in the inter-war years – Stanley Baldwin, three times Prime Minister and the leading figure in the National Government until his retirement in 1937. He consciously projected himself as a country squire. In a celebrated speech he declared:

To me England is the country and the country is England. . . . The sounds of England, the tinkle of the hammer on the anvil in the

country smithy, the corncrake on a dewy morning, the sound
of the scythe against the whetstone, and the sight of a plough
team coming over the brow of a hill, the sight that has been
seen in England since England was a land, and may be seen in
England long after the Empire has perished and every works
has ceased to function, for centuries the one eternal sight of
England.[19]

It is against this background and that of Horne's Southern metaphor
that it is possible to understand the depiction of 'why we fight' in the
handful of films that tackle the question. The England we fight for in
A Canterbury Tale and in its analogues *The Tawny Pipit* (1944) and *The
Demi-Paradise* (1943) is essentially rural, timeless and hierarchical. It
makes an interesting contrast with the 'how we fight' films, which were
at pains to highlight the social change involved in the lowering of class
barriers and often featured townsmen. But the Englishman as urban
man was really celebrated only in the films of Humphrey Jennings, who
provides an interesting comparison with Powell and Pressburger.
Jennings, Suffolk-born, Cambridge-educated, was a left-winger,
influential in Mass Observation, steeped in Shakespeare, Marlowe,
Milton and Blake. His documentaries display the same lambent
photography, mystical quality and feel for landscape as do Powell's
feature films. But for him the recurrent image is St Paul's Cathedral, the
church of the metropolis, and not Canterbury Cathedral, the church of
the older, rural England. In films like *Spare Time, London Can Take It,
Listen to Britain, Fires Were Started* and *Family Portrait* Jennings showed
himself able to come to terms with, to explore and to celebrate the
urban England created by the industrial revolution, an event most other
film-makers preferred to ignore.

The intention of *A Canterbury Tale* was made quite clear by the film's
press book:

> *A Canterbury Tale* is a new story about Britain, her unchanging
> beauty and traditions, and of the Old Pilgrims and the New. As
> the last scene of the picture fades away, to those who see it and
> are British there will come a feeling – just for a moment – of
> wishing to be silent, as the thoughts flash through one's mind:
> 'These things 1 have just seen and heard are all my parents taught
> me. That is Britain, that is me.'[20]

But the reaction of the critics was on the whole one of puzzlement. Richard Winnington in the *News Chronicle* expressed the prevalent view of the film:

> Because they represent the only consistent unification of script, production and direction in British films, Michael Powell and Emeric Pressburger arouse expectancy and generally arrive at something different and individual. Their besetting weakness – lack of coherent purpose in their stories – is more pronounced than ever in this their latest production. . . . Through the fog of a confused and at times vaguely unpleasant story can be seen a steady if dim flicker of what I think was the main idea of Powell and Pressburger – to endow an accidental wartime excursion to Canterbury with the hushed, bated magic of the Pilgrim's Way, to link in mystic suggestion the past and the present. And in an odd, untidy sort of way they infuse a lyric feeling into the pastoral progression of their film. The quality of poetry is not entirely due to the first-rate and refreshing photographic compositions of the Kentish countryside, or the 'village pageant' sequences of Chaucer's pilgrims, or the reading of part of his prologue with a modern bit added, or, as I have suggested, to the story'. It is something to do with Messrs Powell and Pressburger.[21]

The same tone of dissatisfaction ran through the verdicts of the other critics, who praised the photography and the acting, the celebration of the Kent countryside and the visual beauty of the film. But for the most part they found themselves unable to come to grips with the mysticism or the psychology of Colpeper. The *Daily Telegraph* said:

> Michael Powell and Emeric Pressburger have presented the English scene with such artistry and charm, such a wealth of fresh and amusing incident, that if the story had been halfway tolerable this would have been a masterpiece. It isn't and it's not. The story is silly beyond belief. . . . If you can ignore this nonsense, you will enjoy the film for its beauty, for many shrewd and witty touches, and some excellent acting by Sgt John Sweet (US Army), Sheila Sim, Dennis Price and Eric Portman.[22]

The *Manchester Guardian* could not resist the temptation to describe the plot of the film as a 'sticky mess' but added:

Luckily one can ignore the untidiness and improbabilities and enjoy wholeheartedly the sheer pictorial beauty of Canterbury and the Pilgrim's Way.[23]

The *Sunday Times* called it:

an elaborate, beautiful and often witty piece of muddle. The story is half highminded fantasy, half schoolboy thriller.... The exterior work is enchanting and the pictorial beauty of the sequences in Canterbury Cathedral seem to me beyond praise.[24]

C. A. Lejeune in the *Observer* pronounced the final word:

A Canterbury Tale is a remarkable film, in which Michael Powell, the writer, has given Michael Powell, the director, a pretty shabby story and the second Powell has almost managed to get away with it. *A Canterbury Tale* is about a Kentish JP who believes so deeply in the study of his native soil that he pours glue on girls' heads in the black-out lest they seduce the local soldiery from his archaeological lectures. That's the theme, and to my mind, nothing will make it either a sensible or pleasant one. This fellow may be a mystagogue with the love of England in his blood, but he is plainly a crackpot of a rather unpleasant type, with bees in the bonnet and blue-bottles in the belfry. Only a psychiatrist, I imagine, would be deeply interested in his behaviour. And yet, on this horrid foundation, director Powell has built up a film that is in parts moving and even dignified. A man of Kent himself, he has taken his cameras exulting in the green spring of Kent on a sunny April morning. His Canterbury is a place loved and understood; his dialogue often simple and true. His three young people.... who are all in some way influenced by the mystagogue's enthusiasm, have for the most part an unaffected charm, and do suggest pilgrims undergoing an emotional experience.... The piece is an odd example, I should say, of a film that might have reached great heights but hasn't.[25]

As so often, Powell and Pressburger were ahead of their time. They started with the handicap that mysticism is always silly to the unmystical. But beyond that their adoption of a narrative form that was discursive rather than strictly linear and their use of a 'kinky' hero, neither of which would seem remarkable to today's film-makers or cinema-goers, alienated and mystified critics used to more straightforward and traditional fare. Audiences seem to have responded in the same way, for the film was not a success at the box office. In an attempt to retrieve something for an American release, Powell was prevailed upon to cut it and shoot additional sequences for the US market. It was reduced from 124 minutes to 95, and Powell added a framing story, involving Raymond Massey and Kim Hunter, in which Sergeant Sweet tells the story to his wife in New York. It was released in America in 1949 but without success. A British reissue of the cut version in 1948 also failed. Powell's original was reconstructed by the British Film Institute in 1977 and has won increasing admiration.

How far was *A Canterbury Tale* a reflection of what people really were fighting for, and how far was it a middle-class cultural myth? When he toured England in 1933 J. B. Priestley discovered three Englands. The second was:

> the nineteenth-century England, the industrial England of coal, iron, steel, cotton, wool, railways; of thousands of rows of little houses all alike . . . a cynically devastated countryside, sooty dismal little towns, and still sootier grim fortress-like cities.

This was the England of the Midlands and the North and of Horne's Northern metaphor. The third was:

> the new post-war England, belonging far more to the age itself than this particular island. . . . This is the England of arterial and by-pass roads, of filling stations and factories that look like exhibition buildings, of giant cinemas and dance-halls and cafés, bungalows with tiny garages, cocktail bars, Woolworths, motor-coaches, wireless, biking, factory girls looking like actresses, greyhound racing and dirt tracks, swimming pools, and everything given away for cigarette coupons. . . . It is, of course, essentially democratic. After a social revolution, there would, with luck, be more and not less of it. . . . It is a large-scale, mass-production job, with cut prices. You could almost accept Woolworths as its symbol. Its cheapness is both its strength and weakness. It is its strength because, being cheap, it is accessible; it nearly achieves the famous equality of opportunity.

Significantly, Powell and Pressburger turned their backs on these two images in favour of Priestley's first England:

> Old England, the country of the cathedrals and minsters, and manor houses and inns, of Parson and Squire; guide-book and

quaint highways and byways England. . . . We all know this England, which at its best cannot be improved upon in this world. That is, as a country to lounge about in; for a tourist who can afford to pay a fairly stiff price for a poorish dinner, an inconvenient bedroom and lukewarm water in a small brass jug. . . . It has long ceased to earn its own living. . . . There are some people who believe that in some mysterious way we can return to this Old England; though nothing is said about killing off nine-tenths of our present population, which would have to be the first step. The same people might consider competing in a race at Brooklands with a horse and trap. The chances are about the same.[26]

It was this same Priestley who expressed succinctly the war aims of the majority in one of his wartime broadcasts. While for Churchill the aim was victory and, beyond victory, the vague generalized belief that the world would move forward into 'broad, sunlit uplands', for Priestley it was what came after the war that was vitally important. We were fighting, he said, 'not so that we can go back to anything. There's nothing that really worked that we can go back to.' So our aim must be 'new and better homes – real homes – a decent chance at last – new life'.[27]

This was what people fought for, and this was what, in the end, they voted for. As A. J. P. Taylor wrote of the 1945 election:

The electors cheered Churchill and voted against him. They displayed no interest in foreign affairs or imperial might. They cared only for their own future: first housing and then full employment and social security. Here Labour offered a convincing programme. The Conservatives, though offering much the same, managed to give the impression that they did not believe in it.[28]

The result was 393 Labour MPs returned to 213 Conservatives and a reforming government under Clement Attlee which set out to introduce those tangible benefits for which we had fought. The time for mysticism was past.

Notes

1. The memorandum is reproduced in Ian Christie (ed.), *Powell, Pressburger and Others,* London, 1978, pp. 121–4.

2. On the British cinema at war, see in particular Roger Manvell, *Films and the Second World War,* London, 1974, and Charles Barr, *Ealing Studios,* London, 1977.

3. Jeffrey Richards, 'Speaking for England', *Listener*, 14 January 1982, pp. 9–11.

4. C. A. Lejeune, *Chestnuts in her Lap*, London, 1947, p. 95.

5. On Powell and Pressburger, see in particular Christie, *Powell, Pressburger and Others;* John Russell Taylor, 'Michael Powell: Myths and Supermen', *Sight and Sound*, 47, autumn 1978, pp. 226–9; Douglas McVay, 'Cinema of Enchantment: the Films of Michael Powell', *Films and Filming*, 327, December 1981, pp. 14–19; Douglas McVay, 'Michael Powell: Three Neglected Films', *Films and Filming*, 328, January 1982, pp. 18–25.

6. Michael Powell, interview with Gavin Millar on BBC2's *Arena*, transmitted on 17 November 1981. Cf. also Powell's comments in Christie, *Powell, Pressburger and Others*, p. 34; and David Badder, 'Powell and Pressburger: the War Years', *Sight and Sound*, 48, Winter 1978, p. 11.

7. Christie, *Powell, Pressburger and Others*, p. 34.

8. The Anglo-American dimension of the film was introduced deliberately and Powell and Pressburger returned to it in *A Matter of Life and Death* (1946); see Badder, 'Powell and Pressburger: The War Years', p. 11. *A Canterbury Tale* thus also forms one of that group of films that deliberately sought to promote understanding between Britain and America – cf. *Journey Together* (1945) and *The Way to the Stars* (1945).

9. Seeing the film again after its reconstruction by the BFI, Powell remarked: 'It was a failure and hasn't been seen again until recently. Now it looks a wonderful film, I think. I was really thrilled by it. It's got all the things I knew so well. I was born and brought up in and around Canterbury and there's a lot of a little boy growing up in the film. Of course, what I love is this semi-mystical feeling that you get . . . anybody who has lived near Canterbury's old stones must have this feeling.' Badder, 'Powell and Pressburger: the War Years', p. 11.

10. Christie, *Powell Pressburger and Others*, p. 33.

11. *A Canterbury Tale* press book, BFI microfiche. The *Manchester Guardian* (12 May 1944) thought Sweet had 'a casual attractiveness which predicts Hollywood for him'; in fact, he made no more films.

12. Martin Wiener, *English Culture and the Decline of the Industrial Spirit 1850–1980*, Cambridge, 1981.

13. Donald Horne, *God is an Englishman*, Harmondsworth, 1969, pp. 22–3.

14. Russell Taylor, 'Michael Powell: Myths and Supermen', p. 227, reveals that *Puck of Pook's Hill* is one of Powell's favourite books.

15. Sir Arthur Bryant, *The National Character*, London, 1934, pp. 22–3.

16. Wiener, *English Culture*, p. 119.

17. D. W. Brogan, *The English People*, London, 1943, pp. 234–5.

18. A. G. MacDonell, *England, Their England*, London, 1941 (reprint), p. 293.

19. Stanley Baldwin, *On England*, London, 1926, p. 7.

20. *A Canterbury Tale* press book, BFI microfiche.

21. Richard Winnington, *Drawn and Quartered*, London, n.d., p. 22.

22. *Daily Telegraph*, 18 April 1944.

23. *Manchester Guardian*, 16 August 1944.

24. *Sunday Times*, 15 April 1944.

25. Lejeune, *Chestnuts in her Lap*, p. 121.

26. J. B. Priestley, *English Journey*, London, 1976 (reprint), pp. 397–9.

27. J. B. Priestley, *All England Listened*, New York, 1967, pp. 54–8.

28. A. J. P. Taylor, *English History 1914–45*, Harmondsworth, 1976, pp. 722.

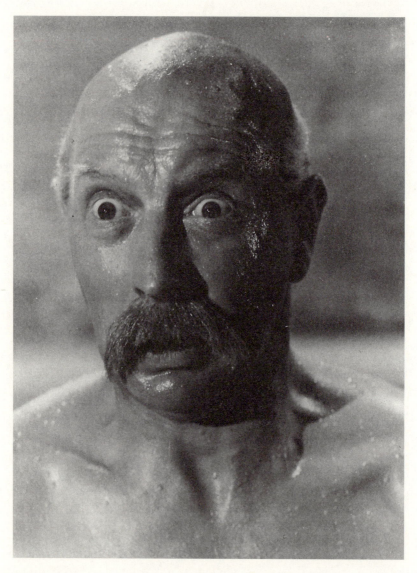

The Life and Death of Colonel Blimp (1943)

5

What a Difference a War Makes
The Life and Death of Colonel Blimp

The original screenplay for the film of *Colonel Blimp* was written by Emeric Pressburger early in 1942.[1] In the first instance it was entitled simply *The Life and Death of Sugar Candy*, 'Sugar Candy' being the nickname of Clive Candy, the leading character in the story. The writer-producer-director team of Michael Powell and Emeric Pressburger planned to shoot the film between July and September of 1942. It was at this stage that they hit upon the idea of approaching the cartoonist David Low to see if they could use his figure of Colonel Blimp as the title and inspiration for their film. 'The thought of dramatizing the life of Colonel Blimp appealed enormously,' Powell records, 'because at that time Blimp was a household word.'[2] And their purpose was to show cinematically that 'Colonel Blimp was the symbol of British procrastination and British regard for tradition and all the things which we knew and which were losing the war.'[3]

For his part Low stipulated only that Powell and Pressburger take full responsibility for the production and, most of all, that Blimp be proved a fool in the end.[4] Since this was also what Powell and Pressburger wished to show, agreement was reached, and the title of the film was changed after production had begun. In one very obvious respect, therefore, the film was unlikely to say anything new. After all, the Blimp cartoons had been in existence since 20 April 1934, and the figure of Blimp had consistently been shown to be a fool in the pages of the *Evening Standard,* where he was regularly to be found. But in the changed circumstances of a Britain experiencing the turmoil of total war the prospect of a film that would make obvious allusions to the figure of Colonel Blimp assumed special significance in the eyes of certain members of the Government of the day. In fact, the cartoon of Blimp disappeared with the *Evening Standard* edition of 27 February 1942 (and did not reappear until over a year later, on 25 June 1943).[5] But if Blimp himself was absent temporarily, accusations of 'Blimpery' remained and indeed reached a peak between the spring and autumn of 1942, when the war was going particularly badly for Britain and when Powell and Pressburger embarked upon and completed the production of their film. 'The months from February to November 1942 were politically the most disturbed time of the war', A. J. P. Taylor has remarked.[6] And this, above all, helps to explain the nature of the official reaction to the film of *The Life and Death of Colonel Blimp* and why the film came to be construed as 'negative propaganda'.[7]

By the beginning of February 1942 the state of public morale was in decline, and it was further depressed by events that occurred in the first weeks of the month. On 13 February three German warships, the *Scharnhorst,* the *Gneisenau* and the *Prinz Eugen,* arrived in Germany from Brest, having successfully evaded the attention of the Royal Navy and the RAF and having navigated the English Channel. Then on the 15 February General Perceval and 60,000 British troops surrendered at Singapore. *The Times* said of the former event that 'Nothing more mortifying to the pride of sea-power has happened in home waters since the seventeenth century.'[8] Many thought the latter to be 'the greatest capitulation in British history.'[9] The Home Intelligence Weekly Report, prepared by a department of Brendan Bracken's Ministry of Information and commenting upon public reactions, declared the week of 16–23 February 1942 to be 'the blackest week since Dunkirk'.[10]

Other, seemingly lesser, events also gave cause for concern in that week. On 23 February, for example, Mr F. W. Pethick-Lawrence, the Labour MP for East Edinburgh, spoke about the war effort in a Commons debate. He opened his speech with the following comments:

> We are all familiar with the personality that the foremost cartoonist of our day has created of 'Colonel Blimp'. I suggest that what . . . critics desire to impress on the Government – and I am in full sympathy with them – is that if the Government are to carry the

country with them in their war effort, they must set about abolishing 'Blimpery' in all fields of life. What is the essence of 'Blimpery'? It has, no doubt, two main characteristics. In the first place, there is the refusal to entertain new ideas, and in the second place, the determination to keep the bottom dog permanently in his place.'[11]

Thereafter Pethick-Lawrence went on to cite certain instances in which he felt such 'Blimpery' might be seen at its worse: in the operations of the Colonial Office, where 'the administration of the Colonies was a scandal' and had been so for several years, as many people had pointed out; over India; and in the case of the coal mines. Despite income tax and the rationing of food, petrol and other articles, he argued, there was still an immense amount of 'luxury expenditure and wasteful self-indulgence'. All sorts of expensive foods could be bought and consumed by persons 'whose wealth remains intact'. And on that issue he maintained:

Everyone who is in touch with the workers knows how detrimental it is to the vigour of the war effort when they see what is happening among a certain class of people. I say, without any doubt, that 'Blimpery' is still rampant in certain circles, and it is up to the Ministers concerned to put a stop to it.

However, he reserved his most vigorous onslaught for criticism of the Army. There, to begin with, he asserted that:

The traditional view in the Army of the common soldier is that he is just a common soldier and as such can be equally well employed upon any task which needs to be done at the moment. It may be sweeping floors or handing round Brussel sprouts in the officers mess.

He did not doubt that there were 'wise heads' in the War Office or that there were 'enlightened' commanding officers who knew better, had much better judgement and responded more aptly to the needs of the moment. But 'Blimpery' existed all the same. He quoted damaging passages from a manpower survey prepared by Beveridge for the Ministry of Labour that condemned the Army for its failure to use men with engineering skill according to their worth and recommended that the services generally needed to scrutinize the use of all the manpower available and not just that of skilled men.

Subsequently Pethick-Lawrence cited examples provided by his own constituents to argue that men from the ranks were prevented, as often as not, from proving their worth as officer material. While there was a genuine desire to give commissions to competent men 'who start from humble positions in life', nevertheless in many cases this purpose was frustrated by 'purely financial considerations'. With respect to clothes alone the initial cost of obtaining a commission greatly exceeded the Government allowance for the same, and a man could thus incur debts directly he took a commission. The recurring expenses of keeping up with 'convention and tradition' added to the burden and meant that such a man had 'the greatest difficulty in providing for himself and his family at home'. In all it resulted in the reluctance of many men to take up a commission because they would be considerably worse off than they were by staying in the ranks.

It was a pretty bleak picture that Pethick-Lawrence painted, though not without foundation. Finally, he called upon the new Secretary of State for War to be rid of such 'Blimpery'. Indeed, he reserved some ironic comments for the man who had taken up that position only on 22 February, the day before the debate. Pethick-Lawrence knew him well, believed him to be 'a forcible and fearless man' who would cut through red tape, if anyone would, and possessed 'great courage'. Pethick-Lawrence hoped that he would 'prove equal to the task of getting rid of "Blimpery" wherever it manifests itself in the Army', though he also clearly doubted the wisdom of the appointment. The man in question was Sir James Grigg, who would indeed have a lot to say on the matter of 'Blimpery' and the Army.

However, on the day of the debate in the Commons it was Stafford Cripps, in his first speech as Lord Privy Seal and Leader of the House, who rose to reply to Pethick-Lawrence. He asked the House to wait and see, promised that things would be done and invited one and all to 'the funeral of that person whom I hope we may now describe as the late and not lamented Colonel Blimp'.

Some measures were taken to deal with the matters that Pethick-Lawrence had mentioned. Cripps himself tried, albeit unsuccessfully, to overcome the constitutional deadlock in India. And in March 1942 he announced a new round of cuts in civilian consumption that were greeted as 'real steps towards total war', though Home Intelligence also reported that many people felt that they did not go far enough in meeting the popular demand for 'equality of sacrifice'.[12]

Furthermore, the charge of 'Blimpery' continued unabated and, if anything, gained momentum despite Cripps's burial of the Colonel and his subsequent disappearance from the *Evening Standard*. By the end of March Home Intelligence, once again, pointed out that its regional summaries indicated a distinct swing in public opinion towards what might loosely be called the 'left'. This current of feeling among the population was not necessarily of a political character, nor indeed was it necessarily channelled along Labour Party or socialist lines. But it was 'directed against the Conservative Party' in so far as this represented 'the so-called "Men of Munich", "the old gang", "Colonel Blimp", and similar die-hard types'. It was, first of all, a feeling of revulsion against 'vested interests', 'privilege' and the like, which were also blamed for 'ills of production'; secondly, it amounted to a general agreement that 'things are going to be different after the war.'[13]

With such sentiments much in evidence, not least among the reports produced by one of its own departments, it is perhaps not surprising that the Ministry of Information was not particularly enchanted when Powell and Pressburger came along with a script which overtly sought to capitalize on the name of Colonel Blimp. Blimp was a household word for all the wrong reasons. Bracken and Jack Beddington, Director of the Ministry of Information's Films Division, did not look kindly upon the idea.[14] The script was read and thought 'defeatist'. Laurence Olivier was denied release from the Fleet Air Arm to play the part of Blimp, and official help, by way of the provision of arms, trucks, uniforms and so on, was out of the question. Not that this deterred Powell and Pressburger from proceeding with production of the film: Roger Livesey was engaged for Blimp and various devious means were employed to overcome the other obstacles.

In truth, though, the production did not merit the rough treatment it received at the hands of the Ministry of Information. As the testimony of the script and subsequent film bear witness, *The Life and Death of Colonel Blimp* was not unduly critical, and it removed most, if not all, of the political sting in the tail of Low's original cartoon creation. If anything, the filmic rendition of Colonel Blimp singled the character out as being greatly at odds with the times – one of Low's intentions, of course – but hardly as a representative of any type to be found in the British Army by the advent of World War II.

The script makes that abundantly clear and shows, from the outset, the best of intentions.[15] An opening page declares:

> This film is dedicated to the New Army of Britain, to the new spirit in warfare, to the new toughness in battle, and to the men and women who know what they are fighting for and are fighting this war to win it.

Subsequently, the script devotes considerable care and attention to detail – a feature which is beautifully evident throughout – in order to ensure that the characteristics of Clive Candy (Blimp) are precisely delineated. He is given a credible pedigree, for example, which doubtless owed much to the presence of the military adviser on the film, Lieutenant-General Sir W. Douglas Brownrigg, KCB, DSO. It read:

> Clive ('Sugar') Candy, VC, CB, DSO. Late Wessex Light Infantry; served South African War 1899–1902; European War 1914–1918; Major-General, retired pay, 1935; re-employed Base Sub-Area Commandant in France, 1939; retired pay, 1940; Zone Commander Home Guard, 1940–1942.

And in one of the most revealing passages, relating to Candy's position by 1942, the script notes (my emphasis):

> A few words are necessary here to explain Clive's position. He was 26 or thereabouts in 1902, so he would have been over the top age for a major-general in 1939 and far over in 1941. It is essential to retain this basic age of Clive in order to portray him as the kind of old fellow who becomes a Blimp. *But it is equally important not to give the impression that our Armies were commanded in 1939 by men who were old, as well* as 'not up to it'. In fact this was not the case and our generals' ages ranged from 47 to 58. The solution is: Clive was retired in 1935. At the outbreak of war he was one of the first to seek employment and was given a Base Sub-Area to command (probably a coastal town such as Boulogne or Entretat). This would be extremely likely and would fit well into the story. After the collapse and evacuation he would be for a few weeks still on full pay, still active, waiting for another job. But he doesn't get it. He is once more on the retired list and, being as keen as mustard, he is very bitter at first.[16]

Powell's and Pressburger's intentions were obvious. Clive Candy was to be portrayed as Blimp and all he symbolized, but he was not meant to represent the men who commanded Britain's 'New Army', and its character was to remain unimpugned.

How far though were these ambitions realized in the film?

Britain's 'New Army' is personified by Lieutenant 'Spud' Wilson (James McKechnie) and his men. From the start of the film, set in September 1942, it is made clear that he is thoroughly equipped to wage 'total war', and he has prepared his men accordingly. As an Army motorcyclist arrives at their encampment, bringing details of a Home Guard exercise that they are to join, the motorcyclist is knocked to the ground as a result of a precautionary ambush laid by Spud's men. 'What's the ruddy idea?' the motorcyclist demands. 'Total war, isn't it?' Spud's men instinctively reply. Spud has instilled the need for vigilance and alertness, even in the midst of mock manoeuvres. Subsequently Spud himself demonstrates the same qualities and harps upon the theme of the exigencies of total war.

He decides to jump the gun on the Home Guard exercise. 'War' starts at midnight, but he intends to 'make it like the real thing'. The 'biggest toughs' from the platoon are to be recruited for his own exercise: 'We attack before war is declared. . . . Yes, like Pearl Harbor.' He sets off to capture the 'enemy' leaders, including Clive Candy (Roger Livesey), before the exercise proper has swung into motion. He does so, after he has found them lounging in the Turkish baths of the Royal Bathers' Club, Piccadilly (the entrance of which is appropriately bedecked with propaganda posters from the period, including the one with the notorious slogan 'Your courage, your cheerfulness, your resolution, will bring us victory').

There Spud confronts Candy, and the might which Spud urges in taking control of the club ('All right, boys, this is it. Brute force and ruddy ignorance') is pitted in heated argument against the right of Candy's protests ('But war starts at midnight'). Candy demands to know what authority Spud has for making his pre-emptive strike. Spud curtly replies: 'These guns and these men.' Candy accuses Spud and his men of behaving like a band of 'awful militia gangsters' and insists once again that 'War starts at midnight'. 'You say war starts at midnight,' Spud retorts, but 'How do you know the enemy says so as well?' War is not run according to 'National Sporting Club rules', Spud comments, before attempting to excuse his actions on the grounds that 'In forty years' time, at least I shall be able to say I was a fellow of enterprise.' In a fit of anger at such 'impudence', Candy struggles with Spud. They fall into the baths, and with a neat visual flourish the film goes back in time to Candy's own impetuous youth and begins to recount the highlights of his life story from that point onwards.

It is a classic confrontation of the old and the new, but the contemporary allusions are clear. Candy is Blimp; furthermore, he is situated in Blimp's best-known setting of a Turkish bath, and he is made up to look exactly like the cartoon figure. Spud represents the men who command the 'New Army'.

Spud, however, at this early point in the film, is always in danger of being painted as the villain of the piece. His apparent philosophy of 'Might is right', his peremptory commands, his precipitate actions, his harsh demeanour and the accusations levelled against him by Candy all hint of Nazi methods and thuggery. Indeed, in a reprise of the opening scenes later in the film he threatens to teach Candy 'Total war . . . Nazi methods, you know'. But he is soon redeemed. In their punctilious fashion Powell and Pressburger reveal his saving graces. He is an able leader and has a close rapport with his men. In fact, he has come up through the ranks (as his girlfriend makes clear) and speedily at that, doubtless as a result of his skills. One moment he is 'a private in training', the next he is 'getting a commission' (obviously, he suffers none of the setbacks that Pethick-Lawrence outlined in Parliament). He has a warm relationship with his girlfriend, 'Johnny' Cannon (Deborah Kerr), and she, furthermore, is Candy's MTC driver. The closeness of this relationship proves him fallible, since he reveals to her, in advance, his plans to capture Candy, whom she tries to warn of the danger. But it also works in Spud's favour, for Johnny helps to awaken Candy to Spud's attributes. Because of Candy's intervention, no charges are brought against Spud for ruining the Home Guard exercise, and by the end of the film Candy and Johnny stand together, proudly watching 'Spud with his men, marching into London'. In the final analysis Powell and Pressburger paint a sympathetic portrait of Lieutenant Spud Wilson, 2nd Battalion, the Loamshires – not surprisingly, in view of the dedication in their script.

Most of their sympathy is reserved, however, for the figure of Clive Candy. Gone is the opprobrium which infused Low's depiction of Blimp. Candy is Blimp, certainly, but Powell and Pressburger's Blimp is not scorned nor disdained. He is a more amiable, lovable and generally understandable character. He is proved a fool, to be sure, and out of touch with the immense changes going on around him, but those are his worst sins. He is quite harmless, and Powell and Pressburger show, particularly in the flashback scenes, that he is meant to be construed as a bit of an outsider and loner throughout.

On returning from the Boer War, for instance, where he has won the VC, he sets out for Germany to correct anti-British propaganda. British military intelligence advises him not to go and would rather have a conversation about Arthur Conan Doyle's latest Sherlock Holmes adventure, *The Hound of the Baskervilles,* in the *Strand* magazine. But Candy determines to go on a whim, and merely because his friend's niece's governess's sister wrote suggesting he might be of help. Once in Germany he has second thoughts, and on meeting the lady in question, Edith Hunter (Deborah Kerr), he counsels her in turn to observe good manners in a foreign country. Referring to the war from which he has recently returned, she replies: 'Good manners cost us 6,000 men killed and 20,000 wounded and two years of war, when with a little common sense and bad manners there would have been no war at all.'[17] Whereupon Candy is goaded into action and inadvertently compelled to defend himself in a duel. His opponent is an Uhlan officer, Theo Kretschmar-Schuldorff (Anton Walbrook). Both men are averse to duelling but proceed to inflict minor wounds upon each other and land up in the same nursing home. Clive, of course, befriends Theo, who woos and wins Edith. Clive realizes what Edith means to him only after she has set upon becoming Theo's wife.

By the time of World War I Clive and Theo are engaged in mortal combat. Clive's increasingly outdated principles are coming to the fore. 'We don't use the same methods [as the Germans]', he asserts, but behind his back and without his knowledge a South African working for Candy and the British Army does. He extracts from a group of captured German soldiers the information that Clive wants. When the war is won Clive sees the victory as a vindication of his belief that 'Right is right after all . . . clean fighting, honest soldiering have won.' Then he seeks out his friend Theo, now a prisoner of war in an English camp, who rebuffs the offer of renewed friendship. Before embarking upon the return trip to a defeated and desolate Germany, however, he apologizes and enjoys dinner with Clive and some of his now eminent colleagues. Once more, Clive proves different. He leads most of them in declaring his belief that 'The reconstruction of Germany is essential to the peace of Europe' and affirms: 'We want to be friends.' But Theo's former camp commandant, also a guest, sits quietly at the end of the table and declines to join in with the spirit of enforced *bonhomie*.

He knows better. So does Theo. On returning to his fellow officer prisoners, Theo tells of his experience: 'They are children, boys playing cricket. They win the shirts off your backs and want to give it back.' 'This childlike stupidity is a raft for us in a sea of despair,' he decides finally. 'We'll soon have Germany on her feet again.'

In the event, by 2 November 1939 Theo is back in England as a refugee from Hitler's Germany. His wife has died; his two boys have become 'good Nazis'; and Theo is being scrutinized under the Aliens' Act by a man who assures him, 'This time we mean business.' He is allowed to stay but not to practise his skills, even in Britain's cause. Circumstances dictate that he is no longer needed in quite the same way as before. By contrast, Clive is back on the active list – but not for long. He is soon dealt a double bow, which curtails his potential contribution as well. Both become outsiders.

The radio talk that Clive is destined to deliver on 16 June 1940, in the *Postscript* series, is dropped at the last moment and J. B. Priestley does one instead.[18] And Clive is put on the retired list once again – 'axed . . . they don't need me any more.' He is dumbfounded. But his friend Theo, wiser and more experienced, explains the reasons. He reads Clive's talk on the topic 'Dunkirk – Before and After', which was intended as a contribution to a discussion on 'the cause of the retreat and its aspects for the future'. It is clearly defeatist.

'You commented on Nazi methods, foul fighting, bombing refugees and so on,' Theo says, 'by saying that you despised them and that you'd sooner accept defeat than victory if it could only be won by these methods.' 'So I would,' replies Clive. But Theo persists: 'You've been educated to be a gentleman and a sportsman. But this is not a gentleman's war. This time you're fighting for your existence against the most devilish idea ever created by the human brain, Nazism, and if you lose, there won't be a return match next year, or for 400 years.' The heart of Theo's message is contained in his statement: 'It's a different knowledge they need now, Clive. The enemy's different, so you have to be different too.' And though initially reluctant to accept the force of these home truths and arguments, even from his close friend, Clive finally faces the inevitable and settles for a role in the Home Guard. He has not changed – far from it: he could never do that – but he is more willing to play the part which circumstances impose upon him.

This, then, is the story which on first reading the Ministry of Information found 'defeatist'. And indeed there are 'defeatist' elements in it, not least in the characterization of Candy, as we have seen. But they are in the script, not of the script. Its purpose was clearly to subject them to scrutiny, if not condemnation, and to suggest that they had been supplanted by new-found values which better served the current situation. For all that they loved him, Powell and Pressburger sought to interpose some distance between their Blimp and the viewer. He was to be sympathized with but not identified with, his sentiments understood but not endorsed. In fact, officialdom obviously grasped many of these nuances, though that did not stop it from damning the venture. But, to repeat, the official reaction owed perhaps as much to factors other than Powell and Pressburger's production.

Before the film had even completed production the official machine rolled into action. It was the Secretary of State for War, James Grigg, doubtless intent upon doing something about the persistent charges of 'Blimpery' in the Army, who sparked the whole thing off.[19] And, frankly, to judge from the documentation in the 'Colonel Blimp File',[20] it is difficult to believe that the film would have caused such a furore without Grigg's initially hostile intervention. For he was dead set against the film from the outset, for reasons which are obvious, and cast it in a sufficiently bad light for Churchill's anger to be aroused in turn.

Grigg's long note to Churchill of 8 September 1942 shows that to be the case. Although the film was well into production, he felt it of the 'utmost importance' to get it stopped. He produced a synopsis of the plot and noted that 'the producer claims that the film is intended as a tribute to the toughness and keenness of the new Army in Britain and shows how far they have progressed from the Blimpery of the pre-war Army.' But 'whatever the film makes of the spirit of the young soldier of today,' Grigg continued, 'the fact remains that it focuses attention on an imaginary type of Army officer who has become an object of ridicule to the general public.' There were other minor objections but clearly the public opinion factor weighed most upon his mind. His claim was that the 'Blimp conception of the Army officer' was 'already dying from inanition' and that the film would give it a 'new lease of life'.

The die was cast. Although nobody had as yet seen the film, since it was still in production, on 10 September 1942 Churchill dubbed it a 'foolish production' and 'propaganda detrimental to the morale of the Army' and asked his Minister of Information to propose measures to stop it 'before it goes any further'. 'Who are the people behind it?' he asked.

Bracken was not daft. He told Churchill who was responsible but said, rightly, 'The Ministry of Information has no power to suppress the film.' The Ministry had tried to discourage its progress 'by withholding Government facilities for its production', but that had not done the trick. And in his eminently sensible reply of 15 September, he pointed out that in order to stop the film 'the Government would need to assume powers of a very far-reaching kind.' For a start, Government would need to be invested with the power to suppress all films if they expressed 'harmful or misguided opinions', and then it would need to insist upon 'a degree of control over films which it does not exercise over other means of expression, such as books or newspaper articles'. In short, such measures would demand nothing less than the 'imposition of a compulsory censorship of opinion upon all means of expression'. Bracken knew full well that such could never be the case. Britain was, after all, a democracy at war. And, as he put it so succinctly and mildly: 'I am certain that this could not be done without provoking infinite protest.'

It was a tactful response. The ball was back in Churchill's court. But Churchill persevered: 'We should not act on the grounds of "expressing harmful or misguided opinions" but on the perfectly precise point of "undermining the discipline of the Army",' he said on 17 September. Impasse was reached. And it was broken only by a War Cabinet minute of 21 September, for that recorded some measure of agreement. When the film had reached 'rough-cut stage' it would be seen by representatives of the War Office and the Ministry of Information. If they took the view that it was 'undesirable', it would be withdrawn by 'friendly arrangement' with the film's backers. The results of that preview were nothing if not revealing. A War Cabinet minute of 10 May 1943 recounts:

> The Secretary of State for War said that the film had now been seen by representatives of the War Office and the Ministry of Information, who took the view that it was unlikely to attract

much attention or to have any undesirable consequences on the discipline of the Army. In the circumstances, he had reached the conclusion that the right plan was to allow the film to be shown.

So Grigg withdrew his objections; the War Cabinet endorsed the course of action that he now advocated; and the film was released in Britain.[21] Churchill was adamant, however, that the film should not be allowed to go abroad at least, and he urged Bracken to hold it up 'as long as you possibly can'. This Bracken did, for several months, though he protested that it was an 'illegal ban' and served only to draw attention to the film in a way that they had strenuously sought to avoid. It was a 'wonderful advertisement', and the film was enjoying an extensive run because there were notices 'in all sorts of places' stating, 'See the banned film.' Churchill's views proved vociferous, though (not for the first time) unavailing.[22] By August 1943 approval was secured to release the film overseas.

Why, though, did Grigg of all people change his mind at that crucial meeting in May 1943? Was it just that reports on the completed film compelled him to alter his misguided opinions regarding its intentions? Or was it also that circumstances had changed sufficiently for him to feel confident it could do none of the harm he had originally ascribed to it? The tide of war had, after all, turned in Britain's favour in November 1942. What had been largely a catalogue of military defeats and setbacks by that point changed at last with the Anglo-American landings in North Africa and Montgomery's victory at Alamein. On the home front there was, by the spring of 1943, considerably less talk of 'Blimpery'. And, as Bracken put it in a memorandum to Churchill of 9 July 1943: 'The prestige of the British fighting man stands higher in the world than it has ever done.' Perhaps, then, in the final analysis *The Life and Death of Colonel Blimp* was just another victim of wartime circumstance.

Notes

1. Ian Christie (ed.), *Powell, Pressburger and others,* London, 1978, p. 105.

2. Michael Powell, interviewed by David Badder for 'Powell and Pressburger: the War Years', *Sight and Sound,* 48, Winter 1978, p. 10.

3. Powell, interviewed by Kevin Gough-Yates for the booklet *Michael Powell: in Collaboration with Emeric Pressburger,* London, 1970, p. 8.

4. Lawrence H. Streicher, 'David Low and the Sociology of Caricature', *Comparative Studies in Society and History,* 8, 1965–66, p. 17. See also David Low, *Low's Autobiography,* London, 1956, pp. 273–4.

5. Streicher, 'David Low and the Sociology of Caricature', pp. 13–18.

6. A. J. P. Taylor, *English History 1914–1945,* Oxford, 1965, p. 542.

7. For an overview on the British propaganda effort, see Michael Balfour, *Propaganda in War 1939–1945,* London, 1979, and Nicholas Pronay and D. W. Spring (eds.), *Propaganda, Politics and Film, 1918–1945,* London, 1982.

8. Quoted in Patrick Beesly, *Very Special Intelligence,* London, 1977, p. 123.

9. Taylor, *English History 1914–1945,* p. 540.

10. Quoted in Paul Addison, *The Road to 1945,* London, 1977, p. 198, which provides much of the information used here on Home Intelligence.

11. *House of Commons Debates,* vol. 378, cols. 304–14, 23 February 1942.

12. Addison, *The Road to 1945,* p. 161.

13. ibid., pp. 162–3.

14. See Powell in Badder, 'Powell and Pressburger: the War Years', and Gough-Yates, *Michael Powell.* Bracken and Beddington soon anyway had their own ideas on what might make a 'really good film about the Army', as Vincent Porter and Chaim Litewski demonstrate in *'The Way Ahead:* Case History of a Propaganda Film', *Sight and Sound,* 50, Spring 1981, pp. 110–16.

15. See the script of *The Life and Death of Sugar Candy* held in the British Film Institute Library, London (S3034: 1942), Parts I and II.

16. Typewritten addenda to ibid., dated 5 July 1942, p. 5.

17. Though it is not dealt with here, the role of the woman in the film is particularly interesting; see Christie, *Powell, Pressburger and Others,* pp. 117–18, for some astute observations.

18. J. B. Priestley did indeed do a *Postscript* on that date, relating to the Local Defence Volunteers. Two weeks beforehand, on 5 June 1940, he had given the first of what was to become many *Postscripts,* an inspiring and patriotic talk about Dunkirk.

19. As Powell well recognizes in Badder, 'Powell and Pressburger: the War Years', p. 11, where he comments that 'Beddington and Bracken were probably laughing like hell in their offices, but they had to do what they were told and follow the policy of the War Office and the Cabinet.' Powell had, after all, participated in the Ministry of Information's Ideas Committee; see Porter and Litewski, *'The Way Ahead . . ',* p. 110.

20. File PREM 4 14/15, cited in Addison, *The Road to 1945,* and reprinted verbatim in Christie, *Powell, Pressburger and Others,* pp. 106–111.

21. As the BFI microfiche on the film shows, the critical response was divided, though most critics reacted adversely to publicity claims that the film set standards against which 'all entertainment, past, present and future will be judged'. Nor did the critics respond favourably to the film's length, which, at 163 minutes, many felt served only to obscure its message. C. A. Lejeune, writing in the *Observer* of 13 June 1943, thought the film's length 'absurd' and its inevitable fault 'unclarity of purpose', while conceding that it was 'handsome' and 'frequently a moving piece'. The *Evening Standard* of 28 June 1943 found it 'not a great picture' but 'exceptionally good entertainment'. The *Manchester Guardian* said it was a 'consistently entertaining film, nowhere boring and yet hardly anywhere satisfactory as a piece of narrative or a piece of fiction'. Dilys Powell in the *Sunday Times* of 17 September 1943 wrote: 'the Blimp of this intellectually humane film is an honourable man, an incurable dreamer, a soldier holding in the midst of totalitarian war to the rules of a game which to

his romantic, if imperceptive, mind was never deplorable'; but, once again, 'the moral of his career is left uncertain; with one voice the film censures his beliefs, with another protests that they are the beliefs of all upright men.'

22. On 17 October 1942, for example, he tried to close down the Army Bureau of Current Affairs and informed the Secretary for War: 'I hope you will wind up this business as quickly and as decently as possible, and set the persons concerned to useful work.' But the attempts proved unsuccessful. See Addison, *The Road to 1945,* pp. 150–1, and Arthur Marwick, *The Home Front: the British and the Second World War,* London, 1976, p. 127.

Fame is the Spur (1947)

6

Lest We Forget
Fame is the Spur

T he Boulting Brothers' film of Howard Spring's novel *Fame is the Spur* was not a popular success. It took five months to make and cost over £350,000, but, contrary to some critics' confident predictions and unstinting praise, it was not a box-office hit. It was, however, an overtly 'political' film, as was well recognized at the time of its release in 1947. Its historical backdrop was broad, no less a canvas than Britain from the 1870s to the 1930s. Its preoccupations were many – the early days of the Labour movement, the Suffragettes, the first Labour Government, the hunger marches, the National Government and not least one man's rise to fame and fortune as a Labour politician in the midst of it all and his final decline. But despite the film's historical setting and allusions, the Boulting Brothers clearly felt they had a message to impart, in the immediate aftermath of World War II, to a Britain experiencing the Labour Government which came to power in July 1945.

Writing about the film in 1970, Raymond Durgnat noted that the film traced the 'rise and moral fall' of a man whose 'principal motivation was not even the substance of power, but its emptier shadow'. He spotted what many commentators had noted before him (and, indeed, what some had said was plainly evident in Spring's original novel of 1940) – that the character of the aspiring Labour politician, played in the film by Michael Redgrave, was nothing short of a thinly veiled portrait of Ramsay MacDonald. In this regard, he argued, it was a 'tardy broadside'. But Durgnat did not stop there. He proceeded to outline how he thought the film was relevant to post-war Britain. It was, he said, the first film to condemn the Attlee administration; its story 'caught the mood of disappointment and discontent which, despite the introduction of the Welfare State, attended austerity'; and, in all, the Boultings were 'belabouring the Labour Government for its lukewarmness'.[1]

Somebody really should have informed the Labour Government (and the Boultings) of that fact. Attlee, Bevin, Cripps and a number of others from the Cabinet dutifully trooped along to see the film shortly after its release in October 1947, and appear to have missed the point. Certainly, Cripps was heard to remark: 'Every man who sees this picture will want to go away and re-examine himself.'[2] But for the most part everybody seems to have agreed, as *Tribune* reported, that the message of the film was: 'It should not happen again'[3] – an unsurprising opinion, since it clearly accorded with the Boultings' intentions.

Nor did their story seek to capture the 'mood of disappointment and discontent' in the country for the simple reason that by the time Nigel Balchin's screenplay was completed in July 1946,[4] just one year after Labour took office, there was little justification for believing any such mood existed. If it did, it had assuredly not manifested itself, during the course of that first year, in disappointment with the Labour Government. After the 1945 election, as Arthur Marwick points out, 'Labour continued to do well in the country, increasing its majority in the first few by-elections, all in Labour-held seats, and doing very well in the first round of local government elections.'[5] Austerity was bad, of course, and getting worse; rationing, controls and shortages were inevitably unpopular. But, generally speaking, the country accepted the difficult post-war circumstances 'with sense and restraint',[6] and it was some time before the Government was held directly responsible for failing to improve the quality of everyday life and was criticized for it.

There was, it is true, some measure of discontent, at least on the industrial front. Within two months of taking office, for example, the Labour Government was confronted with a wave of unofficial dock strikes, which spread across the country from Merseyside. But Attlee's 'characteristically brisk action', as two commentators have described it, dealt with the immediate problem and kept the nation's food supplies going in October 1945.[7] The Cabinet was called in on 9 October; a decision was taken to put the Army into the docks, and the strike was broken. Of course, as these same two commentators go on to observe, Attlee's response on that occasion very much 'set the pattern for his premiership'. As the 1940s progressed and industrial disputes loomed larger and more protracted, Attlee's pragmatism hardened, and 'by 1948 strike-breaking had become almost second nature to the Cabinet'. But the fact of the matter is that in the first year or two of office Attlee's Government achieved genuine and popular success in the field of industrial relations. His personal standing remained such that even in June 1948 a BBC radio broadcast that he delivered played no small part in helping to bring the then striking dockers back to work.[8]

Furthermore, from the outset the Government had clearly set about fulfilling its election promises. They were by no means effected at once, of course, and some were changed considerably in the process of legislation. But the 'peaceful revolution' which Attlee sought was undoubtedly set in motion.[9] Within the first eighteen months of office alone, the National Insurance Act and the National Health Service Act were passed, though the National Health Service did not come into being until July 1948. The programme of nationalization was embarked upon and took in the Bank of England in May 1946 and the coal mines in January 1947.

In short, then, a good deal was achieved during the opening two years of the Labour Government, when the Boultings' film of *Fame is the Spur* was being scripted and produced. And the Boultings did not seek to use their film to criticize the Labour Government for any supposed lukewarmness on its part during that time, nor indeed generally to condemn it. The film was not 'political' in that sense. What the Boultings consciously sought to do with their film was to highlight what Attlee and many others in the Labour Party described as the 'greatest betrayal in the political history of the country'.[10] They were interested, quite simply, in writing history of a sort with their film, and their intentions are clarified by a comparison between the completed film and Spring's original novel.

Howard Spring's novel was nothing if not long and ambitious.[11] It centres upon the character of Hamer Shawcross and weaves a fictitious life story around him in the years between 1877, when at the age of 12 he witnesses the funeral of the 'Old Warrior' who has come to occupy the role of grandfather in his family, and 1939, when he is 74 and himself a grandfather. Born illegitimate, he is brought up in a 'respectable' working-class home by his mother and stepfather. But he moves from these humble origins in Ancoats, Manchester, to a position of some power in the Labour Party. His political career flourishes; he enjoys high office and ends up as Viscount Shawcross of Handforth. His career is contrasted with, and regularly crosses, those of his two childhood friends, Arnold Ryerson and Tom Hannaway. Arnold has none of Hamer's learning (albeit self-taught) or skill at political oratory, but he proves to be a gifted and capable Labour Party organizer at the trade union and grass-roots level. Tom's talents lead him in a completely different direction. He turns out a successful businessman, builds up a chain of shops, accumulates considerable wealth and influence, wins a seat as a Conservative and lands a knighthood.

All three men marry, but once again the focus of attention is Hamer and his household. Hamer's wife, Ann Artingstall, is the daughter of a local businessman, who tires of his commitments and lifestyle, comes to prefer more obvious and immediate pleasures and finally sees his business empire largely bought out and supplanted by the enterprising Tom Hannaway's endeavours in that field. Ann greatly aids and abets her husband's progress in his chosen career, but her own powerfully held principles compel her along a path that sets her at odds with her husband. She chooses to support the Suffragette cause and champions votes for women, which Hamer does not condone. Private and public conflicts ensue, and Ann is jailed for engaging in certain 'illegal' protests. Along with other Suffragettes, she is forcibly fed and physically abused, but in Ann's particular case her naturally delicate health deteriorates and she dies while convalescing abroad with Hamer.

In the meantime their son Charles has begun to enjoy many of the benefits which money can buy, such as private schools and a university education, and which Hamer especially sought out for him. His life, however, is blighted by a traumatic wound which he sustains while fighting in the Great War. His path crosses that of Alice, the daughter of Arnold and Pen Muff, who by contrast wins her way to university on a scholarship. She is naturally intelligent and writes well; she is also politically committed. Charles and Alice fall in love, but he feels threatened by her success, and they are estranged, just as Charles in turn is estranged from his father.

Eventually Charles and Alice are reconciled. They set off to join the

Republican cause in the Spanish Civil War, but Charles is killed en route. Alice returns to join Hamer and has Charles's baby. Her parents are dead, and she stays with Hamer. Hamer, Alice and the baby are together in 1939 as Europe embarks on another war.

Though concerned in the main with the lives of his fictional characters, Spring also makes reference throughout to historical events and personalities. They are woven into the narrative with fascinating, if sometimes far-fetched, results. Even before we embark upon Hamer's story, for instance, his grandfather recounts the incidents which he witnessed at the Peterloo Massacre in 1819 and bequeathes to the young Hamer a sabre which he took from a dragoon there. (The sabre, in fact, becomes a symbol and an inspiration for Hamer; the three parts of Spring's book are entitled 'Sabre on the Wall', 'Sabre in the Hand', and 'Sabre in Velvet'.) As a young man working in Suddaby's bookshop in Manchester Hamer meets Engels; as an up-and-coming politician he meets Keir Hardie and argues with him. With the outbreak of World War I it is Hamer who suggests that the Labour Party should go in with the Government, and in 1931 it is Hamer who suggests a Coalition Government be formed. Ann becomes involved with the Suffragettes; Arnold leads the hunger marches; and Alice, it transpires, was not only responsible for leaking the Zinoviev Letter but also instrumental in writing it.

Spring was clearly intrigued with historical issues, and doubtless his copious historical allusions helped to make his novel a best-seller. But he was as much intrigued with the difference between the public and private persona. And this is most evident in his treatment of Hamer. For Spring consistently confronts Hamer, and the reader, with the evidence of Hamer's diary. Hamer's actions and statements, particularly in public, are both contradicted and explained by Spring's references to the 'inner man', as gleaned largely from a reading of Hamer's diary. It is a useful and successful literary device, for it enables Spring both to build up a fully rounded picture of Hamer and, at the end of the day, to redeem him in the eyes of the reader. For all Hamer's political compromises and personal failings, he is depicted finally as a sympathetic figure and afforded considerable respect. Indeed, the novel is infused with a sense of forgiveness and redemption at its end, as first Charles and then Alice are reconciled with Hamer. 'Take them by and large,' says Alice, and 'we needn't blush for those who made us.' At the last Alice and her child are left in Hamer's charge.

The film has none of this air of reconciliation and redemption about it – quite the opposite, in fact – and it is also in many other important respects greatly at odds with the spirit and the letter of Spring's novel. The film is concerned rather with betrayal – the acts and consequences of Hamer's betrayal of his political ideals – and that alone.

Given the inordinate length of the novel, the film inevitably compresses a great deal, and many of Spring's characters and incidents are omitted. Hamer (Michael Redgrave), Ann (Rosamund John), Arnold (Hugh Burden) and Tom Hannaway (Bernard Miles) still occupy centre stage, but much else is discarded. Interestingly, the Boultings clearly sought, at least initially, to find a filmic equivalent to Spring's recourse to Hamer's diary as 'historical evidence', and the first 'cut' of their film made extensive use of flashback sequences to achieve this end and to confront the viewer with pictures of Hamer as he was and as he became. But they were compelled to re-edit their film for final release in order to bring it down to a certain length.[12] Consequently, after one early flashback to show the events at Peterloo, the film progresses in a comparatively straightforward chronological fashion, selecting highlights from Hamer's life to show his passage from youth to old age.

Hamer is inspired by the tale of Peterloo (depicted very much as the shooting script intended, so that 'What we see is what the boy sees – a romantic version of the old man's tale')[13] and by the cry of 'Bread and Liberty' which was uttered then and which Hamer hears again as a lad from street-corner speakers in Ancoats in 1870. He treasures the sword which his grandfather has given him and is prone to fantasizing about the power he might also wield as an orator. Already his vanity and visions of grandeur are evident.

As a youth, in Suddaby's bookshop, Hamer reads the works of Owen Meredith, and Jean Jacques Rousseau in the French. He does not meet Engels there, but he does encounter Ann, and he introduces her, in an earnest and pompous manner, to the works of Karl Marx. Hamer's intellect is clearly being developed, thanks largely to his own efforts, but so is his capacity for self-aggrandizement. And when he rekindles his friendship with Arnold, who by now is standing as a Labour candidate for Parliament, Hamer is sufficiently vain as to make the initial mistake of thinking that he is being sounded out as a potential candidate instead of just being recruited by an old friend for a difficult campaign.

For Arnold is standing as Labour candidate in the solidly Tory seat of St Swithin's, where the Earl of Lostwithiel (Sir Seymour Hicks) is in control and is paving and paying the way for his son Lord Liskeard (David Tomlinson) to secure the seat. Arnold, furthermore, is a poor speaker with little obvious charisma, and it is no surprise when he loses. But Hamer, when speaking on Arnold's behalf, demonstrates great prowess on the platform and goes down well with many of the crowds. Even at this early stage, however, the seeds of doubt are sown about Hamer's true intentions. On being told that he has delivered a good speech, Hamer instinctively replies: 'Oh, it was nothing.' 'Maybe,' he is told candidly, 'but it sounded all right.'

Subsequently, when Liskeard goes to the Lords on his father's death, Hamer contests the seat himself. He proves successful and becomes its first Labour MP. He marries Ann, writes a book entitled *Crusade Against Poverty,* and his career really takes off.

From that point on the film pitches Hamer into a series of situations which test his worth and credibility and from which he emerges with increasingly less credit and esteem, even in the eyes of those nearest and dearest to him. He almost loses Ann's affections over his refusal to espouse the Suffragette cause. They are reconciled on her death bed, though not before she has expressed her fears that he may change his mind about 'what needs doing'. And, slowly but surely, he alienates Arnold.

This process begins when he speaks to striking miners in Wales, at Arnold's request once again, and uses his Peterloo sabre to great effect during the course of a passionate and stirring speech, in which he urges: 'I want you to help me convict and punish the murderers. They're still abroad in this land – not killing perhaps with the sword, but with the slower weapons of starvation and cold.' He succeeds in inciting them to riot, which the pacifist Arnold has not wanted to see happen, and as a result one of their number is killed. On being accused by reporters, after the event, that 'The whole thing arose from a speech of yours', Hamer is distinctly worried and asks them to 'nail that lie at once'. 'Is it likely that responsible men like Ryerson and I would advocate useless violence?' he pleads.

Hamer alienates Arnold further when, on the eve of World War I, they discuss the Labour Party's likely position. Arnold says he has been 'preaching non-violence' all his life and would like to see the Party 'stick to our principles'. Hamer too has endorsed those principles and has made speeches on the theme of 'Europe and peace'. But he is all for going in with the Government 'to increase our prestige' and because 'Nobody's such a fool as to let his principles interfere with his practice.' He supports the Government's stand and is increasingly drawn into the parlour politics waged at the parties given by Lady Lettice Lostwithiel (Carla Lehmann). At one such party Hamer is prompted by the Minister of Mines to go back to South Wales and to put an end to a strike of miners who see the war as the 'bosses' war'. But Hamer's credibility with these men has suffered. Arnold is in jail as a pacifist, and this time Hamer is scorned.

Power is what Hamer is after, and power of a sort is what he achieves as Minister of Internal Affairs in the Labour Governments of 1924 and 1929. But it serves only to widen the gap between him and Arnold, to emphasize their points of difference and to epitomize what the Boultings clearly intended to be read as the two major strands in Labour Party thinking during those years. In 1929, for instance, Arnold invites Hamer to speak yet again, this time to the hunger marchers he is leading into London. Hamer declines, claiming in a letter, 'All my experience leads me to deprecate mass action and to favour the constitutional use of the machinery of Government.' Finally, in 1931, on the eve of the formation of a coalition National Government which Hamer has advocated (indeed, instigated), Hamer and Arnold part decisively and go their own ways. Arnold castigates Hamer for his willingness to contemplate a coalition. He believes Hamer has 'sold the unemployed' by accepting a cut in the dole and has reneged upon the principles for which they all fought in the early days. Hamer retorts: 'Arnold, my dear fellow, there's far too much sentimental talk about "the old days" in this Party. We're no longer a little bunch of enthusiasts speaking at street corners. We're the men responsible for the welfare of this country. This isn't a personal affair. It's a matter of finance and high policy.' Once again it becomes a matter of pragmatism versus principles over a question which genuinely did split the Labour Government in its day and is personified by the fictional characters represented on the screen. Hamer offers his hand in friendship, but Arnold declines to take it, stating quite simply: 'No. There's no ground of friendship for us now.'

In the novel the two men shake hands, though they still part as implacable opponents. And it is from this point on that the Boulting Brothers film diverges most noticeably from Spring's novel.

The National Government is formed in August 1931 and goes to the country in October of that year. It wins, of course, and Hamer is returned once again for St Swithin's but this time as a National Labour MP. In the novel Spring makes great play of revealing the results of the election (and, not surprisingly, he is accurate). But for Spring's Hamer there then comes a moment of reckoning. He has already appreciated that 'Clear of all evasion and self-deceiving', what he has wanted is 'nothing more than the fame that now [is] his.' And now he is well aware of the 'savage wounding blows' that he and a few colleagues have dealt out to his Party, for all that he thought it was necessary at the time to help save the country. So he decides he will not serve in any future Cabinet and writes a letter to his Prime Minister stating, 'I have made up my mind not to accept office again.' Thereafter he happily remains a constituency MP and finds the peace and reconciliation with his family of which we have spoken.

But in the Boulting Brothers' film there is no redemption, merely retribution. Their Hamer stays at his Cabinet post in 1931, survives the election but loses popularity in his constituency and is thrown out finally in the election of 1935. Since in the film he has no children, there is no comfort to be found in that quarter. His life ultimately proves barren and fruitless. The letter that Hamer writes to his Prime Minister is therefore that much more poignant:

> Thank you for your most kind letter. I am too old a hand to be disturbed by political defeat. But I am now nearly seventy-five; accordingly, I shall not seek re-election, and the question of finding me a seat does not arise. I am deeply touched by the suggestion in your last paragraph. As you know, I have been in the past an opponent of the system of hereditary titles. But as I have no children, it would perhaps be possible, if His Majesty so pleased to confer such an honour on me, to accept it without sacrifice of principle.

Whereupon his vanity takes the better of him, and he ponders which title would sound best and writes out a list from which to choose.

It is a logical step for a man who has become enamoured of the charmed circles within which the likes of Lady Lattice moves. She is one of the few friends remaining to him, the only source of some joy and comfort. And on a visit to her country mansion, where he was treated as a trespasser in his youth but is now warmly welcomed, he is moved to comment upon the 'grandeur and spirit of England, expressed in wood and stone' and revels in the tranquillity it brings.

Old age has truly caught up with him. The last we see of the film's Hamer is the image of a frail old man, capable only of delivering rambling speeches but intent still upon seeing whether they have been reported in the press. He too is increasingly afflicted by his conscience, and in a final speech, delivered at a Lord Mayor's banquet in the City of London, he is haunted by the visions which are conjured up before him of Arnold and Tom, the two people he has known since child-hood. Arnold is a gaunt and haggard spectre, Tom a leering and enticing figure. At home that evening Hamer reminisces. He is prompted to try to wrest the Peterloo sabre from the handsome scabbard to which he consigned it as a showpiece many years before. But he can no longer do so; it has rusted in. A broken man and a pathetic figure, he is helped to bed by his servant.

To the end the Boultings relentlessly hounded their Hamer. Spring allowed his character some respite, and Hamer's son Charles threw the sabre into the sea on his ill-fated voyage to Spain. Its job done, it no longer served a useful purpose. But it served the Boultings' purpose to keep the sabre on view as a haunting symbol of his betrayal and to leave the audience with a visual image of that.

Hamer had, quite simply, been weighed in the balance and found wanting. The film had surveyed his political career and come down resoundingly against him. But in the process of situating this character within a particular context and in comparing him with his fellows the film had also captured many of the nuances and facets of political life. The pictures it drew – of Arnold, the solid, dependable and principled Party worker; of Ann, the thoroughly middle-class and idealistic 'modern' woman; of Tom, the rags-to-riches Conservative businessman; and of the Lostwithiels, the traditional yet by no means uncaring Tories – were often treated, like the historical topics and issues that it broached, in a simplistic fashion. Yet the film was convincing for all that and was nothing if not novel in its choice of subject matter.

The Boulting Brothers' film, then, set its face grimly against its principal character of Hamer Radshaw and allowed him no redeeming characteristics. He was not meant to be construed in any sense as the archetypal 'hero'. This hardly made Michael Redgrave's task as an actor very easy, nor indeed was it likely to recommend the film as a commercial proposition. Although there were critics who dearly liked the film, it is perhaps no surprise that there were also critics who, while recognizing its purpose, found the film unremitting and despondent.

A. E. Wilson in the *Star* was typical in this respect. He noted that it was 'a long and worthily intentioned film', but he found it 'very sombre in tone, with hardly a touch of humour and only a hint of sentiment to relieve it'.[14] Harold Conway in the *Evening Standard* thought it a 'penetrating and rather bitter portrait' but doubted whether 'this fine picture, with its atmosphere of drama and grimness, will prove good box office throughout the country'. He did, however, applaud the Boulting Brothers 'for their courage in making it, and doing so with such unswerving integrity'.[15] The *Observer* considered it 'very serious and rather long'.[16] The *News of the World* concurred, but thought the direction 'intelligent' and that overall it amounted to a 'spacious and imaginative production'.[17] The *Daily Telegraph* believed it to be 'as somniferous as a political speech, indeed it is one'.[18] But the *Daily Worker* found the film a political speech to its liking. It was 'magnificent ... not a second is wasted' and it urged that 'all Labour leaders should see the film twice'.[19]

Very few critics failed to comment upon the political import of the film. Richard Winnington in the *News Chronicle* thought that the 'MacDonaldesque effigy supplied by Michael Redgrave is the film's central and incurable flaw'.[20] And some, like the *Sunday Times* critic, felt that the arrival of *Fame is the Spur* meant that henceforth films would be judged on 'political rather than on human and artistic grounds'. This would lead to a sorry state of affairs, since films should speak with 'a voice above politics'.[21] For others such as the *Evening News,* though, it meant that the Boultings had broken the age-old maxim 'Keep politics off the screen', and it declared, 'Thank goodness for a movie that has something to say.' 'Although it deals with past events,' the *Evening News* continued, 'its subject is so timely today.'[22] And the *Daily Mail* agreed that the film's theme was 'of permanent interest, perhaps never more so than now'.[23] 'Its controversial appeal is obvious,' concluded the *Daily Mirror.*[24]

In the event, of course, the film turned out to hold little appeal for the mass of cinema-goers. It was relevant, but in box-office terms it proved to be neither remarkable nor rewarding. It was political but not popular. Still, if nothing else the Boultings had succeeded admirably in putting a controversial political subject on the screen, and that, as the *Evening News* critic had suggested, was no small achievement.

During the 1930s, for instance, such a project would not have been entertained. Then politics, and particularly 'references to controversial politics',[25] were quite definitely barred from the screen by the British Board of Film Censors. And in a notable 1936 speech to the Cinematograph Exhibitors Association, the President of the BBFC, Lord Tyrrell, had reiterated the BBFC's belief that subjects dealing with 'political controversy' should not be introduced into the cinema, since 'Nothing would be more calculated to arouse the passions of the British public.'[26]

During World War II a good deal more flexibility and latitude was introduced, of necessity, into the censorship system, which resulted in several films on overtly political themes, such as Thorold Dickinson's *The Prime Minister* (1941) and Carol Reed's *The Young Mr Pitt* (1942), albeit well shrouded in antiquity and hardly of a controversial nature.

But the Boultings were to benefit in the immediate post-war period from the continued display of latitude on the BBFC's part. When in July 1946 they submitted the scenario of *Fame is the Spur* for pre-production scrutiny by the BBFC's readers, it was found that there were no insuperable problems, though it was noted of the 1880s sequences that 'The class differences of the time are shown by the contrast between the Earl of Lostwithiel and Hamer and his friends. The balance is heavily in Hamer's favour – all simple poverty – while the Tory Earl bribes his way into politics. The worst landlord in England, he is a drunkard, a crook and a brute.' Of the Peterloo Massacre the readers said, 'The actual scenes of fighting with the mob must be reduced to the minimum.' The word 'bloody' was to be deleted from the script, and it was thought that the scenes of the rioting Welsh miners suggest extremes of violence very reminiscent of the famous montages in the Russian films *Potemkin* and *Odessa* [sic] many shots of which the Board cut'. Finally, they added that 'forcible feeding should not be overstressed as torture' in the scenes of Ann's imprisonment as a Suffragette.[27]

The Boultings succeeded, then, in convincing many people of the worthiness of their political intentions, with the exception, perhaps, of those people who counted most, the bulk of the cinema-going population.

Notes

1. Raymond Durgnat, *A Mirror for England,* London, 1970, pp. 67, 70.
2. Reported by Harold Conway in the *Evening Standard,* 10 October 1947.
3. 'Fame is the Spur', *Tribune,* 562, 17 October 1947, p. 1.
4. Two Cities Films Ltd, *Bulletin,* 15 July 1946 (*Fame is the Spur* microfiche, British Film Institute Library, London). The shooting script was by Roy Boulting. My thanks to Roy Boulting for letting me borrow his shooting script of the film and for being so kind and helpful in providing me with information, both in interview (26 February 1982) and by letter (9 February 1982).
5. Arthur Marwick, *British Society since 1945,* Harmondsworth, Middlesex, 1982, p. 103.
6. ibid., p. 110.
7. Peter Hennessy and Keith Jeffery, 'How Attlee stood up to strikers', *The Times,* 21 November 1979. The authors go on to say: 'Attlee enjoyed several advantages over his successors. He presided over a nation conditioned by the discipline of war, both from forces' life abroad and experiences of the siege economy at home.' Their researches have lately been published in fuller form in *States of Emergency. British Governments and Strikebreaking since 1919,* London, 1983.
8. See Kenneth Harris, *Attlee,* London, 1982, pp. 422–3.
9. Paul Addison, *The Road to 1945,* London, 1977, p. 278.
10. The Boultings proved to be accommodating in other ways. Spring's character was, of course, called Hamer Shawcross, but the name was changed in the film to Hamer Radshaw. It was changed 'very simply', as Roy Boulting puts it, 'on legal advice. The present Lord Shawcross (then Sir Hartley Shawcross) was a member of the Labour Government, and we were told quite forcibly that to keep the original name of the character in Howard Spring's book would almost certainly take us into the law courts' (letter to the author of 9 February 1982). It is also interesting to note (see chapter 10) how apposite Roy Boulting's 1951 film of *High Treason* becomes in the light of the release of Government papers from that period, which show that the Attlee administration was obsessed with the idea of a communist conspiracy and 'attempts to disrupt the nation's economy' in its last year of office.
11. The novel of *Fame is the Spur* has been reprinted regularly since it was first published in 1940. The last occasion was in January 1982, as a tie-in with a BBC dramatization. The television production was poor, but Spring's novel re-entered the 'top ten' paperback lists. Spring served in British Intelligence between 1915 and 1918, and in 1941 he was one of the two writers assigned by Bracken to accompany Churchill and to produce a 'record for posterity' of his signing, with Roosevelt, of the Atlantic Charter.
12. The first 'cut' of the film ran for 2 hours 10 minutes, but the Rank Organization thought it too long and insisted upon the 'very substantial cuts' that were subsequently made to bring it in at an initial release length running to 116 minutes. Roy Boulting recounts, 'The finished film, then, proved a great disappointment to John and myself. So much indicative of the slow and insidious process of corruption had to be removed.' Marion Howard Spring records that she and her husband saw the film and that they too were 'disappointed with the result, it was not a bit like the novel' (*Howard,* London, 1967, p. 176).
13. Both the shooting script and the completed film show how 'romantic' the boy's vision was meant to be: 'with men and women dancing, and a fantastic Sam Bamford

with a hat full of leaves and later, dragoons of enormous size, all on grey horses like tin soldiers, and grandfather in shining armour, avenging his sweetheart.... The setting is quite unnaturalistic, and belongs to the pages of a child's fairy book.'

14. *Star,* 10 October 1947.

15. *Evening Standard,* 10 October 1947.

16. *Observer,* 12 October 1947.

17. *News of the World,* 12 October 1947.

18. *Daily Telegraph,* 13 October 1947.

19. *Daily Worker,* 11 October 1947.

20. *News Chronicle,* 11 October 1947.

21. *Sunday Times,* 12 October 1947.

22. *Evening News,* 9 October 1947.

23. *Daily Mail,* 10 October 1947.

24. *Daily Mirror,* 10 October 1947.

25. See the list of barred subjects reprinted in Neville March Hunnings, *Film Censors and the Law,* London, 1967, pp. 408–9.

26. Reprinted in the British Board of Film Censors *Annual Report* for 1936 (BFI Library, London).

27. *BBFC Scenario Reports,* 1946–7, pp. 27, 27a (17 and 23 July 1946; bound volume, BFI Library).

The Guinea Pig (1948)

7

Old School Ties
The Guinea Pig

It is a commonplace that total institutions – hospitals, prisons, schools – can be used in fiction as microcosms of the nation. Equally it is said that the public school system is the cornerstone of the class structure and of the deep-rooted social divisions which differentiate British society from that of other countries. We might legitimately expect, then, that a film set in a public school would be open to interpretation both as direct comment on the public school system *per se* and, more broadly, as comment on the state of the nation. The British film industry did, in fact, produce films set in public schools at two different and formative periods of change in British society – *The Guinea Pig* in 1948 and *If* ... in 1968. An examination of these two films is extremely enlightening about the attitudes towards society, class and education that were prevalent in the film industry during the eras which produced them.

The Guinea Pig was the work of the twin Boulting Brothers, Roy directing and John producing the film. The Boulting Brothers were among the more progressive elements in the film industry. Raymond Durgnat classifies them as 'moralists'.[1] Since founding Charter Films in 1937, they had produced and directed a series of films which had thoughtfully examined serious issues and had won them critical acclaim – *Pastor Hall* (1940) (resistance to Nazi tyranny), *Thunder Rock* (1942) (pacifism), *Brighton Rock* (1947) (crime and guilt). They had identified themselves with Labour by producing *Fame is the Spur* (1947). In *The*

Guinea Pig, based on a hit play by Warren Chetham Strode, they set out to examine the role of the public school in the post-war world and, in broader terms, the new society for which the Labour Government was striving. Bernard Miles, another progressive film-maker whose *Chance of a Lifetime* (1950), a film about workers taking over the running of a factory, was rejected by both major circuits, contributed to the screenplay and appeared in the film as the 'guinea pig's' father. Interestingly, both the play's author and the film's producer and director were at public schools – Sherborne and Charterhouse respectively.

The play was directly inspired by the recommendations of the Fleming Report. The first steps towards the creation of the welfare state had been taken during the war. The Butler Education Act (1944) provided for secondary education for all up to the age of at least 15, with a change of school at 11. The Act did not specify the nature of this change, but it was understood to involve a process of selection which would separate children into two groups – those who went to grammar schools and those who attended secondary moderns. In 1942 R. A. Butler, President of the Board of Education, set up a committee under Lord Fleming to consider how links between the public school system and the general education system could be improved. The committee's report (1944) concluded that some measure of integration between the two could be achieved by giving up to 25 per cent of places at all public schools to children selected from the state system by the local authorities. The Headmasters' Conference unanimously accepted the recommendation, but the scheme never really took off. The Government would not provide the money for the state pupils, insisting that this was a matter for the local authorities, and the local authorities were reluctant to spend money on the scheme. But the report had the effect of deflecting Labour's opposition to the public schools, despite the commitment to comprehensive education which had become party policy at the 1942 Labour conference.

Chetham Strode's play examined the experiment by following the progress of Cockney council school boy Jack Read through Saintbury School between 1944 and 1948. He is the 'guinea pig' of the title, though the Americans, with characteristic directness, retitled the film *The Outsider* for its US release, giving it a more obvious class resonance. The film version shot exteriors at Haileybury and Mill Hill, and Saintbury was constructed in the studio, its buildings and layout modelled directly on Sherborne's.

The arguments for and against the Fleming experiment are advanced at various stages in the film by the characters who represent progressive and reactionary standpoints. Lloyd Hartley (Cecil Trouncer), the old housemaster, is a dyed-in-the-wool traditionalist. He is opposed to the experiment, believing that the classes cannot mix successfully. Nigel Lorraine (Robert Flemyng), the young housemaster, supports the experiment. He is a meritocrat who has faith in the public school system but wants to open it up to worthy lads who cannot afford the fees. He believes in preserving the best of the past but adapting also to meet the needs of the present. He is a pipesmoking ex-army officer and former Oxford rugger blue who lost a leg in the war. It is perhaps worth noting that another pipesmoking ex-army officer, devoted to his old school (Haileybury), was at the same time heading the post-war Labour Government. The difference of opinion between Hartley and Lorraine becomes so intensive that Lorraine resigns, though he later withdraws his resignation.

The same argument is rehearsed at a higher level in the school when the governors meet to discuss the War Memorial Fund. The bishop wants a new school hall built with the money. But the headmaster, who shares Lorraine's progressive viewpoint, wants to place a commemorative plaque in the chapel and to allocate the rest of the money to scholarships in order to bring poor boys to Saintbury and to send them on to Oxford and Cambridge. The governors object that this influx of poor boys is likely to lower the tone of the school.

Both conflicts, that between Lorraine and Hartley and that between the governors and the headmaster, are resolved by divine revelation of a kind. Hartley, who is retiring because of heart trouble, takes a walk through the school hall and sees the inscription of the sixteenth-century founder's bequest, setting Saintbury up as a grammar school for use by poor boys. He realizes that he has lost sight of the reasons for the existence of the public schools. He intervenes in the debate at the governor's meeting to support the headmaster, and the scholarship proposal is carried. Hartley then asks Lorraine to take over from him as housemaster because he can make the necessary change within continuity which is required. Lorraine agrees, and the reconciliation is cemented by Lorraine's marriage to Hartley's daughter Lynne, who shares his ideas.

Interwoven with the debate about the merits of the experiment is the progress at the school of 'guinea pig', Jack Read. It follows more or less the standard format for the public school story, as summarized by E. C. Mack:

A boy enters school in fear and trepidation, but usually with ambitions and schemes; suffers mildly or seriously at first from loneliness, the exactions of fag-masters, the discipline of masters and the regimentation of games; then makes a few friends and leads for a year or so a joyful, irresponsible and sometimes rebellious life, eventually learns duty, self-reliance, responsibility and loyalty as a prefect, qualities usually used to put down bullying or overemphasis on athletic prowess; and finally leaves school with regret for a wider world, stamped with the seal of an institution which he has left and devoted to its welfare.[2]

But added to this is a crucial dimension not usually present in this standard format – class.

The film opens with Jack Read (Richard Attenborough), the bright son of lower-middle-class parents who keep a tobacconist's shop in Walthamstow, boarding the train with the new boys headed for Saintbury. Packed into a carriage, the boys talk excitedly of their prep schools and are silenced when Jack reveals that he comes from Middleton Road School, Walthamstow. We see the school through Jack's eyes in an eloquent sequence of point-of-view shots of the stately buildings. Although one boy befriends Jack and shows him the ropes, the others mock his accent and his manners, and his early days are unhappy. His misery culminates in the Founder's Ceremony, when all the new boys have to bow to a statue of King Henry VIII. As he bows, Jack is kicked on the bottom. Asked to bow again, he refuses, gives a two-finger salute to the founder and is dumped in the 'Rubbish Box'. He denounces the ceremony to Hartley as an excuse 'for kicking you up the arse'. A special censors' dispensation had to be obtained for the use of this four-letter word, not hitherto heard on the screen.[3] The Lord Chamberlain had permitted it on the stage, seeing it, apparently, as having the same deliberate shock value as Shaw's 'Not bloody likely' in *Pygmalion* and as an economical and pointed way of demonstrating the gulf between the classes. The Film Censor followed the Lord Chamberlain's lead.

Jack has not understood that the kicking is a ritual initiation ceremony, and he sees it as the last straw. He tries to run away but is dissuaded by

Lorraine. Lorraine explains to him the educational, as distinct from the social, advantages of going to Saintbury. He encourages Jack to stand up against what he does not like and tells him that the boys are not snobs – they have just been brought up in a different environment. It is hard to accept Lorraine's explanation of the boys' behaviour, since their attitude to Jack, like Hartley's, is the purest snobbery. But Jack accepts it and agrees to make a go of it. We see him being initiated into the mysteries of fagging, beating, Latin and rugby. At home at Christmas for the holidays, he tells his father that he is unhappy but wants to stick it out. Significantly, he defends the school and its traditions against charges of snobbery, demonstrating that his socialization is well under way.

This socialization continues back at school when he settles a vendetta with another boy, Tracey, in a boxing match fought in the gym instead of in a rough-and-tumble fistfight outside. The two boys end up friends, and the value of rules over anarchy is demonstrated. By the end of the film Jack is the perfect public schoolboy, accent eradicated, manners impeccable. He wants to become a teacher, and Lorraine arranges for him to receive one of the new scholarships to Cambridge.

The standpoint of the film is patently one of consensus, of the modification of existing institutions to accommodate a wider spectrum of the population, of evolutionary rather than revolutionary change. It is an extension of the principle by which the public schools in the nineteenth century had been employed to merge the aspiring upper middle class with the upper class to produce a single ruling elite with a common set of references and a uniform style. Similarly, the franchise had been progressively extended until it had even been granted to women. Now such schools are also to accept the deserving sons of the lower middle class. If the aspirations of dispossessed groups can be accommodated, then there will be no need to abolish or indeed even undermine institutions such as the public schools.

But the consensus is weighted on the side of conservatism, as the film clearly shows in dealing with Jack's family. One of the factors leading to Hartley's conversion is his discovery of a congruence of view with Jack's father (Bernard Miles). The Reads turn up on Commemoration Day, the living embodiment of continuity and tradition. Mr Read is shown round the school by Hartley, and as they talk, Read, a former sergeant-major, indicates that he knows the value of discipline. He thanks Hartley for taking his son on and praises the public school system for providing not just an education but also team spirit, self-confidence and good manners. Seen from the vantage point of today, the Reads look like deferential lower-middle-class Tories with more or less the same views as the old-style High Tory reactionary that Hartley represents. The Reads are totally supportive of Jack, and Mrs Read is prepared to go out to work to earn the money needed to send him to university, with its obvious educational and social advantages. They are not the sort to rock the boat.

Jack himself is transformed so that there is no trace of the original Cockney urchin. 'Gosh, sir, jolly good show,' he declares on learning he has got a scholarship to Cambridge and he leads the cheers for Hartley at his retirement ceremony. There can be little danger to the system if outsiders can become so totally integrated with the traditions. The film aims to show that both sides can learn from each other, a classic consensual stance, but the evidence suggests that it is the poor boys who do most of the learning.

The film does poke a little fun at the stuffiness of the single-sex school. Jack is found whistling at girls from a nearby girls' school, and Hartley asks him severely if he behaves like that at home. Jack replies innocently that he does, and Hartley is outraged. When Jack is seen walking in the woods with a girl, Hartley is furious and denounces and beats him. But Lorraine defends Jack's behaviour as natural. When Tracey tells his mother that he has painted a nude, she is shocked. 'It's a man,' he replies, 'Oh, that's all right,' says mother.

In sanctioning some change and urging the public schools to unbend a little *The Guinea Pig* reflects a considerable advance in the cinema's attitude to the public schools. For the cinema, education meant the public schools. Although the inter-war years were an era of virulent criticism of the public schools in literature, beginning with Alec Waugh's *The Loom of Youth* in 1917, none of this found its way on the screen. Writers like H. G. Wells, George Orwell, E. M. Forster and Graham Greene castigated the public schools, depicting them variously as hotbeds of philistinism, snobbery and homosexuality, as promoters of conformism and authoritarianism or as soulless machines which turned out identikit people ill-equipped emotionally or educationally to deal with the real world. But the cinema's view of the public schools was summed up by the enormously popular *Goodbye, Mr Chips* (1939), James

Hilton's gentle and sentimental celebration of the lifetime's teaching career at Brookfield of the venerable Latin master, Mr Chipping (Robert Donat). The same year saw a similar cinematic tribute to another dedicated schoolmaster, Charles Donkin (Otto Kruger), in *Housemaster,* based on the novel and play by Ian Hay. In both films much-loved, slightly eccentric old teachers defended tradition, repelled innovation and preserved continuity.

The importance of the watershed represented by the war is to be seen in a brace of films made after it in which the cosiness of Chips's Brookfield and Charles Donkin's Marbledown is replaced by the bleakness and repression of schools, depicted by Hugh Walpole in *Mr Perrin and Mr Traill* (1948) and Terence Rattigan in *The Browning Version* (1951). The films of these two works can be regarded almost as direct ripostes to *Chips*. Anthony Asquith's *The Browning Version* makes direct reference to *Chips,* and in Lawrence Huntington's *Mr Perrin and Mr Traill,* although the novel was published in 1911 and therefore pre-dated *Chips,* Marius Goring's Vincent Perrin is made up to look very like Robert Donat's Chips. Both Andrew Crocker-Harris (Michael Redgrave) in *The Browning Version* and Vincent Perrin in *Mr Perrin and Mr Traill* are elderly failures, unloved, pedantic disciplinarians with tormented private lives. Their schools are joyless prisons, Perrin's Banfields being described by one character as 'a decaying tooth'. The next stage is the comprehensive criticism of the system in *If* ... (1968).

It was not until the mid-1950s that the cinema got round to depicting a grammar school, and a co-educational one at that, in Cyril Frankel's *It's Great to be Young* (1956). Scripted by Labour stalwart Ted Willis, it takes that familiar theme of school fiction – the schoolboy rebellion. But the rebellion is merely the desire to play a little jazz in the school orchestra, and the film's moral is the familiar one of the need to compromise between excessive concern for academic achievement and the desire for free expression. The imagery of the film however, is still rooted in the public schools; Angel Hill Grammar School boasts venerable, ivy-covered buildings, masters in gowns and mortar boards and white-flannelled cricketers at play on lazy summer afternoons. The pupils are well scrubbed, well mannered and well spoken middle-class children, their conversation liberally sprinkled with Greyfriars banter ('Keep cave, you chaps', 'Cheese it', 'Good-oh', 'Scrag him', 'Thanks awfully', 'Oh, lor').

It was 1961 before the first serious film to deal with a secondary modern, *Spare the Rod,* appeared. A melodramatic but well meaning British equivalent of the American *Blackboard Jungle* (1955), this film has a progressive ex-naval man (Max Bygraves) combating bad facilities, poor teachers, parental indifference and the poverty of working-class expectations. Similar problems and conditions occur in the subsequent secondary school dramas, *Term of Trial* (1962) and *To Sir With Love* (1967). It is significant that the cinema should have turned its attention away from the public schools in the 1960s, for that was the decade that was to see the Labour Government implement its policy to introduce comprehensive education as part of the process of achieving a truly egalitarian society. It had been reaffirmed as party policy at the 1959 party conference, and by 1974 two-thirds of all schools had gone comprehensive. The ethos of the 1960s was established by working-class youth, and the cinema was at last to catch up with the literary criticism of the public schools in Lindsay Anderson's *If* . . . .

Back in 1948, however, the critical reactions to a film about the public schools make fascinating reading and are as revealing about the critics and their standpoints as about the film. The communist *Daily Worker* noted:

> There is a positive idea contained in the story – that any boy will make good if given proper scope for his abilities. The trouble is, the film takes for granted the inherent superiority of the public school. . . . While (gently) criticizing snobbery, the film itself reeks of snobbery, and its patronizing attitude to the 'guinea pig' and his parents is as insufferable as it is unintentional. . . . Nevertheless I must admit that the film is capably directed and acted and has many pleasant touches of human observation.[4]

Joan Lestor, writing in the pro-Labour *Reynolds' News,* agreed:

> Where I think the Boulting Brothers have erred is in caricaturing the Walthamstow family in order to emphasize the conflict. Perhaps it is because they shirk the deeper issues involved that they make the boy from Walthamstow . . . incredibly uncouth. It is taking the easy way out to mark your class boundaries by making one side say 'Pleasedtermeetyer' and wear comic hats on festive occasions. . . . Knowing the makers and actors in this picture to have no particle of snobbery or patronage in their make-up, I'm sure offence was not meant. I am fairly sure it will be taken. . . .

The solutions are too easy, the superficial boundaries too easily overlooked. The Walthamstow boy's advent has the indirect effect of giving a fillip to the more progressive forces. He himself learns the value of tradition. Is it as simple as that?[5]

The Times, on the other hand, thought it:

a rational and intelligent film. The author would not pretend that he has vindicated the Fleming Report . . . but at least he sets out to examine the problem as fairly as he can, and if success is snatched from the jaws of failure, and the public school system is vindicated, the uneasiness implicit in the title remains. The school and its life are presented with a fine plausibility, although the supreme importance of house politics is overlooked, and when the false, misleading note rings out, and Saintbury is less Saintbury than Greyfriars, the acting is usually good enough to hush it up quickly. . . . The film picks its way surefootedly among the treacherous cross-currents of English social life and has the courage to recognize that, unfortunate though it may be, class distinctions still exist.[6]

The *Daily Telegraph* agreed that:

a subject both topical and timeless is tackled with intelligence, sympathy and that rarest of qualities these days good humour.[7]

The *Graphic* felt that the film had been written:

with great sensitivity and an admirable lack of bias. . . . It will, I am sure, reassure most people that the Fleming recommendations are practical and altogether worthwhile. I am sure, too, that most people will find it as satisfying an entertainment as they have seen for a long time. It is full of warmth and humour and often is extraordinarily moving.[8]

As ever, the Liberal *Manchester Guardian* saw both sides of the argument and came down in the middle:

This is not, goodness knows, the first film about a British public school, but it is the first of them to be so truthful. . . . Saintbury, one is convinced, might exist and might besides be a fairly sensible educational establishment. And when one hears the film (like the play from which it was adapted) damned both for brandishing the 'old school tie' and for being 'socialist propaganda', then one is inclined to believe that it has, indeed, found the just, truthful, middle way.[9]

But reviewers were divided not just in their attitudes to the treatment of the Fleming recommendations. but also according to whether or not they themselves had been to public school, confirming thereby a great divide that still existed in British life.

The *Evening Standard* critic, admitting that his knowledge of public schools was confined to reading the *Magnet* and the *Boy's Own Annual* reported:

> So convincingly has this tale been told that it has left me with a fresh understanding of public school life and these unanswered questions: is it likely that so class-conscious a housemaster would have changed his general views even if he were satisfied with the conduct of one working-class boy? What would such a boy's reactions be to his old environment when he returned with his new accent and new manners? Does the public school system account in any way for Mr Shaw's remark that 'the whole strength of England lies in the fact that the enormous majority of the English people are snobs'? Now any picture that raises problems of this kind should be seen. But *The Guinea Pig* is far more than just a quiz programme. For it has been made with such intelligent tenderness that you will be carried effortlessly and absorbed through an important aspect of British life.[10]

The *Daily Express* critic similarly confessed to not having been to public school:

> I am perhaps over-sceptical of the value of fagging and ragging (and even let me whisper it, cricket) as character-building factors. . . . What becomes of him afterwards, when he has learned not to sop up his gravy, to pick up his aitches and to love the Old Place, is one of the unanswered questions of a well made and notably well acted picture which takes itself a shade too seriously. . . . But overtones of caricature and an underlying acceptance of snobbish values made me uneasy.[11]

The critic of *Time and Tide,* on the other hand, had been to public school:

The Boultings have put a public school on the screen convincingly enough to put Messrs Chips, Perrin and Traill to shame. It
is not flawless in detail. No head ever called the governors 'the
school governors' to a housemaster. Above all, no successful
housemaster, however reactionary, would have taken on the first
experimental schoolboy suggested by the Fleming Report without
telling him even one thing or two. But the general atmosphere,
unlike any other in the world, is true and the playing fields, chapel,
fagging, prefects' studies, burnt toast and colts' caps are successfully evocative of the enclosed emotions we never find again
outside them. If *The Guinea Pig* were just a super-school story there
would be small cause for complaint. But there is the socio-
educational problem here to give an extra twist to the guinea pig's
tail and the film never really grasps the problem at any deeper level
than that of *The Bending of the Twig*.[12]

Whatever their political and social standpoints, the critics were in the main
united about the excellence of the film as a film. In a controversial piece
of casting, Richard Attenborough, then aged 24, was cast as Jack, but most
critics found his performance convincing; and the *Sunday Times* thought it
'one of his best performances so far'.[13] But Robert Flemying earned
almost equal praise for his performance as Nigel Lorraine; *Time and Tide*
observed that he had 'the very rare gift of making an educated Englishman's
under-statement as natural and telling as it can be in real life'.[14]

The *Sunday Times* effectively summarized the message which this film
carried for its time: 'The piece has two morals. The first, that the public
schools should unbend a bit. . . . The second moral, that the Common Boy
has something to learn even from the nobs.'[15] In other words, there was
nothing wrong with the public schools or society at large that a little more
tolerance and mutual understanding between the classes would not put
right. So, although it was entering an area of potential controversy and, as
the *Sunday Times* put it, infusing 'into its story quite a bit of social conscious-
ness', at bottom the film was rejoicing, as the cinema industry in its heyday
so often was, in the essential soundness of our institutions.

Notes

1. Raymond Durgnat, *A Mirror for England,* London, 1970, p. 206.
2. E. C. Mack, *Public Schools and British Opinion since 1860,* New York, 1941, p. 201–2.
3. *Evening News,* 21 October 1948.

4. *Daily Worker,* 24 October 1948.

5. *Reynolds' News,* 24 October 1948.

6. *The Times,* 25 October 1948.

7. *Daily Telegraph,* 25 October 1948.

8. *Graphic,* 24 October, 1948.

9. *Manchester Guardian,* 25 October 1948.

10. *Evening Standard,* 21 October 1948.

11. *Daily Express,* 24 October 1948.

12. *Time and Tide,* 30 November 1948. Desmond Coke's *The Bending of a Twig,* a mild satire of public school stories, was published in 1906.

13. *Sunday Times,* 24 October 1948.

14. *Time and Tide,* 30 November 1948.

15. *Sunday Times,* 24 October 1948.

The Blue Lamp (1950)

8

The Thin Blue Line
The Blue Lamp

B oth on the cinema and the television screens in Britain and in
America, the police are ubiquitous. In Britain there are both fictional
and documentary series about urban and rural police officers, male and
female police officers, senior officers and junior officers, plain clothes
and uniformed police officers, the flying squad, the robbery squad, the
fraud squad, the metropolitan and provincial police, the police
complaints department, the special branch. There are now so many
police series that in 1997 the central body controlling ITV output
ordered a reduction in their number in the interests of varied program-
ming. Nevertheless the public love them. The BARB (Broadcasting
Audience Research Board) figures for the week of 5–12 August 1996
reveal that half of the top ten ITV programmes watched by audiences
were police dramas: *The Bill* (11.58 million), *Inspector Morse* (9.42 million),
A Touch of Frost (9.29 million), *Wycliffe* (9.21 million) and *Heartbeat* (8.40
million); one of the top ten BBC programmes was a *policier, Out of the
Blue* (8.13 million).[1] Nothing better reflects the concerns of a society
preoccupied with law and order and the rise of violence and criminality
than the omnipresence of the police on the screen.

The current centrality of dramas focusing on day-to-day police work
stems back directly to one celebrated progenitor, *The Blue Lamp,* directed
by Basil Dearden for Ealing Studios and released in January 1950. It is

impossible to overestimate the importance of *The Blue Lamp* either at the time or subsequently. It was the top British moneymaker of 1950. It won the British Film Academy Award as best British film of 1950 and it catapulted its star Jack Warner to the top of the list of male British box office stars. It also established an image of the police force which persisted for over a decade, only being dented in the 1960s by *Z-Cars* and then overwhelmed in the 1970s by *The Sweeney*.

It was in many ways a revolutionary film in its depiction of the police. The project that ultimately became *The Blue Lamp* originated at Gainsborough Studios. Producer Sydney Box and his script editor Jan Read had the idea of doing a film about the life and work of the average policeman. They called in Ted Willis, who had already helped to script several of Gainsborough's social realist films, *Holiday Camp, Goodtime Girl* and *A Boy, a Girl and a Bike*. Willis recalled in his autobiography:

> Up to that time the British policeman had usually been portrayed as a bumbling simpleton who habitually licked the stub of his pencil, was respectful to the Squire and left the investigation and solution of serious crime to brilliant, educated amateurs like Sherlock Holmes and Lord Peter Wimsey. Sydney decided that there had to be a little more to it than that and Jan and I were asked to do some research and knock together a script.[2]

Willis was correct in his analysis. There has been a long cultural tradition of lovable incompetent bobbies It includes Gilbert and Sullivan's chorus of policemen in *The Pirates of Penzance* lugubriously singing 'A policeman's lot is not an 'appy one' and the popular music hall sketches of beloved comics Sandy Powell and Robb Wilton. In Powell's 'The Lost Policeman' (recorded in 1929), a policeman, informed by a small boy that 'Our Herbert's fallen in the river,' laboriously takes down all the details before contemplating rescuing the child who cannot swim but then reveals that he is lost. In Robb Wilton's 'The Police Station' (recorded in 1931 and later filmed as a short), an amiable and dithering station sergeant does not want to be bothered with a woman who confesses to having poisoned three husbands ('You'll have to try and break yourself of it'). There were popular music hall songs: 'Policeman 92X', 'If you want to know the time, ask a policeman', 'The P.C.', 'Send for a P'liceman', 'It's part of a policeman's duty'. Two of the most famous were Charles Penrose's 'The Laughing Policeman' (recorded in 1926) and Harry Fay's 'P.C. 49' (1910). Penrose's song about a fat and jolly red-faced bobby unable to stop laughing was a perennial entry on the BBC record request programme *Children's Favourites* throughout the 1950s. Fay's song, recalling the tribulations of a policeman who relates how children threw mud at him, navvies punched his nose and suffragettes stripped him, gave its title to a popular radio series of the late 1940s and early 1950s about an accident-prone silly ass policeman Archibald Berkeley-Willoughby whose catchphrase was 'Oh, my Sunday helmet'.[3]

The music hall image of the slow-talking, dull-witted, good-hearted bumbler was transferred to the screen. The American Keystone Kops established a popular slapstick image of disaster-prone policemen and a succession of British comedy stars donned the blue uniform usually to play comic constables: Jack Hulbert (*Jack's the Boy,* 1932), Gracie Fields (*Looking on the Bright Side,* 1932), Stanley Holloway (*Sing as We Go,* 1934 and *Squibs,* 1935), Will Hay (*Ask a Policeman,* 1939), George Formby (*Spare a Copper,* 1940), Norman Wisdom (*On the Beat,* 1962), the 'Carry On' team (*Carry On Constable,* 1960) and Cannon and Ball (*The Boys in Blue,* 1983).

In terms of serious drama, it was the case that Sherlock Holmes had established the dominance of the omniscient private detective who solved the cases that baffled Scotland Yard. There was the occasional gentleman police inspector (Sir Gerald Du Maurier in *The Scotland Yard Mystery,* 1934, Hugh Williams in *The Dark Eyes of London,* 1939 and Sebastian Shaw in *The Flying Squad,* 1940). But the dominant image of the regular police force was that established by Gordon Harker's lugubrious and canny but indelibly comic cockney police officer. He played detective Sergeant Elk in the films of Edgar Wallace's *The Frog* (1937) and *The Return of the Frog* (1938) and detective Inspector Hornleigh in a series of thrillers based on the popular radio series *Inspector Hornleigh* (1938), *Inspector Hornleigh on Holiday* (1939) and *Inspector Hornleigh Goes to It* (1941).

This consistent lovable comic image was a way of defusing discontent. For there was a longstanding suspicion and hatred of the police, 'the plague of blue locusts,' in some sections of the working class. But one reason why the police were so often comic was that they were working class and before the 1940s the working classes in films were invariably comic. The amateur sleuths were serious because they were gentlemen and they certainly dominated the screen. There were long-running series of Sherlock Holmes films in both Britain and America in the 1920s,

1930s and 1940s, a succession of Bulldog Drummond films both in Britain and America in the 1930s and two Peter Wimsey films (*The Silent Passenger,* 1936 and *Busman's Honeymoon,* 1942), all of them featuring gentlemen sleuths.

The Blue Lamp was to change all this and present the working-class copper as hero. Ted Willis spent six weeks researching his script, working out of Leman Street and Paddington Green Police Stations, accompanying policemen on the beat, visiting their homes, sitting behind the counter in the station and in the charge room. He spent much of his time with Inspector Mott who 'had spent years in his East End manor, seemed to know every crack in every pavement, and was instantly recognised and greeted respectfully by half the population.'[4] Willis recalled that he sorted out personal problems, dealt firmly with disturbances of the peace, acted as a combination social worker, father confessor and law enforcer. He was the model for P.C. George Dixon who became the central figure in *The Blue Lamp.* Once the research was complete, Willis and Jan Read wrote the script. But at that point Lime Grove Studios were sold to the BBC and Gainsborough ceased production. However the script was taken up by Michael Balcon at Ealing. He gave it to Ealing regular, T. E. B. Clarke. Willis and Read were disappointed but Willis admitted later that Clarke, who had been a policeman, 'honed, refined and improved our material and added much more that was uniquely his own.'[5]

The film exactly fitted the ethos of Ealing. From 1942 onwards Ealing films had a collective ethos. The people were the hero. Throughout Ealing's films there were two structuring themes. First, the idea that there *was* such a thing as society and it was made up of communities, organic, cohesive, rooted in shared values, traditions and experiences, tolerant, restrained, decent and civilized, a society that needs defending and is worth protecting. The second is the concept of public service, shared activity in defence of the community and its values, a concept celebrated in Ealing films about the fire service (*The Bells Go Down*), the probation service (*I Believe in You*) and nursing (*The Feminine Touch*).[6]

Basil Dearden, an expert exponent of the Ealing ethos in such films as *The Bells Go Down* and *The Captive Heart,* was assigned to direct and Jack Warner, who had convincingly played an East End policeman in *It Always Rains on Sunday* (1947), was asked to play P.C. George Dixon.

Friends advised against it as Dixon is killed half way through the film. But Warner accepted the role, recalling in his autobiography:

> I realised that the murder of the policeman, far from eliminating him, really gave him a martyr's crown as a man never to be forgotten and that any audience would readily understand the spirit of the film and the message it conveyed.[7]

Dearden cast Dirk Bogarde, whom he had seen on the stage in *Power Without Glory,* as Tom Riley, the delinquent gunman, telling him 'You *could* play the snivelling little killer. Neurotic, conceited, gets the rope in the end,' and Bogarde considered the result 'the first time I came near to giving a cinema performance of any kind of depth,' discovering with this film that 'the camera actually photographed the mind process.'[8]

The shooting script was submitted to the British Board of Film Censors in 1949 and they thoroughly disapproved. Scriptreader A. Fleetwood Wilson wrote: 'A sordid, vicious unpleasant story. I deplore this type of film being produced in this country. I feel certain in my own mind that it does a great deal of harm to those of the younger generation who are criminally minded. No doubt they will watch this film and try to improve on the methods used, causing the downfall of the youngsters,' and Mrs. Norah Crouzet thought 'it is a pity that a film illustrating London police work should be just another 'American' gangster story.' But she conceded: 'As the company is to have police co-operation, one can reasonably hope for a factual treatment without sensationalism. It would be disastrous to treat this dangerous subject of adolescent criminals with any glamour. On the other hand, whilst it is necessary to show the criminals as mean, cowardly sneak-thieves, there should not be too much emphasis on cruelty towards women; and though the background is sordid, there should not be any prostitution or eroticism.' The list of deletions proposed by the censors centred on the elimination of eroticism, violence and bad language.[9]

The film was indeed made with the full co-operation of the Metropolitan Police, and is dedicated to the police service. It was shot at several police stations, notably Paddington Green. The actors were coached in police procedure and etiquette by serving officers and Warner recalled that he and other actors were regularly mistaken for real policemen during filming.[10] Rushes were viewed and inaccuracies corrected by Sir Harold Scott, Commissioner of the Metropolitan Police. Scott later wrote in his autobiography:

> *The Blue Lamp* ... gave a faithful picture of the policeman's life
> and work in the form of an exciting crime story, much of the
> detail of which was taken from actual happenings in recent crimes.
> This film has been shown all over the world and had been a valu-
> able means of spreading a knowledge of the efficiency and high
> tradition of the Metropolitan Police.[11]

The film coupled Ealing's wartime documentary style, complete with
location shooting, a narrator and an air of authenticity with a view of
society as essentially moral and communal. The view of England and
the English, of the life of service and duty under discipline that had
characterized Ealing's wartime films passed in peacetime from the war
against the enemy without – the Germans – to the war against the
enemy within – the criminal. Before *The Blue Lamp,* there had been no
British examples of the police procedural thriller that was becoming
popular in America. *The Blue Lamp* remedied that defect but in a very
British style. It remains a first-rate, fast-moving thriller, set and filmed
in a now historical London, which aside from bomb damage is still
essentially Victorian. The car chases, through Ladbroke Grove, excit-
ingly shot and edited, remain highly effective.

The narrator identifies the public concern which was the background
to the film's success with the upsurge of crime, which is identified as
resulting from post-war malaise, family breakdown and broken homes.
He highlights a new criminal threat – the juvenile delinquent. The
opening of the film – a graphic car chase and the shooting down of a
man who tackles fleeing armed robbers – will have reminded audiences
of the Alex D'Antiquis case, when a passing motorcyclist, a father of
six, was gunned down while trying to stop a getaway after a bungled
jewel robbery in Charlotte Street, London, in 1947. Similarly, the
shooting of Dixon will have recalled the shooting of P.C. Nathaniel
Edgar in Southgate in 1946. He was the first policeman to be shot on
duty in many years.[12] Both *The Daily Mirror* and *The News of the World*
mentioned these cases in their reviews of the film.[13]

The shooting is followed by a montage of headlines and then the
narrator declares, quoting an Old Bailey judge, that the best weapon
against crime is the bobby on the beat. He is incarnated in the film by
P.C. George Dixon, played by Jack Warner as the epitome of the respectable working class. He is also the ideal bobby: solid, dependable, decent,
wise, kindly, experienced, commonsensical, dedicated to the job. He

smokes a pipe, tends his begonias, calls his devoted wife (Gladys Henson) 'Ma'. Their only son was killed in the war and their only daughter lives in Canada. They take in as a lodger a new young cop Andy Mitchell (Jimmy Hanley) who becomes a surrogate son, learns the job from George and at the end is seen patrolling the same beat and replicating George. The mood is one of continuity, tradition and service.

Dixon knows his patch and his people, helps them solve their problems informally but also tackles guntoting tearaways. The film establishes the texture of everyday police routine: dealing with drunks, lost children and dogs, requests for directions, domestic disputes. But the central thread of the film is the career of three juvenile delinquents, Tom Riley (Bogarde), Diana Lewis (Peggy Evans) and Spud (Patric Doonan). First of all they mug a jeweller, visiting his mistress in order to get his keys, they then rob the jeweller's shop knocking down a policeman as they flee; and finally Riley shoots George Dixon in the course of a robbery of a cinema, the Coliseum. The remainder of the film traces the police investigation, headed by Detective Inspector Cherry (Bernard Lee), to solve the robbery and the shooting. Riley is tracked down to White City Dog Track and captured.

Bogarde gives an electrifying performance as Riley, a new kind of criminal, a new kind of male, a new kind of youth, the antithesis of everything Ealing stands for, the threat to settled order and stability. He is neurotic, erotic, arrogant, revelling in violence and power, caressing his gun like a phallic symbol, beating up his girlfriend, shooting down an unarmed policeman. He sets the pattern for a series of such threatening young males who emerge in postwar cinema, notably Richard Attenborough in *Brighton Rock,* Laurence Harvey in *I Believe in You* and James Kenney in *Cosh Boy*.[14] The juvenile delinquents are self-centred individuals out for kicks and personal gain. The police, in line with Ealing's collective ethos, are a community. They are the epitome of British life, deeply rooted in the local community and committed to protecting it. George and Andy are members of the police choir and the police darts team, at home in the camaraderie of the canteen which, like the prisoner of war camp and the platoon barracks during wartime, is given a conscious U.K. dimension, with the presence of a Welshman (Taffy Hughes) and a Scot (Jock Campbell) to complement the cockneys. 'Mustn't grumble' is the constant stoical refrain here as in the war and 'the nice cup of tea' is invariably offered at times of crisis, again like the war. The community of the police is linked both to the wider community (the finale at the White City Dog Track has the crowd including professional criminals, bookies and punters joining forces with the police to trap Riley) and to the family (Jack Warner/Gladys Henson/Jimmy Hanley) forming a settled unit to contrast with the violent broken home that produces Diana Lewis. The shooting of George Dixon is deeply shocking and his death unexpected. It reduced contemporary audiences to tears. But it is both redemptive and sacrificial, the price of duty and an extension of that wartime imperative to dramatize the need for sacrifice if victory is to be obtained. *The Daily Mail* noted the link in describing it as a 'team film' which 'ranks with the better war documentaries.'[15]

The Blue Lamp garnered almost universal critical praise for its writing, its directing and its acting. Both *The Star* and *The Times* called the film 'a handsome tribute' and *The Manchester Guardian* 'a sincere tribute' to the police.[16] It was seen as 'human'; *The Daily Mail* calling it 'a thoroughly human glimpse of the man on the beat – as well as a comforting impression of the efficiency that lies under the kindliness,' and *The News of the World* praised its 'warm humanity and realistic humour.' Its humanity was linked to its distinctive Britishness by *The Daily Telegraph* which noted that it was not characterized by 'the clockwork organization and febrile brilliance' of the best U.S. thrillers 'but then it wouldn't be quite British if it had.' Instead it was characterized by its 'humanity and humour'.[17]

The Daily Mirror called it 'flawless and factual' and *The Evening News* backed up this impression by reporting that it had been shown to an audience of London policemen: 'They roared over the professional jokes, chuckled knowingly at the peccadilloes of civilians and 'froze' stiff during the hair-raising car chases.' Nevertheless, many saw it as propaganda.[18] *The Daily Mirror* reported Sir Harold Scott as saying: 'We're hoping to win recruits with this film.'[19] *The Daily Herald* suggested it was selective in its depiction of police life: 'The understaffed, overworked, poorly housed London bobby is not shown, nor is the cynicism and attitude of compromise that spring from these evils hinted at . . . it ignores the idea that married quarters for young policemen, better pay and better pensions would do all the recruiting required.'[20] *The Daily Worker* denounced 'the glorification of the copper' in *The Blue*

Lamp and other films as 'a symptom of how successful has been the debauching of public taste. While police-protected Fascists incited people to race violence ... and police broke up May Day ceremonies ... the public flocked to see policemen singing carols and growing begonias, all mother's boys together.'[21]

Although George Dixon died in *The Blue Lamp,* he was to enjoy a spectacular resurrection. Ted Willis had persuaded Sydney Box to assign to Read and himself the stage and fictional rights to their script. So Willis first turned *The Blue Lamp* script into a novel, published in 1950 and illustrated with stills from the film. Then he and Read turned the story into a stage play. Jack Warner was eager to do it and impresario Jack Hylton staged it at the Grand Theatre, Blackpool, in 1952 for the summer season. But Hylton, who clearly had not realized the mythic significance of Warner as Dixon, flatly refused to allow his star to play the role of a character killed half way through and cast Warner as Detective Inspector Cherry, who clears up the murder. Bonar Colleano and Susan Shaw played Tom Riley and his girlfriend and in a fascinating throw-back to the 1930s, Gordon Harker played Dixon. The play subsequently transferred to the West End.

But Willis realized the mythic significance of Warner as Dixon better than Hylton and in 1955 he revived Dixon as the central character of a BBC Television series, *Dixon of Dock Green.* Warner resumed the role and was to play it continuously until 1976, appearing in 434 episodes and becoming a British institution. He wrote the words of the series signature tune 'Just an ordinary copper' to a tune provided by his old cabaret partner Jeff Darnell. The centrality of Dixon to British popular culture is emphasized by the fact that both Warner and Willis titled their autobiographies 'Evening All' after Dixon's celebrated catchphrase. A fictional autobiography of George Dixon, reworked by Charles Hatton from Willis' scripts, was published in 1960.[22] When in 1958 the Dixon character was awarded the British Empire Medal, a widow from Bristol sent Warner the ribbon of the B.E.M. awarded to her late policeman husband for bravery during the Blitz, saying that he was like her husband: 'To me, Dixon is real.' In its heyday *Dixon of Dock Green* regularly attracted an audience of 14 million.[23]

The series was written by Ted Willis for the first seven years. What was the secret of its success? Willis said: 'I had what every writer in television dreams of. I had an absolutely integrated cast, led by Jack

Warner. The chemistry was perfect between them. They became a kind of rep company; the personalities took over the parts and the parts took over the personalities. It was marvellous to see. We also had a marvellous director Douglas Moodie, and, though I do say it myself, we had some pretty good scripts.'[24] Willis had a panel of twenty policemen of all ranks who supplied him with story ideas and this gave the series an authentic feel which convinced the public.

Willis was an excellent scriptwriter. A working class lad from Tottenham who left school at fourteen, he was for fifty years a prolific writer in every narrative form. A life-long Socialist, he learned his craft during the war writing scripts on topical themes for the Unity Theatre, wartime documentaries and the theatre unit of the Army Bureau of Current Affairs. He did not, however, consider himself a 'Socialist writer':

> A great deal of my work is pure entertainment. But there has been a strand in my work that deals with social issues. My play *Hot Summer Night* dealt with intolerance between the races – and also a deeper kind of intolerance, the intolerance of a man towards his wife. *Woman in a Dressing Gown* dealt with the social issue of divorce and its impact on people. *Dixon* at its best always carried a social message.[25]

Like his literary idol Dickens, Willis had an ear for dialogue, a flair for characterization, a strong dramatic sense, an essential optimism and a deep and abiding humanity. Critics, particularly from the 1960s onwards, accused him of sentimentality but he pointed out that 'sentimentality was a vital strand in working class culture. It still exists. Perhaps not to the same extent as it did. But if you think of the songs that working class people like, they are usually very sentimental. They cry easily. And I'm a very typical representative. I cry easily.'[26] It is then perhaps as Dickensian that we should see Dock Green but that does not make it inauthentic for Britain in the 1950s was still in many respects profoundly Victorian.

Dixon became perhaps the best representative of an image of the police force which, as Clive Emsley argues, had developed in the 19th century:

> Here was an institution which Englishmen could boast of as being peculiarly English in that, in contrast to European police organizations, it was generally unarmed, non-military, and non-political; it

suited well the liberal Englishman's notion that his country's success derived from institutions, ideas and practices which provided models for the world. The police constable, to many middle-class Victorians, became the personification of an idealized image of the English legal system – impartial and functioning with solemnity and clockwork regularity.[27]

In his 1955 analysis of English public attitudes sociologist Geoffrey Gorer found to his surprise, since there were few attitudes subscribed to by two-thirds or more of the population, that three-quarters of the population expressed 'an enthusiastic appreciation of the English police.' He had expected many people to see them as 'the servants of the capitalist class.' Instead he found enthusiasm for them ('the best in the world') which he describes as 'peculiarly English and a most important component of the contemporary English character. To a great extent, the police represent a model of behaviour and character, an aspect about which many respondents are articulate.'[28] The qualities the police were seen to embody and were repeated over and over again by Gorer's respondents were reliability, courage, devotion to duty and fundamental decency. They could have been describing George Dixon.

The emotional restraint associated with the whole Dixon saga is also seen as quintessentially English. Charles Barr testifies to this in his sensitive analysis of the scene in *The Blue Lamp* in which Ma receives the news of George Dixon's death:

> I remember, before seeing *The Blue Lamp,* having known about this particular scene through a critic's scornful reference to it . . . as the epitome of falsity, a crude and patronising stiff-upper-lip stereotype. But it's not like that at all. It is observed and organised very precisely, finding a balance between 'English' restraint and the unembarrassed expression of grief that can't be contained: the scene does end on an image of weeping. In position and feeling alike, it is right at the centre of the film. I would go further and say that it is central to the twenty years of Ealing production, in the same double sense, and that the response of impatient irritation is not hard to understand. The scene has an obstinate 'weight' to it that is hard to discount, a representative quality which transcends the particular context . . . and makes it a definitive enactment of certain codes of behaviour and expression, which whether we welcome this or not, are deeply rooted in our culture.[29]

While on television for over twenty years, Jack Warner came to incarnate 'just an ordinary copper patrolling his beat,' his role in the cinema was subject to upwards revaluation. Warner was certainly associated with the image of the police in the public mind and when after *The Blue Lamp,* he played policemen in *Emergency Call* (1952), *The Ladykillers* (1955), *The Quatermass Experiment* (1955) and *Jigsaw* (1962), it was always as an inspector or superintendent. This is symptomatic of what happened to the police film in the 1950s.

The Blue Lamp was one of the last of Ealing's 'the people as hero' films. As Britain exchanged its reforming post-war Labour government for a Conservative government in 1951, so cultural assumptions and attitudes changed. The wartime 'people as hero' films were replaced by films celebrating officer and gentleman heroes of the Second World War: *Angels One Five, The Cruel Sea, Sink the Bismarck, Battle of the River Plate, The Dambusters, Reach for the Sky* etc. Similarly in the police films, there was a new concentration on senior officers and suddenly police inspectors and superintendents were being drawn from the ranks of actors previously associated with the roles of officers and gentlemen: John Mills (*Tiger Bay* 1959; *Town on Trial* 1957), David Farrar (*Lost,* 1955), Nigel Patrick (*Sapphire,* 1958) and particularly Jack Hawkins who appeared in two of the most significant police films of the 1950s: *The Long Arm* (1956) and *Gideon's Day* (1958). They contrast interestingly with *The Blue Lamp* because *The Long Arm* is an Ealing film and *Gideon's Day* was scripted by T. E. B. Clarke. Both centre on senior officers and are symptomatic of a reassertion of hierarchy in the culture of the 1950s with the return to power of the Conservatives.[30]

The Long Arm, directed by Charles Frend from a Janet Green/Robert Barr script, is a carefully constructed and rivetingly staged police procedural thriller, detailing the work of Criminal Records and forensics, methodical detailed detective work and the dedication and intuition of the professional policeman, in this case Chief Superintendent Halliday (Jack Hawkins). Halliday has a semi in Bromley, a long-suffering wife and a son whom he neglects for his duty. It is the exposition of the burden of command, dedication and service but focused here on an individual. He has to solve a series of safecrackings and track down a hitherto unknown criminal mastermind who with his equally ruthless wife is perfectly prepared to kill to escape arrest. The film is at pains to establish the home life of the victim of their escape from one robbery, whom we later see dying in hospital as he gives information to the police. Here there is no sympathy for the criminals who are hard, greedy and ruthless.

Hawkins plays almost exactly the same role in *Gideon's Day,* based on the novel by J. J. Marric. Published in 1955, it was the first of a series of 21 Scotland Yard police procedural novels by the prolific John Creasey writing under a pseudonym. Commander George Gideon of Scotland Yard was modelled on Commander George Hatherill, a friend of Creasey, and Creasey regularly visited the Yard for authentic detail. The novel was filmed in Britain for Columbia by John Ford, who declared: 'Scotland Yard is the British equivalent of the Wild West,'[31] and he sought with some success to turn the Metropolitan Police into the equivalent of the U.S. Cavalry in ethos and structure. T. E. B. Clarke was recruited to provide the script, probably because of *The Blue Lamp,* and worked with Ford to create a very faithful screen adaptation of the novel, which pioneered the multi-plot approach which became a commonplace of American TV cop shows in the 1980s but was way ahead of its time in the 1950s.

The hand of Ford can clearly be seen in the way Detective Inspector Lemaitre, Gideon's assistant in the book, has been replaced by a team who effectively duplicate the officers' mess of a frontier fort and are played by veterans of earlier Ford films: Detective Sergeant Frank Liggott (Frank Lawton) plays the equivalent role of George O'Brien's Captain Sam Collingwood in *Fort Apache*: John Loder, complete with the bowler hat and rolling gait of Victor McLaglen, is cast as Detective Sergeant 'Duke' Ponsford. There is the inevitable Irishman, Paddy (Barry Keegan) and there is Michael Trubshawe in full uniform and medals as Sergeant Golightly. Ford said:

> We'll have Michael Trubshawe as Gideon's assistant. I like the quirk of that officer's moustache on a three-stripe sergeant. And give him a long row of ribbons. This character had a fine war record.

Clarke objected that the C.I.D. and the uniformed branch worked separately and did not mix, to which Ford replied: 'They do in this picture. Mike Trubshawe wears uniform.' Clarke commented: 'And they did. And nobody queried it. Accuracy is fine so long as it is not allowed to become a despoiler of entertainment.'[32] Also added to the novel's characters is an eager beaver young P.C. Simon Farnaby-Green, the equivalent of the young subalterns in *She Wore a Yellow Ribbon,* who begins by giving Gideon a ticket, arrests a murderer and ends up escorting Gideon's daughter home from a concert.

To complete the cavalry analogy, Ford imported Anna Lee, archetypal soldier's wife in *Fort Apache,* to play Kate Gideon. The scene in which Gideon unannounced arrives with his team for lunch and they take over the kitchen is pure Ford. The film also builds up the home life, with the running theme of Gideon trying to get home for supper before his daughter's first concert and then attend the concert, but missing both because of his duties. Hawkins' Gideon is the definitive Scotland Yard officer: tough, dedicated, honest, professional. During the course of his day, he unmasks a sergeant for taking bribes from drug-pushers, saves his informer from a razor gang, hunts down an escaped mental patient who rapes and murders an 18 year old girl, breaks up a payroll robbery gang and finally deals with a gang of aristocratic amateurs who rob a safety deposit. For a Ford film, there is an uncharacteristic element of cruelty: a sex murderer; a safety deposit night manager ruthlessly shot down; Gideon terrifying a female prisoner with a description of hanging. Like *The Long Arm* it testifies to the hardening of society, the fragmentation of community and the greater problems facing the thin blue line.

But there is a change in the nature of police officers at the end of the 1950s and it epitomizes the changes in society. It is encapsulated in the arrival among the ranks of senior officers of Stanley Baker. This marks a distinct shift in class and cultural indicators. Baker's previous incarnation in films had been as a tough and ruthless criminal (*Hell Below Zero, Campbell's Kingdom, Checkpoint*) but he showed qualities that appealed in particular to two notable expatriate American directors, fugitives from McCarthy, Cy Endfield and Joseph Losey who were looking for a different kind of hero from the officer and gentleman of British films and saw qualities of toughness and proletarianism in Baker. These were highlighted in three police films: *Violent Playground* (1957), *Hell is a City* (1960) and *Blind Date* (1960). Interestingly after his spell on the side of the law, Baker returned effortlessly to playing criminals who demonstrated many of the same qualities as his policemen. He did this most notably in *The Criminal* (1960), *A Prize of Arms* (1962) and *Robbery* (1967). Baker is not just a proletarian police officer but also a provincial: *Violent Playground* is set in Liverpool, *Hell is a City* in

Manchester and *Blind Date,* though set in London, has Baker as a Welsh policeman. These films pre-figure the first great television challenge to the Dixon image – *Z-Cars.*

Violent Playground (1957) was the first of a series of Michael Relph – Basil Dearden social problem dramas made after they left Ealing. It concerns juvenile delinquency and like their subsequent dramas on racism (*Sapphire*) and homosexuality (*Victim*), it adopts a crime structure with a police investigation. In this case, it is a series of arson attacks which is eventually traced back to the leader of the teenage gang, Johnny (David McCallum). The perspective is liberal and in the case of the latter two films, the leading policeman (Nigel Patrick and John Barrie) gives voice to liberal sentiments. In *Violent Playground,* the central figure has to be won over to a liberal perspective. Stanley Baker plays Detective Sergeant Jack Truman who to his horror is appointed juvenile liaison officer. He protests 'I'm clumsy – I'm tactless – I'm brutal' but the experience of dealing with the Murphy family leads him to a greater understanding of the problems of parentless families growing up in teeming estates. He falls in love with Cathy, the older sister who is trying to raise the children, and takes in hand the streetwise children Patrick and Mary to stop them drifting into crime. But he is unable to save brother Johnny, the juvenile gangleader, who is behind the arson attacks and when unmasked, takes a classroom full of children hostage at gunpoint. Cathy persuades him to give up but it is agreed by all that he must be punished for what he has done. At the end, Truman, who is by now a 'true man', reveals that his father and grandfather were shepherds and he leads off a mixed race child by the hand, symbolic of his assumption of his role in guiding and protecting the young.

Baker then took on the role of Detective Inspector Harry Martineau in *Hell is a City* (1959), a Hammer film made for Associated British and directed and written by Val Guest. Tough, hard-edged and fast-moving, it transfers the vendetta between policeman and criminal common in American films to a British location with complete success. The only flaw is the casting of an American actor (John Crawford) as the villain, Don Starling, a role that should have been played by a British tough-guy actor to match Baker. The film opens with the escape of murderer/ rapist/robber Don Starling from jail, killing a warder and Martineau's vow to catch him. Martineau and Starling grew up together, went to school together but ended up on opposite sides of the law, indicating that character and not environment make criminals. Martineau though tough is a moralist. He pursues Starling because he is evil, and he refuses an affair with goodhearted barmaid Lucky Lusk because he is married, albeit unhappily. Martineau is working-class and there are class tensions within his marriage to snobbish middle-class Julia who denies him the children he desires. The film centres on the pursuit of Starling who leaves a trail of robbery and murder behind him. Eventually after a rooftop chase Martineau captures Starling, who is hanged. The last shot is of a brooding Baker walking the streets alone, the guardian of law and order. With its well-staged action scenes and atmospheric location shooting, it has all the pace and power of its American equivalent.

Joseph Losey's *Blind Date* (1960), directed by a McCarthyite refugee and scripted by two others (Ben Barzman and Millard Lampell) is a tightly constructed and elegantly shot thriller, centring on the investigation of the murder of a kept women Jacqueline Cousteau whose boyfriend, Dutch artist Jan Van Rooyen, is the prime suspect and is questioned by Detective Inspector Morgan (Baker). In a twist ending, the murdered woman turns out not to be Van Rooyen's mistress. His mistress is the jealous wife of the highranking diplomat who kept Jacqueline, Lady Helen Fenton (Micheline Presle). She had posed as Jacqueline, whom she murdered, and set up Jan as the suspect. In the end, she confesses, because contrary to her plan, she had fallen in love with him. Characteristic of Losey, it explores the idea of betrayal but there is a strong class element injected. Baker's Inspector Morgan is a tough, dogged, honest Welsh cop, the son of a chauffeur ('I'm not a gentleman') and suffering from a permanent cold. He has to deal with Assistant Commissioner Sir Brian Lewis and public-school educated, bowler-hatted Inspector Westover who weekend together and are anxious to protect Sir Howard Fenton from involvement in the case. But Morgan, convinced that Lady Fenton is the culprit, breaks her and charges her.

The class element was introduced deliberately by Losey who told James Leahy:

> I wanted to use Stanley as a Welshman who ... is a natural antagonist to the English ... and who was also working class, but who found himself caught up in a British class-structure, of the most rigid old boy kind of set-up, where unless he behaved in certain ways, his chances of promotion were slight ... it's influence, knowing the right people. Being the right person. Doing the

right thing . . . The people who were distributing it . . . and some of the people who had a part of the financing, were very concerned about the attitude toward the police, which they hadn't encountered before . . . that it was not in good taste, that it was not true, and so on. As a matter of fact, I think that the Baker character is highly flattering to the police.[33]

In several respects, these Baker films look forward to the next two significant developments in the police image, both on television. The provincial settings of *Violent Playground* and *Hell is a City,* the location shooting, authentic detail and social problem element prefigure *Z-Cars* and the tough-guy working-class anti-establishment cop anticipates *The Sweeney.*

Z-Cars marked a major departure in television depictions of the police. It was part of BBC Director-General Sir Hugh Greene's calculated bid to energize the corporation and bring it into line with contemporary cultural developments. In its first incarnation, *Z-Cars* ran for 170 episodes between 1962 and 1965. Thereafter in January 1966 several of the cast transferred to a new police series, *Softly, Softly,* centred on the regional crime squads. *Z-Cars* was revived in a twice weekly early evening format in 1967 and ran for a further ten years. The series in its first incarnation coincided exactly with the 'British New Wave' in the cinema and shared many of its characteristics: black and white photography, northern locations, accurately observed working-class characters and milieux. Troy Kennedy Martin and John McGrath, the original scriptwriter and director of *Z-Cars* had a precise vision of what they wanted. McGrath said: 'We placed a conscious emphasis on narrative-society, real and recognizable, but *in motion*. No slick tie-ups. No reassuring endings, where decency and family life triumphed.' *Radio Times* emphasized this view in its description of the series:

> Life is fraught with danger for policemen in the North of England overspill estate called Newtown. Here a mixed community, displaced from larger towns by slum clearance, has been brought together and housed on an estate without amenities and without community feeling.[34]

This makes it the antithesis of *Dixon* and this is something contemporary critics picked up on,[35] consistently comparing *Dixon* unfavourably with *Z-Cars*. It is true that audiences for *Z-Cars* rose from 9 to 14 million within the first eight weeks of its run and attained 16.65 million viewers by 1963 but by 1965 the audience had dropped back to 11.9 million. It should be remembered however that *Dixon* was still drawing audiences of 13 million even at the height of *Z-Cars'* popularity and it continued to run until just before *Z-Cars* itself came off.

Much of the criticism of *Dixon* is unfair. It was not untrue. It was selectively true. It represented the spirit of an earlier, more communally based society which was being superseded by a new more mobile, more fragmented, more materialistic and more individualistic society. If *Z-Cars* reflected those changes, the continued popularity of *Dixon* represented a hankering for that older world. Further evidence that this hankering for a settled, moral order, established values and a dedicated, uncorrupt police force was real is provided by the popularity on ITV of *No Hiding Place,* which ran for 236 episodes between 1959 and 1967. It was a London-based police series, centred on the archetypal officer and gentleman copper, the snuff-taking Chief Superintendent Lockhart, played by Raymond Francis. When ITV cancelled the series in 1965, there was such an outcry from the public that it was brought back and ran for a further two years. Simultaneously in 1965–66 *Gideon's Way* ran on ITV, bringing to the television screen the hero of J. J. Marric's Scotland Yard novels, already filmed with Jack Hawkins in 1958. John Gregson played the role on TV.

Z-Cars seemed to be making a conscious reference to *The Blue Lamp* by opening its first episode with the aftermath of the shooting of a bobby on the beat. The reaction is the introduction of crime patrols in cars, to be staffed by the hardest men they can find. They are in the first instance the rugby-playing Scot Jock Weir, the Lancastrian Bob Steele, the Yorkshireman Fancy Smith and the Ulsterman Bert Lynch. There was a Liverpudlian desk sergeant, Sergeant Twentyman. The series was set in Lancashire in a Liverpool overspill town, Newtown, based on Kirby, and with a nearby port, Seaport. The initial episode of 'Four of a Kind' saw the recruiting of the crews for Z Victor One and Z Victor Two, and interwove pub fight, teenage runaways and a psychiatric patient with an axe. It also highlighted the domestic problems of the police, whose lives were far removed from the settled domestic routine of Dixon: Sergeant Watt's wife has left him because of the job and P.C. Steele and his wife have had a fight over his late return home. That event is reported, not seen, but the stain of the hotpot on the wall and Mrs. Steele's black eye testify to it. It was this which caused the

Chief Constable of Lancashire to demand, in vain, that the series be taken off for bringing the police into disrepute. But the police grew to approve of it for its realistic depiction of police work. Two of the leading characters in *Z Cars* were the permanently bad-tempered Superintendent Charlie Barlow (Stratford Johns) and his faithful and phlegmatic assistant Detective Sergeant John Watt (Frank Windsor), both portrayed as northerners. They were carried over to *Softly Softly* when the first run of *Z-Cars* ended.

It seems likely that Barlow and Watt provided the inspiration for the tough, permanently bad-tempered individualist Detective Inspector Jack Regan (John Thaw) and his faithful, even-tempered assistant Detective Sergeant George Carter (Dennis Waterman) in *The Sweeney*. After *Z-Cars* this was the next breakthrough cop show. Created by Ian Kennedy Martin and produced by Euston Films for Thames TV, *The Sweeney* ran for 52 episodes from 1975 to 1978 and set a new standard in *policiers*. Interestingly Troy Kennedy Martin and Allan Prior, stalwarts of *Z-Cars,* were among the regular writers for *The Sweeney*. It was set and filmed in London, reflecting the cultural shift in the 1970s from the North back to the Metropolis, and featured the exploits of the flying squad, whose cockney rhyming slang nickname was the Sweeney Todd. Regan, like John Watt, is separated from his wife because of the pressure of the job. Regan is a tough-talking, hard-drinking, disrespectful individualist, continually passed over for promotion for following his instinct. He is willing to bend the rules to get his man and is usually vindicated in the outcome. He had been fourteen years in the force before joining the flying squad and is contemptuous of university-educated intellectual coppers ('penpushers with 2nd class honours degrees'). His philosophy is summed up by the defiant 'I am not a gentleman, and I don't like losing.' He is far cry from Jack Hawkins, John Mills and Nigel Patrick.

The Sweeney was full of car chases and large-scale punch-ups and there was a sense that there was little difference in style and ethos between police and criminals, who behaved and spoke and lived in a similar fashion and shared the same proletarian habits (the pub, the football match), could handle themselves in a fight, were tough professionals, but happened to be on opposite sides in a war.

Unlike *Z-Cars, The Sweeney* had two cinematic spinoffs: *Sweeney!* (1976) and *Sweeney 2* (1978), which had more violence, nudity and bad language than the television series and in which both Regan and Carter are single.

Sweeney! is a prime example of the paranoid thriller that flourished in the wake of Watergate, the idea that high level conspiracies are at work involved in illegal activities and cover-ups. In this version, the American press agent of the Labour Government's Energy Secretary is secretly working for the multi-national oil companies and seeking to ensure that the OPEC meeting in London lowers rather than raises the oil price. He uses prostitutes, assassins, blackmail and murder to achieve his ends. Regan, despite having his flat bugged and his telephone tapped and being the subject of several assassination attempts, uncovers the conspiracy and by his tenacity forces the resignation of the minister and the deportation of the press agent, Elliott McQueen. He seeks to arrest him before his deportation but McQueen is mysteriously gunned down, presumably by his employers.

Sweeney 2, scripted by Troy Kennedy Martin, pits the Sweeney against a gang of well-organized, professional, violent bank robbers, based in Malta. The fleeing robbers shoot innocent people who get into the way and also their own wounded comrades. Eventually they are broken, but when the last two survivors are trapped, one is killed and the other commits suicide. It is a violent film, which is basically exploring the conflict between two very professional violent clans or tribes, one on the side of the law, and one not, and the macho culture which they share: drink, sexism and virile banter.

The same kind of all-male canteen culture is explored in Lynda LaPlante's *Prime Suspect* (1991), a detailed police procedural thriller about the search for a serial killer of prostitutes. The difference here is that the leading figure is a woman, Detective Inspector Jane Tennison (Helen Mirren), who has to fight entrenched chauvinism to lead the murder hunt but does so successfully and wins the respect of the men, though her domestic relationship breaks up as a result of the pressure and her partner moves out. The novelty of the film is the feminist slant, showing how hard it is for a woman to make her way in the force. *Prime Suspect* generated several sequels, all starring Helen Mirren. The first three *Prime Suspects* all focused on sex crimes: the hunt for a serial killer of prostitutes; the rape and murder of a mixed-race teenager by a pornographer; the systematic abuse of teenage rent boys by authority figures, among them police officers.

Alongside these social realist police dramas, there has continued to be a succession of more traditional, civilized, intuitive and reflective senior officers starring in series based on popular novels: Detective Chief Inspector Wexford (George Baker), Detective Inspector Morse (John Thaw), Chief Superintendent Adam Dalgleish (Roy Marsden) and Detective Superintendent Charles Wycliffe (Jack Shepherd), all of them provincial rather than metropolitan.

It is interesting to note that each of the principal developments in police series has grown out of a cinematic trend. *Dixon of Dock Green* was a byproduct of *The Blue Lamp* and of the ethos and approach of Ealing Studios and began and ended with moral homilies to camera. *Z-Cars* emerged from the British 'New Wave': the provinces, drama/documentary, social realism. *The Sweeney* was inspired by American police films like *Coogan's Bluff, Dirty Harry* and *Magnum Force* and focused on intuitive individualists dealing with crime on their own terms. But they also highlighted the much greater violence that was now a feature of society.[36] This is reflected in the statistics for reported woundings. In 1920, there were 791; in 1930, 5,177; in 1960, 14,142; in 1980, 95,044.

Television definitively took over from cinema in the depiction of the police. During the 1960s and 1970s, the British police were conspicuous by their absence from the cinema screen. Admittedly the 1960s was the decade of the spy thriller. But the sidelining of the police was also a reflection of the way in which the cinema was moving from a conformist to an oppositional stance, from a national to a sectional medium, pitched at the under-30s, a third of whom by 1997 had a criminal record. There were one or two exceptions. The underrated *The Informers* (1963) was an excellent thriller in which disgraced police inspector Nigel Patrick goes underground to locate the people responsible for his downfall. In *Bunny Lake is Missing* (1965) Laurence Olivier gave a performance of monumental calm as an old-fashioned methodical police inspector investigating a missing child. Two *Z-Cars* alumni took a much more disenchanted view of the police in the cinema. David Greene's *The Strange Affair* (1968) starred Jeremy Kemp, the erstwhile P.C. Bob Steele of *Z-Cars,* playing a paranoid police sergeant who blackmails an idealistic young recruit (Michael York) into helping him frame a drug smuggling ring. It is set in a degenerate London, people by trendy pornographers, psychopathic criminals and corrupt policemen. Sidney Lumet's powerful and claustrophobic *The Offence* (1972), scripted by John Hopkins from his own play, centred on Sean Connery as a hard-bitten detective tormented by thoughts of murder, rape and evil he encounters every day. During the tough questioning of a suspected child rapist (Ian Bannen), he is forced to confront his own similar feelings, beats the suspect to death and is arrested.

The majority of crime films at this time centred on criminals and their crimes, with the police at best peripheral. The planning and execution of robberies, the psychology and interplay of criminals and the buzz of violence were their principal features: *The Criminal* (1960, *Payroll* (1961), *The Frightened City* (1961), *A Prize of Arms* (1962), *West 11* (1963), *Night Must Fall* (1963), *He Who Rides the Tiger* (1963), *Robbery* (1967), *The Italian Job* (1969), *Get Carter* (1970), *Villain* (1971).[37]

Nothing could be more symptomatic of the complete reversal of values and sympathies after the 1960s than the spate of retro movies, rewriting the history of the post-war decades so that figures who were regarded as socially or culturally deviant and were condemned by the legal system in one way or another are revalued, revealed as hapless victims of an oppressive system or heroic rebels against repressive and outdated bourgeois values. Thus there have been sympathetic cinematic depictions of real life criminals of the 1940s, 1950s and 1960s, such as Craig and Bentley (*Let Him Have It*, 1991), Ruth Ellis (*Dance With a Stranger*, 1984), Stephen Ward (*Scandal*, 1989) and Karl Hulten and Elizabeth Jones (*Chicago Joe and the Showgirl*, 1989). In addition, there has been a trend for casting pop idols as famous real-life criminals, thus transforming these criminals into cultural heroes: Roger Daltrey in *McVicar* (1980), Phil Collins in *Buster* (1988) and Martin and Gary Kemp in *The Krays* (1990). Thus cinema confirms its acceptance of a minority, youth-orientated role, whereas majority views, values and aspirations are now reflected in television, which explains why the police in every guise and form dominate the television screen.

Notes

1. *Radio Times* 7–13 September 1996.
2. Ted Willis, *Evening All: Fifty Years Over a Hot Typewriter,* London, 1991, p. 70.
3. On music hall songs and the police see Christopher Pulling, *They Were Singing,* London, 1952, pp. 87–105.
4. Willis, *Evening All,* p. 71.
5. Willis, *Evening All,* p. 73.
6. On Ealing Studios, see Charles Barr, *Ealing Studios,* London, 1993 and Alan Burton, Tim O'Sullivan and Paul Wells eds., *Liberal Directions: Basil Dearden and Postwar British Film Culture,* Trowbridge, 1997.
7. Jack Warner, *Evening All,* London, 1979, p. 133.

8. Dirk Bogarde, *Snakes and Ladders,* St. Albans, 1979, pp. 159–60.

9. Anthony Aldgate, *Cinema and Society: Britain in the 1950s and 1960s,* Open University Study Guide, Milton Keynes, 1992, pp. 68–70.

10. Warner, *Evening All,* p. 134.

11. Sir Harold Scott, *Scotland Yard,* London, 1954, pp. 90–1.

12. Robert Murphy, *Smash and Grab,* London, 1993, pp. 94–5.

13. *Daily Mirror* 18 January 1950; *News of the World* 22 January 1950.

14. Andy Medhurst, 'Dirk Bogarde' in Charles Barr ed., *All Our Yesterdays,* London, 1985, pp. 345–54.

15. Sue Harper and Vincent Porter, *Weeping in the Cinema in the 1950s,* Mass-Observation Archive, Occasional Papers 3, Sussex University, 1955, p. 10; *Daily Mail* 20 January 1950.

16. *The Star* 20 January 1950; *The Times* 20 January 1950; *Manchester Guardian* 20 January 1950.

17. *Daily Mail* 20 January 1950; *News of the World* 22 January 1950; *Daily Telegraph* 23 January 1950.

18. *Daily Mirror* 18 January 1950; *Evening News* 19 January 1950.

19. *Daily Mirror* 18 January 1950.

20. *Daily Herald* 20 January 1950.

21. *Daily Worker* 30 December 1950.

22. George Dixon, *Dixon of Dock Green,* London, 1960, revealed that Dixon was born and brought up in Dock Green, the son of a painter and decorator. He was educated at the local Board School and eventually followed his maternal uncle, a village bobby, into the police force.

23. Willis, *Evening All,* p. 190.

24. Author's interview with Ted Willis, 17 July 1991.

25. Author's interview with Ted Willis.

26. Author's interview with Ted Willis.

27. Clive Emsley, 'The English Bobby' in Roy Porter ed., *Myths of the English,* Cambridge, 1992, p. 118.

28. Geoffrey Gorer, *Exploring English Character,* London, 1955, p. 213.

29. Charles Barr, *Ealing Studios,* p. 98.

30. Jeffrey Richards, *Films and British National Identity,* Manchester, 1997, pp. 128–46.

31. T. E. B. Clarke, *This Is Where I Came In,* London, 1974, p. 194.

32. Clarke, *This Is Where I Came In,* pp. 194–5.

33. James Leahy, *The Cinema of Joseph Losey,* London, 1967, pp. 79–81.

34. Stuart Laing, 'Banging In Some Reality': the original 'Z' Cars' in John Corner ed., *Popular Television in Britain,* London, 1991, p. 129.

35. Laing, 'Banging In Some Reality', pp. 130–1.

36. Alan Clarke, 'You're Nicked! television police series and the fictional representation of law and order' in Dominic Strinati and Stephen Wagg eds., *Come On Down: Popular Media Culture in Postwar Britain,* London, 1992, pp. 232–53; and Alan Clarke 'This is not the boy scouts! Television police series and definitions of law and order' in Tony Bennett, Colin Mercer and Janet Woollacott eds., *Popular Culture and Social Relations,* Milton Keynes, 1986, pp. 219–232.

37. Robert Murphy, *Sixties British Cinema,* London, 1992, pp. 210–18.

The Ladykillers (1955)

9

Cul-de-Sac England
The Ladykillers

When Ealing Studios were sold to the BBC in 1955, in the very month that *The Ladykillers* was released, a plaque was installed which declared: 'Here during a quarter of a century were made many films projecting Britain and the British character.' It is reasonable to assume, then, that *The Ladykillers* was consciously projecting something distinctively and desirably British. To find out what this was we need to examine the film and to set it in the context both of Ealing films and of contemporary British society.

The projection of Britain was an aim dear to the heart of the studio's dynamic and imaginative production chief, Sir Michael Balcon. One of the greatest of all British film producers, he was responsible for a distinctive body of work which raised not only the quality but also the standing of British films both nationally and internationally. 'My ruling passion has always been the building up of a native [film] industry with its roots firmly planted in the soil of this country,' he wrote in his autobiography.[1] With the onset of World War II he became concerned as much with the social and political role of cinema as with its economic and cultural importance. Abroad, in particular, he saw 'British films, truthfully reflecting the British way of life' as the 'most powerful ambassador we have'. In 1945 he outlined a programmatic schedule for post-war film-making which demonstrates a high level of civic responsibility and patriotic pride:

Never in any period of its history has the prestige of this country, in the eyes of the rest of the world, mattered so much as it does now. The political intervention of Britain in the affairs of liberated countries colours the attitude not only of Government towards Government, but of people towards people. And to these people German propaganda with the varying degrees of skill has presented the British in many guises: blood-soaked Imperialists, punch-drunk degenerates, betrayers of our Allies, grovelling servants of fabulous Jewish plutocrats – the list is familiar, and laugh at it as we may, let us not delude ourselves that its authors have been entirely ineffectual in their purpose. Clearly the need is great for a projection of the true Briton to the rest of the world. . . . The world, in short, must be presented with a complete picture of Britain . . . Britain as a leader in Social Reform in the defeat of social injustices and a champion of civil liberties; Britain as a patron and parent of great writing, painting and music; Britain as a questing explorer, adventurer and trader; Britain as the home of great industry and craftsmanship; Britain as a mighty military power standing alone and undaunted against terrifying aggression. We do not set ourselves up as a master race if we remind the world that Britain has this background; we merely seek a place of recognition among nations who have too long been presented only with the debit side of our account.[2]

There is evidence of the partial implementation of this aim at Ealing in the series of films set in the Commonwealth (*The Overlanders, Where No Vultures Fly, West of Zanzibar*), in a Dickens adaptation (*Nicholas Nickleby*), in films dramatizing the work of the police (*The Blue Lamp*), hospitals (*The Feminine Touch*), the Church (*Lease of Life*) and the probation service (*I Believe in You*), in films dealing with problems posed by the post-war reintegration of returning prisoners of war (*The Captive Heart*) and reconciliation with Germany (*Frieda*). However, perhaps it is worth noting that two of the most spectacular of Ealing's films dealt with noble defeats (*Scott of the Antarctic* and *Dunkirk*), suggesting a view of Britain as perennially gallant loser rather than triumphant victor.[3]

But for most people Ealing's post-war output means the celebrated Ealing comedies. There is no doubt what view people have of the Ealing comedies and of the world they project. It is a world that is essentially quaint, cosy, whimsical and backward-looking; it venerates vintage steam trains (*The Titfield Thunderbolt*), old Clyde 'puffers' (*The Maggie*) and run-down seaside piers (*Barnacle Bill*). It is a world that enshrines what are seen as quintessentially English qualities: a stubborn individualism that is heroic to the point of eccentricity ('It's because we're English that we are sticking to our right to be Burgundians,' says a character in *Passport to Pimlico*); a hatred of authoritarianism and bureaucracy coupled with a belief in tolerance and consensus; a philosophy that can be summed up by the slogan 'Small is beautiful; old is good'. It is for all these reasons that the films have been so popular in the United States, whose philosophy is, of course, their antithesis ('Large is beautiful; new is best'), and have helped to shape American attitudes towards Britain. It is also the reason why non-Ealing comedies, admittedly made by ex-Ealing personnel, are often grouped together with the genuine article – films like *Genevieve* (vintage cars) and *The Smallest Show on Earth* (rundown fleapit cinema). That some of the Ealing comedies conform to this image cannot be denied. But it is too sweeping and incomplete a definition of the studio's entire comedy output, and it takes no account of, for instance, the wickedly elegant *Kind Hearts and Coronets,* which is by any reckoning one of the most distinguished Ealing comedies. Nevertheless, Balcon believed that 'the comedies reflected the country's mood, social condition and aspirations.'[4] To test this assertion we must examine the similarities and differences in the comedies and find out what the film-makers thought they were doing and how far audiences agreed with them.

In what circumstances were the films produced, and by whom? In the days when Basil Dean ran Ealing (1931–38), he had had painted on the studio wall the slogan 'The studio with the team spirit'. It was a slogan Balcon tried to live up to after he took over from Dean. There was a permanent staff at Ealing, and Balcon ran the studio by committee, with regular round-table meetings to discuss projects and current productions. If there was a consensus in favour of a particular production, Balcon would back it even if he had misgivings himself. It was Monja Danischewsky, publicity director at Ealing, who coined the much quoted phrase 'Mr Balcon's Academy for Young Gentlemen', and the role of a paternalist headmaster in which he was cast was one that Balcon goodhumouredly accepted in his autobiography.[5] 'Ealing', wrote Danischewsky, 'had the air of a family business, set on the village green of the queen of London suburbs.'[6] If Balcon was the head of this family, it also had a resident nanny in the Brazilian-born director Alberto Cavalcanti, who helped to integrate the documentarists recruited by Balcon into the mainstream of feature film-making.[7] It is perhaps small wonder, then, that Ealing films were often set in tightly knit little communities animated by a spirit of co-operation.

What was the attitude of this community of film-makers? Balcon recalled it in 1974 in an interview with John Ellis:

> We were middle-class people brought up with middle-class backgrounds and rather conventional educations. Though we were radical in our points of view, we did not want to tear down institutions. . . . We were people of the immediate post-war generation and we voted Labour for the first time after the war: this was our mild revolution. We had a great affection for British institutions: the comedies were done with affection. . . . Of course, we wanted to improve them, or, to use the cliché of today, to look for a more just society in the terms that we knew. The comedies were a mild protest, but not protests at anything more sinister than the regimentation of the time. I think we were going through a mildly euphoric period then: believing in ourselves as having some sense of, it sounds awful, national pride.[8]

The period spanned by the Ealing comedies, from *Hue and Cry* (1947) to *Barnacle Bill* (1957), covers the terms of office of both Labour and Conservative Governments. The Attlee Government (1945–51) implemented Labour's plans to create a 'brave new post-war world' with the introduction of the welfare state, the nationalization of key industries and the granting of independence to India. The Labour victory in 1945 had not been exactly a landslide in percentage voting terms: 47.8 per cent of those who actually voted cast their votes for Labour, but 39.8 per cent voted Conservative, and 20 per cent did not vote at all. In the 1950 election 46.1 per cent voted Labour, and 43.5 per cent voted Conservative. In the 1951 election 48.8 per cent voted Labour and 48 per cent voted Conservative, but, as a result of the inequitable British electoral system, the Conservatives won a majority of seats and formed the Government. They were to remain in power for the next thirteen years. It is clear that the country was more or less evenly divided between Labour and Conservative voters. But what matters more than precise voting figures is that great intangible the national mood, and popular culture is a valuable indicator of it. In 1945 there was a desire for change. Labour duly met this desire through the introduction of much needed reforms, but rationing, shortages and restrictions persisted. The generation which had won the war wanted the welfare state, but it also wanted fun and spending money. The Conservatives stayed in office for thirteen years by maintaining the welfare state but dismantling restrictions, ending rationing and promoting affluence. So having veered leftwards and sanctioned major social changes, the country veered rightwards, settling down to enjoy the fruits of peace and turning its back on further change.

The first half of the 1950s was an era of peace, prosperity and order. The crime rate was falling. There was full employment and rising productivity. The greater availability of consumer durables blunted class antagonisms. The coronation of Queen Elizabeth II in 1953 was seen as ushering in a 'new Elizabethan age', as the Empire was transmuted into the Commonwealth, a worldwide brotherhood of nations, and as Britain continued to notch up memorable achievements: the Hunt expedition's conquest of Everest in 1953, Dr Roger Bannister's first four-minute mile in 1954 and, in 1956, Britain's tenure of all three speed records, air, land and sea. The cinema meanwhile was reliving the epic deeds of World War II with such popular recreations of British gallantry as *The Dam Busters* and *The Battle of the River Plate*.

Critics have seen the period from 1951 to 1958 as one of 'complacency and inertia', as 'extraordinarily dead', a 'doldrums era'.[9] It is a curious fact that the British film industry ran out of steam at about the same time as the Labour Government. Just as World War II had energized British society, so it had revitalized and stimulated the British film industry. This revival continued into the late 1940s, when British cinemas enjoyed their highest-ever attendances and British films their finest artistic flowering. David Lean, Carol Reed, Thorold Dickinson, Michael Powell and Emeric Pressburger, Frank Launder and Sidney Gilliat and the Boulting Brothers were producing their best work. Then in the early 1950s, just as Labour and the enthusiasm for change were fading, these careers either ended or entered periods of stagnation and decline. As Vernon Bogdanor and Robert Skidelsky wrote in 1970:

> Perhaps the period of Conservative rule will be looked back upon as the last period of quiet before the storm, rather like the Edwardian age which in some respects it resembles. In that case its tranquillity may well come to be valued more highly than its omissions.[10]

But tranquillity is rarely the matrix of cultural excitement. As Orson Welles observed in one of the British cinema's post-war masterpieces, *The Third Man:*

> In Italy for thirty years under the Borgias they had warfare, terror, murder, bloodshed – but they produced Michelangelo, Leonardo da Vinci and the Renaissance. In Switzerland, they had brotherly love, 500 years of democracy and peace, and what did that produce? . . . the cuckoo clock.[11]

The Ealing comedies, then, were produced against a background first of post-war change and later of post-change complacency. What they have in common was isolated by Balcon.[12] They are not vehicles for established comedians. They are in the main original screen stories and not adaptations. They all deal with people in recognizable settings who are plunged into extraordinary situations. They are essentially wish-fulfilment fantasies. This is a view shared by Ealing writer T. E. B. Clarke, who calls them 'what if?' films: what if part of London declared itself independent (*Passport to Pimlico*)? What if a village tried to run its own railway line (*The Titfield Thunderbolt*)? What if someone discovered a foolproof way of smuggling gold out of the country (*The Lavender Hill Mob*)? All Clarke's comedies involve a fantastical premise realistically worked out.[13] There is a dream-like quality to many of the Ealing comedies: William Rose, in fact, dreamed the idea of *The Ladykillers* and *Passport to Pimlico* takes place during a midsummer heatwave which breaks at the end, giving the film something of the quality of a fever-dream.[14]

The important thing to remember about films like the Ealing comedies is that they are susceptible to different interpretations from different angles at the same time. Also the audience may respond to a film in an entirely different way from that which the film-makers expected. John Ellis offers a class interpretation of the films:

> Ealing's comedy does not deal with resentments or guilt so much as with aspirations and Utopian desires. It is not primarily concerned with satire, which can be identified with the playing out of class resentments. . . . Ealing's comedy style was new in that it dealt with the Utopian desires of the lower middle class rather than its resentments.[15]

He sees the comedies as dealing almost exclusively with the lower middle class, as affirmations of the idea of community solidarity denied by the facts of a competitive, status-conscious, middle-class life. This affirmation of community can take two forms, producing both 'progressive' comedies (*Passport to Pimlico, Whisky Galore*), which disrupt the social order to maintain the well-being of the community, and 'reactionary' comedies (*The Titfield Thunderbolt*), which spring from a respect for ideas swept aside by the forces of history. Ellis believes this concentration on the lower middle class to be a reflection of the background of the Ealing personnel and of the radicalization of their generation by the Depression. But it is a limited radicalism, constrained by Balcon's strict moral attitude and national pride. Ellis concludes that 'no real revolution can be advocated and no serious criticism of national institutions of power.'

The changes in the nature of the comedies he sees as a reflection of the changing preoccupations of the petty bourgeoisie. Thus the early Ealing comedies reflect their revolt against post-war restrictions (*Passport to Pimlico, Whisky Galore*) and their aspirations to higher status via class and wealth (*Kind Hearts and Coronets, Lavender Hill Mob*). But the later Ealing comedies, made during the emergence of the consumer society, attack the lack of social conscience reflected in the closing of railway lines (*The Titfield Thunderbolt*) and the rise of the American multinationals (*The Maggie*).[16]

The lower-middle-class bias of the characters in the Ealing comedies is undeniable, with a draper's assistant killing off a ducal family (*Kind Hearts and Coronets*), small shopkeepers declaring UDI in part of London (*Passport to Pimlico*), a bank clerk and a small manufacturer planning the perfect crime (*The Lavender Hill Mob*). But a purely class-based interpretation of the films is too restricted and too restrictive. It makes more sense to consider class as one dimension of a broader socio-political interpretation.

Given the admitted Labour allegiance of the Ealing film-makers, it is arguable that the early Ealing films (1947–51) constitute a programmatic attack on the evils that Labour wished to eradicate: entrenched aristocratic privilege (*Kind Hearts and Coronets*), the power of money (*The Lavender Hill Mob*), monopoly capitalism (*The Man in the White Suit*) and colonialism (*Whisky Galore*). *Passport to Pimlico* (1949) is perhaps the arch-Labour film, pointing to the evils of a blanket removal of restrictions and seeking to reconcile the public to its lot.

Dedicated to the memory of rationing, the film is informed by a desire to return to the wartime spirit of unity and co-operation as the best means of facing and overcoming the problems of the post-war world. The first part of *Passport to Pimlico* shows greed and self-interest surfacing in society to submerge the community interest when Pimlico Borough Council throws out greengrocer Arthur Pemberton's scheme for turning a bomb site into a lido for local children and decides instead to sell it for profit (the evils of the unrestrained free market economy). When an unexploded bomb goes off, revealing a Burgundian treasure and a charter of independence, all restrictions and regulations are abolished, and black marketeers flood in. Naked self-interest rules. At this point an enemy appears to unite the people. In 1939 it was Hitler. In 1949 it is Whitehall, which seeks to bludgeon the inhabitants of Pimlico into surrender. Miramont Place, Pimlico, declares itself independent and fights the war again in miniature. In the end the bureaucrats are beaten by communal effort and self-sacrifice. A compromise is agreed by the two sides, and Pimlico re-enters the United Kingdom, to everyone's relief ('You never know when you're well off until you aren't'). The ration books are redistributed, for, as the message clearly states, rationing and restriction are better than the unrestrained growth of free enterprise.[17] The film captures exactly the mood of J. B. Priestley's 1945 novel *Three Men in New Suits, in* which a returning soldier says: 'Instead of guessing and grabbing, we plan. Instead of competing, we co-operate.'[18]

Balcon was giving a too literal and one-dimensional reading of the comedies when he wrote in his autobiography:

In the immediate post-war years there was as yet no mood of cynicism; the bloodless revolution of 1945 had taken place but I think our first desire was to get rid of as many wartime restrictions as possible and get going. The country was tired of regulations and regimentation, and there was a mild anarchy in the air. In a sense our comedies were reflections of this mood . . . a safety valve for our more anti-social impulses. Who has not wanted to raid a bank (*The Lavender Hill Mob*) as an escape to a life of ease; commit mayhem on a fairly large scale to get rid of tiresome people in the way (*Kind Hearts and Coronets*); make the bureaucrat bite the dust (*Passport to Pimlico* and *The Titfield Thunderbolt*)?[19]

The key phrase here is 'a safety valve for our more anti-social impulses', for the role of the wish-fulfilment fantasy is not just to reflect but also to defuse discontent, producing heady images of the abolition of rationing (*Passport to Pimlico*), as much whisky as you want (*Whisky Galore*) and money unlimited (*The Lavender Hill Mob*) before returning the characters to earth and reality at the end. The fantasy projection purges the resentment and makes people happier with their lot. Significantly, the first Ealing comedy, *Hue and Cry,* premiered at the height of the appalling winter of 1946–47, lit up cinemas with its exuberance and humour and took people's minds off the fuel shortage.[20]

But times change, and if the early Ealing comedies can be seen as an affirmation of Labour's programme, the later ones can be seen as a retreat from it. Interestingly, the early Eating comedies were more or less remade in the Conservative era (1951–58) and show interesting and instructive changes. *Whisky Galore* (1949), in which a Scottish island community fools and frustrates an English laird in order to keep a cargo of illicit whisky, is reworked as *The Maggie* (1954), in which the crew of an old Scottish 'puffer' fools and frustrates an American laird to keep its ship. *Passport to Pimlico* (1949), in which a small urban community defies the attempts of Whitehall to suppress its independence, becomes *The Titfield Thunderbolt* (1953), in which a small rural community defies the attempts of British Railways to close its branch line. *Kind Hearts and Coronets* (1949), in which a shop assistant wipes out all those who stand between him and a ducal title, becomes *The Ladykillers* (1955), in which a group of criminals fail to wipe out a little old lady and polish off each other instead. The changes in emphasis, locale and personnel are significant. In *Whisky Galore* an entire community undermines the English colonial power; in *The Maggie* the community has shrunk to a crew defending a vintage boat, and the enemy is an American businessman. A full-scale revolt has become the small-scale defence of a relic of the past, a Scottish analogue of *The Titfield Thunderbolt.* In *Passport to Pimlico* a committee of shopkeepers under a democratically elected leader fight the monolithic power of Whitehall over an inner-city area; in *The Titfield Thunderbolt* a semi-feudal rural community, led by its traditional leaders, the vicar and the squire, defends a rural branch line against British Railways, one of the great nationalized industries. In *Kind Hearts and Coronets,* a lower-middle-class murderer successfully eliminates the aristocracy; in *The Ladykillers* a little old middle-class lady successfully survives attempts by a criminal gang to eliminate her. The shift of values and sympathies in every case is clear.

But there is a third approach to the comedies which cuts across this socio-political interpretation – the personal and artistic, which relates to the intentions of individuals within the Ealing organization. On this level the films fall into two distinct groups, which bear no relation to chronology. The dominant strain, which is nostalgic and conformist, is that associated with the scripts of T. E. B. Clarke – *Passport to Pimlico* (1949), *The Lavender Hill Mob* (1951), *The Titfield Thunderbolt* (1953) and *Barnacle Bill* (1957). Significantly, he also wrote the Ealing tribute to the police, *The Blue Lamp* (1950) and is himself an ex-policeman. Clarke's films come closest to the popular image of Ealing and conform with Balcon's stated desire not to attack established institutions too forcefully.

The subversive strain is represented by Robert Hamer and Alexander Mackendrick. Both are significantly un-English figures. Hamer, French-educated and a Francophile, a man who set four of his films in France, brought Gallic sophistication, sensibility, elegance and wit to *Kind Hearts and Coronets* (1949), making it in that sense unique among the Ealing comedies. Mackendrick, American-born and Scottish-educated, made four Ealing comedies and deliberately subverted the essential cosiness of the Ealing archetype. He said in interview in 1968:

> The films that I made there were personal and I wrote the scripts of them with the scenarists. . . . Personally I was always very attracted by comedy, because I believe that it alone can say certain things. It allows you to do things that are too dangerous or that a certain audience cannot accept.[21]

Superficially, *Whisky Galore* is similar to *Passport to Pimlico*; in both a small community unites to defeat an intolerant outside force. But an extra dimension is added by the location (Scotland) and the object of the struggle (whisky). In *Whisky Galore* the enemy is Captain Waggett, a pukka British officer who is effectively administering the natives. But he is completely out of his depth, does not understand their mentality and is constantly outwitted. The Scottish community is devious and ruthless, unlike the open, honest, decent bourgeoisie of Pimlico. Its aim is not a community facility (a lido) but instant gratification (whisky). Similarly, *The Man in the White Suit* (1951), one of the few British films to deal with British industry, focuses on the impossibility of reconciling capitalism and progress. It shows unions and management combining to suppress the invention of an indestructible fabric and demonstrates the inability of a sclerotic industrial structure to deal with discovery, change and innovation. If we can see *Whisky Galore,* and to a lesser extent perhaps *The Maggie* (1954), as anti-imperial parables and *The Man in the White Suit* as a critique of the capitalist industrial structure, *The Ladykillers* needs to be examined in the context of Mackendrick's work as a whole as well as in the context of Ealing and of Britain at large.

Scripted by the American William Rose, *The Ladykillers* was directed by Mackendrick shortly before he departed for the United States to direct an acid study of power and corruption in the intense and inbred world of New York press agents and gossip columnists, *The Sweet Smell of Success* (1956). It is hard, in the light of Mackendrick's career, to see *The Ladykillers* as anything other than an irreverent farewell to England – that England of the Conservative mid-1950s that has been character-ized by Arthur Marwick as suffering from 'complacency, parochialism, lack of serious, structural change'[22] – and to Ealing, the well-run 'Academy for Young Gentlemen' with its resident nanny. It is a sardonic recognition of the impossibility of change in either institution. But at the same time it meets perfectly the criteria for inclusion within the dominant Ealing strain that preferred the small and the old, a strain which the public identified as the Ealing world. Whether you take the film as a critique or as a celebration of that ethos, however, depends entirely on your point of view.

One thing which can be agreed, though, is that *The Ladykillers* is the last of the great Ealing comedies. Its plot is simply outlined. Mrs Louisa Wilberforce, a widow living alone in a Victorian house in a cul-de-sac near St Pancras Station, rents her upstairs room to a mysterious 'Profes-sor Marcus', who meets with four oddly assorted friends to play chamber music. The musical quintet is, in fact, a cover to their plans to commit a security van robbery at King's Cross Station. They carry out the robbery with Mrs Wilberforce's unwitting help, but as they are about to leave, she discovers the truth. They plot to kill her but cannot bring themselves to do it and succeed only in eliminating each other. The bodies are dumped on to passing coal trucks. Finally only the Professor is left, and then he is struck down by a signal and also ends up in a coal truck. Mrs Wilberforce tries to turn in the money at the police station, but the police, believing it to be a tall story, tell her to keep the money. She trots happily home.

Artistically the film is wholly satisfying. It has all the ritual formality of a time-honoured ceremony and the internal logic of a remembered dream, with the reiterated drawing of straws for the choice of killer, the succession of deaths, the disposal of the bodies over the railway bridge and their transport thither in a wheelbarrow. The murders themselves are all done off-screen so as not to allow real violence to intrude on the cumulative atmosphere of fantasy. The mood is reinforced by the music. Mrs Wilberforce's departure for the police station at the outset of the film is accompanied by a tinkling musical box rendition of 'The Last Rose of Summer'. The supposed string quintet practises the Boccherini minuet, nostalgic, elegant and gentle, which thereafter accompanies Mrs Wilberforce. A sombre hymn-like tune accompanies the disposal of the bodies.

Within the formal framework of action, music and staging the humour derives both from parody of the horror film (the exaggerated Gothic opening when Professor Marcus, accompanied by shadows, thunder and lightning, first arrives at the house) and of the gangster film (the meticulous planning of the robbery, whose execution is jeopardized by Mrs Wilberforce) and from incongruity. Nothing could be more incongruous than the idea of a criminal gang posing as a string quintet. The juxtaposition of their illegal activities and the genteel existence of Mrs Wilberforce, who is constantly interrupting their planning with offers of cups of tea, requests for assistance to recapture her parrot and insistence that they meet her friends, extracts the maximum humour from the situation.

The cast is uniformly excellent, revealing the strength of the corps of British character actors. Katie Johnson, a long-established Ealing small-part player, could not be bettered as the little old lady. Alec Guinness, complete with straggly hair, buck teeth, black-rimmed eyes, long scarf and fluttering tiptoe movements is the very image of the demented intellectual. His gang are superbly characterized by Cecil Parker as the raffish bogus major, Herbert Lom as the grim, gun-toting, old lady-hating gangster Louis, Peter Sellers as the chirpy Cockney teddy-boy Harry and Danny Green as the dumb ox 'One-Round', a lumpen proletarian moron ('Old Queen who?').

The image of England which the film projects is undeniably parochial, backward-looking and complacent. The setting is a small, enclosed urban community in the shadow of St Pancras Station, that symbol of Victorian exuberance and energy. Everyone knows everyone else. As Mrs Wilberforce proceeds to the police station, she greets all the shopkeepers by name. The police station itself is presided over by Jack Warner, already familiar as the benignly paternalist police officer, having played PC George Dixon in *The Blue Lamp* and later immortalizing him in the subsequent long-running television series.

Mrs Wilberforce herself is the spirit of England. She is the living embodiment of the Victorian age, all lavender and old lace and faded gentility. She is sweet, polite, prim, bourgeois, immaculate and patriotic, a perfectly preserved period piece. She is the widow of a Merchant Navy captain who went down with his ship in the China Seas twenty-nine years ago, having first put his parrots in a lifeboat (the English as a nation of pet lovers).

Her house, at the end of a cul-de-sac, is England, stuffed with Victorian bric-à-brac and suffering from wartime subsidence. Mrs Wilberforce lives there with her memories of the past, recalling her twenty-first birthday in Pangbourne in 1901 when news of the Old Queen's death came through, naming her parrots 'General Gordon' and 'Admiral Beatty' and taking tea with her friends, similarly well preserved old ladies. But she is quite without fear. She shows her steel and causes a street riot when she intervenes to stop a barrow boy from ill-treating a horse, laying into the man with her umbrella. When she discovers the crime, she takes charge like a stern nanny, telling the criminals, who shuffle about like sheepish naughty boys caught out in a prank, 'Try to behave like gentlemen for once.' She insists they join her friends for tea rather than create an embarrassing disturbance. Subsequently Marcus tries to persuade her that no one wants the money back and that they stole it only to help unfortunate dependants. However, Mrs Wilberforce's morality is inflexible. She determines to go to the police even if they send her to prison as an accomplice. She cows them so completely that they wipe each other out rather than kill her and she ends up with the money.

Charles Barr has proposed a fascinating reading of the film:

> The gang are the post-war Labour Government; taking over 'the House', they gratify the Conservative incumbent by their civilized behaviour (that nice music) and decide to use at least the façade

of respectability for their radical programme of redistributing wealth (humouring Mrs Wilberforce and using her as a front). Their success is undermined by two factors interacting: their own internecine quarrels, and the startling, paralysing charisma of the 'natural' governing class, which effortlessly takes over from them again in time to exploit their gains (like the Conservatives taking over power in 1951, just as the austerity years came to an end). The gang are a social mix like Labour's – a mixture of academic (Alec Guinness), ex-officer (Cecil Parker), manual worker (Danny Green), naive youth (Peter Sellers) and hard-liner (Herbert Lom).[23]

Barr is needlessly diffident about advancing such a detailed political reading of the film. For it makes sense if it is viewed in the context not just of what had happened since 1945 but also of what was about to happen to British society. The years 1956–58 were to represent a cultural watershed, energizing society with a cultural revolt which was to lead in due course to political change and to the end of the long period of Conservative rule These years saw on the political front the Suez debacle and the Notting Hill race riots, symptoms of Britain's emergence into a post-imperial, post-Victorian world. But the period also saw the arrival of rock music from the United States, the appearance of the 'angry young men' of literature and the theatre and the first steps towards the development of the distinctive youth culture that was to flower in the 1960s and took the form of protest against established canons of taste, decency and respectability. It was spearheaded by intellectuals and upper-middle-class opinion leaders and rapidly gained a large young working-class following, which in time threw up its own leaders.

Looked at against this background, the gang in *The Ladykillers* represents not only the elements which made up the post-war Labour Party but also those elements in 1950s society that constituted the forces of dissidence around which the youth culture was to coalesce: intellectuals (Guinness), middle-class renegades (Parker), the young (Sellers), the working classes (Green) and criminals (Lom). Just as the Barr interpretation suggests that the gang as Labour Party is contained and suppressed, so the gang as social dissidence is cowed into submission and disposed of. Mrs Wilberforce gets the money and even gives a fiver to the pavement artist whose most prominent creation is a portrait of Churchill. But 1955 is almost the last year in which these dissident elements can be contained, for they are about to burst forth in all directions, and also to penetrate the film industry in the form of the so-called British 'new wave' cinema, which begins with *Room at the Top* (1959).

In locating the ideological position of a film analysing what is not there is just as important as analysing what is there. *The Ladykillers* is marked by a total absence of sexuality and a relative absence of youth. It is, on the contrary, a paean to old age. The absence of sexuality is not in itself remarkable, in that it was usually suppressed in Ealing films, and indeed in British films in general, until the late 1950s. Robert Hamer's films *It Always Rains on Sunday* and *Kind Hearts and Coronets* are notable exceptions within both Ealing and British cinema. The suppression of sexuality is a reflection of the Puritanism of British life. But its counterpart is the penchant which the British have for brisk, no-nonsense old ladies, of whom the archetype is the 'Old Queen' herself and other more recent examples are Dame Margaret Rutherford, Lady Violet Bonham-Carter and Mrs Barbara Woodhouse. The cult of the nanny and the concept of the nanny society is an extension of this. It is perfectly encapsulated in *The Ladykillers,* in which the little old lady reigns supreme, evoking George Orwell's dictum on England: 'It resembles a family, a rather stuffy Victorian family. . . . It is a family in which the young are generally thwarted and most of the power is in the hands of irresponsible uncles and bedridden aunts.'[24]

Youth is represented by Peter Sellers's Harry, who is part of the gang. He, like contemporary youth itself, is emasculated and neutralized in one of the film's key scenes. The gangsters are forced to take part in the old ladies' tea-party. They stand about helplessly, cups of tea and plates of cake in their hands, as they are swamped by the old ladies, and Professor Marcus glumly hammers out on the pianola 'Silver Threads among the Gold'. Similarly, at the start of the film, as Mrs Wilberforce heads for the police station, she pauses to smile at a baby in a pram. Instead of cooing, the baby screams. It is the nascent revolt of extreme youth against a society dominated by extreme old age. Significantly, the cultural revolt of the late 1950s was to be characterized by those elements of sexuality and youth that are suppressed here.

The absence of youth from *The Ladykillers* is particularly striking in view of the close association of Mackendrick with children in films (*Mandy, The Maggie, Sammy Going South, A High Wind in Jamaica*) that express a child's view of the world. In the context of Ealing it is perhaps also significant that while the first great Ealing comedy, *Hue and Cry,* centred on a gang of youngsters foiling a crime ring, the last great Ealing comedy features an old lady foiling a criminal gang.

It is instructive to compare *The Ladykillers* with the American classic black comedy *Arsenic and Old Lace,* memorably filmed by Frank Capra in 1941. It may even have been a memory of this that inspired William Rose, for in a sense *The Ladykillers* is *Arsenic and Old Lace* turned upside-down. In *Arsenic and Old Lace* it is the inhabitants of a venerable nineteenth-century house in Brooklyn, the Brewster family, whose ancestors came over on the *Mayflower,* who are the murderers. Two dear sweet little old ladies, Aunt Abby and Aunt Martha, poison lonely old men because they are sorry for them. The bodies are buried in the cellar by their nephew, who thinks he is Theodore Roosevelt and is digging the Panama Canal beneath the house. They are joined by Cousin Jonathan, a homicidal maniac who looks like Boris Karloff. Eventually the whole family is carted off to an asylum, leaving a sensible, sane, modern young couple (Cary Grant and Priscilla Lane) in charge. The values, then are completely reversed. In America, it is age, tradition and the past that are mad and irrelevant; in Britain they are venerated and triumphant.

The Ladykillers was both a box-office and critical success, winning the British Film Academy award for best screenplay (William Rose) and best actress (Katie Johnson) for 1955. But there is no evidence to suggest that the critics who reviewed it saw it as a critique of England. The reviews concentrated on the acting, which was universally praised, and on the difficulty of making a comedy about murder. Most critics agreed that *The Ladykillers* had succeeded in avoiding the pitfalls triumphantly. The *Sunday Times* thought it 'captivating'; the *Evening Standard,* 'the most stylish, inventive and funniest British comedy of the year'; the *Daily Telegraph,* 'one of the funniest comedies of the year'; the *Daily Herald,* 'wonderfully funny'; the *Daily Worker,* 'accomplished and polished'.[25] *Tribune* said, 'It made me laugh more frequently and more heartily than any this year', and the *Daily Mirror* said it had 'lots of laughs with a thrill or two'.[26] Rather more substantial comment came from the *Manchester Guardian,* which thought it 'a thoroughly typical Ealing work – except that it is even better than most', and C. A. Lejeune in the *Observer* called it 'an entertaining piece of harmless nonsense'.[27] This suggests that the film was seen as being squarely in the mainstream, whimsical Ealing tradition. If the cinema-going public reacted in the same way, it seems likely that it took what Mackendrick intended as a satire on the Ealing view of England as a celebration of that view. They identified, in other words, with the old lady and not with the frustrated and exasperated gang who are her victims. Mrs Wilberforce's world is an apt metaphor for mid-1950s England, a cul-de-sac slumbering peacefully but shortly to be violently awakened.

Notes

1. Michael Balcon, *A Lifetime of Films*, London, 1969, p. 48.
2. *Kinematograph Weekly*, 11, January 1945, p. 163.
3. The best analysis of Ealing Studios and its output is to be found in Charles Barr, *Ealing Studios*, London, 1977.
4. Balcon, *A Lifetime of Films*, p. 158.
5. Monja Danischewsky, *White Russian – Red Face*, London, 1966, p. 127; Balcon, *A Lifetime of Films*, p. 138.
6. Danischewsky, *White Russian – Red Face*, p. 127.
7. ibid., p. 134.
8. John Ellis, 'Made in Ealing', *Screen*, 16, Spring 1975, p. 119.
9. Vernon Bogdanor and Robert Skidelsky (eds.), *The Age of Affluence 1951–64*, London, 1970, p. 12; Charles Barr, 'Projecting Britain and the British Character', *Screen*, 15, Spring 1974, p. 116; Raymond Durgnat, *A Mirror for England*, London 1970, p. 140.
10. Bogdanor and Skidelsky, *The Age of Affluence*, p. 7.
11. John Russell Taylor (ed.), *Masterworks of the British Cinema*, London, 1974, p. 192.
12. Balcon, *A Lifetime of Films*, p. 158.
13. T. E. B. Clarke, *This is Where I Came In*, London, 1974, pp. 159–60.
14. Balcon, *A Lifetime of Films*, p. 167.
15. Ellis, 'Made in Ealing', p. 113.
16. ibid., pp. 113–27.
17. Jeffrey Richards, 'Passport to Pimlico', *The Movie*, 28, 1980, pp. 552–3.
18. Quoted by Arthur Marwick, *Britain in the Century of Total War*, London, 1974, p. 158.
19. Balcon, *A Lifetime of Films*, p. 159.
20. Clarke, *This is Where I Came In*, p. 157.
21. *Positif*, 92, February 1968, p. 41.
22. Arthur Marwick, *British Society since 1945*, Harmondsworth, 1982, p. 111.
23. Barr, *Ealing Studios*, pp. 171–2.
24. George Orwell, *Collected Essays, Journalism and Letters*, vol. 2, Harmondsworth, 1971, p. 88.
25. *Sunday Times*, 11 December 1955; *Daily Telegraph*, 10 December 1955; *Daily Herald*, 9 December 1955; *Daily Worker*, 10 December 1955.
26. *Tribune*, 23 December 1955; *Daily Mirror*, 9 December 1955.
27. *Manchester Guardian*, 10 December 1955; *Observer*, 11 December 1955.

I'm All Right Jack (1959)

10

Vicious Circles
I'm All Right Jack

F ilms about industrial relations were few and far between in the
mainstream British cinema from the 1930s to the 1950s. It was a
vexed and contentious issue, for a start, and rarely free of controversy.
As a result, producers and scriptwriters alike were prompted to steer
clear of the matter. Doubtless, they anyway saw little in the subject to
recommend it as a viable and commercial proposition. Those films that
did touch upon the question, however, have inevitably turned out to be
of some interest.

In the 1930s, of course, the 'relations of Capital and Labour' was
one of those taboo subjects which greatly exercised the collective mind
of the British Board of Film Censors. T. P. O'Connor, the second
President of the BBFC, had seen fit to include it as a matter for careful
consideration on his list of basic censorship rules, which was compiled
in 1917.[1] And from the early 1930s, when the BBFC sought to initiate
the pre-production scrutiny of synopses, scenarios and scripts, a good
deal of attention was given to the depiction of industrial relations. This
meant, quite simply, that when a story was deemed likely to transgress
the bounds laid down by the BBFC or to emphasize elements which
the BBFC might not wish to see emphasized it was very quickly ruled
out of court and declared 'not suitable for production'. In the case, for
instance, of a synopsis which was submitted in 1932 under the title *Tidal*

Waters and which purported to deal with Thames dockland life and a watermen's strike, the BBFC readers were clearly worried that the film might be in danger of stressing the 'differences between capital and labour which led to the strike' and that the strike might be construed as the 'prominent feature of the story'. One of their number felt compelled to remark:

> Our attitude to the subject has always been very definite. Strikes or labour unrest, where the scene is laid in England, have never been shown in any detail. It is impossible to show such strikes without taking a definite side either with or against the strikers and this would at once range the film as political propaganda of a type that we have always held to be unsuitable for production in this country.[2]

But the BBFC did not worry for long; its anxiety was soon assuaged. The film company proved co-operative and duly obliged by dropping the project without a murmur.

For the most part the BBFC had nothing to fear from the makers of feature films during the 1930s. They were naturally inclined, as we have seen, to favour images of national harmony and relative tranquillity on all fronts, including the industrial, whenever they chose to mention it. Strikes were overcome, as in Michael Powell's 1934 film of *Red Ensign,* by the simple expedient of the management's addressing the workers with stirring calls to 'pull together' (thereby winning an approving nod from the BBFC and the comment: 'Quite a good story with a strong patriotic note').[3] When depression threatened, as it did the cotton industry in Basil Dean's 1934 production of *Sing As We Go* (a film which, incidentally, did not come before the BBFC for pre-production scrutiny), it threatened both management and workers alike, and it neither soured nor broke their close relationship. Besides, Gracie Fields, who fancied the boss's son anyway, was there to keep everybody happy with a joyful and optimistic song as she led the people out of work, into unemployment and then back to work again when the times got better, as they invariably did.[4]

The workers, for their part, were a pretty resilient lot. In the case of John Baxter's *The Navvy* (retitled *A Real Bloke* on its 1935 release), the answer to being thrown on the dole after twenty-three years of continuous employment was not to 'whine and whimper' but to 'keep his chin up bravely'.[5] New employment was eventually found for men of such calibre and character. Indeed, even George Formby was lucky enough to find another job, despite the fact that he was initially taken 'off the dole', in the 1935 film of that name, because he displayed few redeeming characteristics and showed little inclination to work at all. In reply, for example, to the accusation levelled by the manager of his employment exchange that he was 'afraid of work', George cheekily retorted, 'Me, afraid of work? I could sleep beside it'; on being told that he has 'got out of the way of work', he replied, 'Well, I've managed it up to now, but it's been a struggle'; and on being asked what his trade was, George responded by saying, 'Selling calendars every leap year.'

By the end of the 1930s these stereotypes and caricatures, both comic and heroic, were well and truly established. The worker, the workplace and labour–management relations had some meaning in the British cinema, albeit on a limited and carefully delineated scale of representation. World War II was to extend that scale and to expand the British cinema's horizons considerably. It is a commonplace that the 'People's War', in which the civilian population was sometimes as much in the front line as were the fighting troops, produced the conditions that enabled the British cinema to flourish, not least in the creative sense; 'ironically, despite all the paraphernalia of official wartime censorship, British film-makers were now able to approach topics which they would have been warned off in the thirties.'[6] And that latitude extended also to the depiction of industrial relations – not surprisingly, since during the war, as two commentators have put it, 'trade unions and employers' associations amalgamated with the Government into what was virtually a "corporate state".'[7]

Of course, the successful prosecution of the war effort was paramount. It overrode the film-makers' other considerations and largely dictated where their priorities would lie. Yet among that admittedly small corpus of films which included the likes of *Love on the Dole* (1941), *Hard Steel* (1942), *The Shipbuilders* (1943) and *Millions Like Us* (1943) it is possible to discern signs of a fresh and more open approach to matters certainly of social and also, on occasion, of industrial interest. Some of these films were inclined to look backwards in time and were, ostensibly, retrospective in their concerns, but their pertinence to Britain in the 1940s was amply demonstrated. *Love on the Dole,* for instance, was set firmly in the 1930s and dealt mainly with a problem which had been overcome, for the most part, with the advent of war and nearly full

employment, but for all that it closed with an extract from a speech by
A. V. Alexander, Labour MP and a member of the wartime Government, which stated that: 'Our working men and women have responded
magnificently to any and every call made upon them. Their reward must
be a new Britain. Never again must the unemployed become the
forgotten men of peace.'[8]

The story of *The Shipbuilders* also began in the 1930s, though it
continued into the first years of the war. As Arthur Marwick has
suggested: 'The film quite deliberately shows prosperity brought back
to the Glasgow shipyards by conscious Government action in wartime:
there is a very definite message on behalf of interventionist, Keynesian,
economic policies, as well, of course, as one of the essential unity and
involvement of everyone in the all-consuming war effort.'[9]

Unity was the keynote of *Millions Like Us,* with its tale of girls from
all social groups coming to live together in happy harmony, in the main,
as a result of their work experiences in an aircraft factory. And the
needs of the war effort doubtless accounted for the injection of a
speech as the climax of *Hard Steel,* yet another film to start its plot in
the 1930s and finish after the onset of war, in which the protagonist
successfully inspires some steelworkers to 'co-operate, that's the word'.
'Can you and me co-operate so the mills can give of their best?' he asks
the men. Initially they prove reluctant, since they have grown to dislike
his way of running things, but he slowly wins them round, and to their
increasing applause he concludes: 'We know this war is a war of steel,
and we're going to give the old country the steel she needs, and more
steel, and more, and more. . . .'

The propagandist intentions of both films were obvious and, as ever,
the issues to which they alluded were greatly personalized. But at the
same time they revealed other distinct features. In the case of the
former film there was a clear, and by no means unsuccessful, attempt
to paint a more faithful picture of life on the factory front, and in the
latter instance there was more than a passing hint of the propensity of
the industrial workforce, particularly marked during the period of the
war, to resort to quick unofficial strikes to achieve its ends. Finally, in
common with the other wartime films in the same mould, there was
more detailed characterization, especially in the portrayal of the working-
class figures.

But, surprisingly, although labour emerged from the war with its status much enhanced and also, of course, with a stronger bargaining power than ever before, the film-makers quickly turned their backs on the subject in the immediate post-war years. Michael Balcon spoke in 1945 of the need 'for a projection of the true Briton to the rest of the world' and included 'Britain as the home of great industry and craftsmanship' among his list of topics to be covered.[10] But little of that was actually shown in British films of the post-war era. And indeed it was not until the early 1950s that a handful of film-makers looked once again to industrial themes for their inspiration, and then with ominous consequences.

In 1950, for example, Bernard Miles's film *Chance of a Lifetime* was released. It was, in truth, rather a benign and pleasant piece, which told of the owner and managing director of a small works manufacturing agricultural machinery, who has trouble with his workers and, in a fit of pique, relinquishes the running of the place to their control. The men take over and achieve some success but find that they cannot really function properly without the skill and expertise of their old boss. He is invited back; he returns; there is a new found and closer understanding all round; and the film ends 'a little tritely', as *The Times* critic put it, 'with the conclusion that, if the management needs the men, the men need the management'.[11]

'There is nothing very revolutionary in all this,' *The Times* went on to say, and indeed there wasn't. Milton Shulman maintained that the film 'dared to discuss a vital and important contemporary problem – worker and management relations',[12] but if it was daring, it was daring in a benevolent and paternalistic fashion. The film was imbued with the spirit of consensus, and the most it advocated was that some attention be paid to the idea of worker participation in management, a matter about which by 1950 even the Trades Union Congress was increasingly lukewarm, except in the case of the nationalized industries.

Yet the film caused a furore and in fact was only assured a release as a result of direct intervention by the President of the Board of Trade, Harold Wilson. None of the major cinema circuits wished to show the film, claiming it was 'propaganda' and not 'entertainment'. And the same feelings were amplified by Ministry of Labour officials, who reportedly called it 'propaganda for communism and workers' control in industry'.[13] Wilson disagreed with the views expressed by the Minister of Labour, George Isaacs, about the film, and the Cabinet was persuaded to let him use his powers to 'direct' one of the three circuits to show the film. It was released finally on the Odeon circuit but flopped badly.

The film was not 'communist propaganda', of course, though the charge stuck to the film as it did the rounds of the cinemas, but it was unfortunate enough to come into the reckoning at a time when there was a good deal of talk about 'communist propaganda' and 'communist-fomented' industrial unrest in the country, not to mention the cold war tension abroad. The Labour Government, and Ernest Bevin in particular, were suspicious that industrial strikes and disputes were being caused by political extremists from the moment they came to power. Increasingly these suspicions fastened upon 'communist subversion' until, in the last year of office, they became an obsession. Scotland Yard repeatedly urged that it could find no evidence of any 'communist influence',[14] but despite such assurances the fear of 'reds under the beds' and the 'communist threat' was felt as powerfully in government circles as it was elsewhere.

Not surprisingly, it was also manifested in the cinema. Roy Boulting's 1951 film *High Treason* has, for example, been described as the 'paranoid counterpart' to *Chance of a Lifetime* for its allusions to 'Communist Party schemes to sabotage British industry'.[15] But in fairness its paranoia, such as it was, was no more acute, as we now know, than that being shown by no less a body that the Government at the very time the film was being made. Close analysis of Roy Boulting's film reveals, furthermore, that while it makes reference to the perpetration of dockland espionage by subversive workers, nevertheless the communist cell (not actually identified as such, but the inference is obvious) masterminding the operation clearly feels that it cannot depend upon 'effective strike action' and the like to achieve its ultimate objective. The motley band of disenchanted workers, idealistic intellectuals and renegade civil servants are compelled finally, once they have donned their duffle coats, to resort to physical violence and the attempted take-over of several key power stations throughout the country as the only means to 'paralyse' British industry.

The fault did not always lie then with the worker, communist or otherwise, and indeed it is clear from another film released in the same year (1951), Alexander Mackendrick's *The Man in the White Suit,* that management was capable of deeds pretty near as dark as anything done by the workers or their representatives. When the dedicated young scientist Sidney Stratton (Alec Guinness) produces a fabric that repels dirt and will seemingly never wear out, his idea is tardily but enthusiastically taken up by the mill-owning Birnley (Cecil Parker), who sees a golden opportunity to scoop the market. But other implications soon loom large. Sidney 'falls victim to the restrictive practices of the place' and, as Charles Barr goes on to put it in his excellent critique of the film:

> Everlasting suits mean fewer new ones to be bought and less work for the factories. (A topical parallel: the manufacturers' cartel against long-life light bulbs, on which the Monopolies Commission reported in 1951, the year of the film's release.) The owners hastily get together, sort Birnley out and combine to suppress the invention.[16]

The film's gibes at myopic management, and its comments upon the perils of monopoly capitalism are evident. But if management bears the brunt of the criticism for instigating the moves towards pernicious restraint, the unions are by no means forgotten or exempt from criticism. They are brought in by the owners to help suppress the invention and give their support. 'Capital and labour are hand in hand in this' is the message which emanates from their meeting together later in the story. Yet it is also obvious from the same scene that if these two generally opposing sides are in agreement on this one issue, they still view each other with suspicion, if not outright contempt.

In all, the film conjured up a bleak vision of industry and industrial relations: capital and labour were out to do the country down. But it was a vision that some felt to be not without substance in a period that was distinguished by the 'gathering cold war which affected British industrial relations, with a snobbish and often uninformed management entrenched on one side, with an immobile, unambitious workforce, deeply attached to its long traditions, on the other'.[17] And it was a vision, furthermore, that had gained considerable credence by the time that the Boulting Brothers' *I'm All Right Jack* came out in 1959.

With a series of films beginning in 1956, the Boultings had seemingly changed tack and had started, less earnestly, to take every opportunity to poke fun at various facets of the British way of life and the nation's institutions. Their first film of the bunch, *Private's Progress,* which utilized what was to become a regular band of actors and sparked off a fruitful relationship with writer Alan Hackney,[18] was actually placed in a wartime army setting. But it was as much an assessment of 'national service drudgeries and idiocies' as anything else,[19] and the Army duly took it as an 'insult'.[20] Thereafter the Boultings turned their attention to the law, with *Brothers In Law* (1957), to the universities, with *Lucky Jim* (also in 1957), and to the sillier side of diplomacy, the Foreign Office and colonialism in *Carlton-Browne of the FO* (1959).

The films met with varying degrees of success. *Lucky Jim,* for instance, was a harmless farce. It displayed none of the trenchant wit that is evident in the original novel by Kingsley Amis and it was ultimately little different from the many comedies that seemed to pour out of the British cinema during the 1950s. But the Boultings' other films were distinguished by a marked, if light, satirical touch. And this rich satirical vein was most in evidence when the Boultings set out to tackle *I'm All Right Jack* early in 1959.

I'm All Right Jack was the industrial relations film *par excellence*. It accurately charted the deteriorating state of the 'industrial cold war', to borrow Arthur Marwick's phrase, and reflected the widening gulf between management and the workforce. This gulf had resulted in a perceptible increase in the number of strikes, strikers and working days lost from the mid-1950s onwards. In the ten years before 1955, for instance, there was an annual average of 1,791 strikes, involving 545,000 workers and resulting in 2,073,000 days lost. In the ten years after 1955 there an annual average of 2,521 strikes, involving 1,116,000 workers and resulting in 3,889,000 days lost.[21] But if the growth in the number of strikes signalled the ever-widening gulf between management and workers, there were also signs, in the kind of strikes that ensued, of a gulf developing between trade union leaders and their rank-and-file members. The enhanced status of the unions after the war, their increased bargaining power and full employment all served to stimulate a rise in trade union membership throughout the 1950s. But even during the war itself some workers 'came to feel that their union leaders were no longer fully representing the interests of the rank and file' and 'the estrangement of union leaders from their members stimulated a militant attitude among shop stewards, who frequently arrogated the role of representing labour opinion which union officials seemed to have relinquished.'[22] These rank-and-file frustrations, and the concomitant growth in militancy among shop stewards, were exacerbated in the post-war period[23] and perhaps help to explain why so many of the strikes that ensued during the 1950s were unofficial and not sanctioned by the appropriate union. But whatever the depth of the division between the trade union leadership and the rank-and-file membership by that time, the plain fact of the matter was that the power and prestige of shop stewards had undoubtedly increased in the workplace. And the Boulting Brothers' film of *I'm All Right Jack* had a lot to say on that matter as well.

The film starts with a brief pre-credit sequence which looks back to VE Day in 1945 and sets the irreverent and jocular tone that will dominate throughout. Church bells are ringing; guns are firing; and people are heard celebrating in the streets as Ern, the servant in a London men's club, awakens old Sir John (Peter Sellers) from his slumber to inform him that the war is over. 'That's another one we've come through, Ern,' boasts Sir John. 'That's right, they can't finish us off, can they?' asserts Ern. But Sir John immediately senses the wind of change and orders Ern to close the window: 'It's become damned chilly in here.' And a narrator interjects to tell us: 'Look hard, for this is the last we shall see of Sir John.' He is a 'solid block in the edifice of what seemed to be an ordered and stable society'. And given his impeccable credentials, who would doubt it? He is, after all, a Justice of the Peace, Chairman of the Wroughton Unionist Association, Vice President of his local British Legion, Honorary Chairman of the Regional Board for the Adjustment of Distressed Gentle Women and sleeping partner in that vast financial complex, the City and Threadneedle Trust. But now he is on his way out, for with victory has come a 'new age' and with that new age a 'new spirit'.

We are treated to a glimpse of what that 'new spirit' entails with a shot of a soldier (Victor Maddern, later seen as a factory workman, Knowles) who is celebrating while perched on top of a lamp-post, and whose two-fingered 'Victory' sign is instantly reversed into its vulgar opposite. Whereupon the film breaks into a similarly jokey credits sequence to the accompaniment of some comic cartoons and a bouncy raucous title song from Al Saxon (so typical of British pop music from the era when the film was made),[24] the first verse of which states:

> I'm all right Jack, I'm okay, that is the message for today
> So, count up your lolly, feather your nest,
> Let someone else worry, boy, I couldn't care less.
> You scratch my back, I'll do the same for you, Jack,
> That's the message for today.

The scene is set, then; we are into the 1950s, and the film proper begins.

'Times have changed,' Stanley Windrush (Ian Carmichael) tells his aged father (Miles Malleson), who has retired to a nudist camp. 'In industry nowadays they're crying out for people like me.' He is a 'university man' and his father would prefer to see him going into one of the learned professions, the Church or the Army. The old man cannot see why anybody 'brought up as a gentleman' should 'choose to go into industry'. But Stanley persists. 'Of course, I shall be an executive,' he insists, and sets out for an interview with the Combined Universities Appointments Board, where he is told that all he needs is 'confidence, intelligence, and enthusiasm. . . . Above all, an air of confidence'.

Stanley's two forays as a management trainee do not work out quite as expected, however, and he is ultimately rejected by Detto, the detergent manufacturers and the makers of Num-Yum bars (both heavily lampooned by the Boultings with the aid of mock advertising jingles, outrageous slogans and all). He is clearly incompetent, and industry can do well enough without him. The Appointments Board, after finding him another nine such posts, all of which prove equally fruitless, despairs of him.

While staying with his amiable and aristocratic Great Aunt Dolly (Margaret Rutherford), Stanley is finally offered a job in industry by his Uncle Bertram (Dennis Price), who is a director of an engineering firm, Missiles Ltd, that has just landed a big armaments contract. He is cajoled into taking it with the help of a mutual friend, Sidney de Vere Cox (Richard Attenborough). Aunt Dolly does not doubt that Stanley will just 'supervise': 'After all, you were at Oxford.' Sidney suggests, however, that he join 'on the other side' and become a worker, 'unskilled, of course'. Aunt Dolly is aghast at the suggestion that a nephew of hers should 'throw in his lot with the working classes'. But Sidney proceeds to spell out the potential advantages to Stanley and Lady Dorothy alike. Stanley, for instance, says that he might expect to start with £8 a week if he went in on the management side. Yet if he went in as unskilled worker, Sidney counters, 'Your union would see you never get as little as that.' Aunt Dolly still cannot imagine her nephew 'all muscles and sweat'. 'These days it's the management that does all the perspiring,' Sidney replies, choosing his words carefully.

Aunt Dolly fears he might have to join 'one of those horrid unions' with all that 'violence', but Bertie reassures her that 'that doesn't happen nowadays', and Stanley is convinced. He agrees to join the workforce without mentioning that his uncle is on the board of directors, in case it disturbs the 'industrial peace'. But that is precisely what Bertie and Sidney are hoping for. Stanley is part of their scheme to bring Missiles to a standstill (the others include the imposition of a time-and-motion man and a provocative speech to be delivered to the workers on the theme of 'Export or die'). Bertie intends to sell his shares in the company beforehand; the overseas contract will be transferred at a higher price to Sidney's firm; and a hefty profit will be made and divided between them and the representative of the foreign Government, Mr Mohammed (Marne Maitland), who immediately co-operates when he realizes what is in it for him.

Bertie and Sidney are Big Business incarnate and represent its seamier side, though the implication is clearly that much of business manage-ment is invested with the same traits. They scheme, manipulate, are totally unscrupulous in their transactions and, though they talk piously about the benefits that are likely to accrue to the country from their endeavours, are really concerned only with promoting their own personal interests (which are by no means even class interests, for though Bertie is definitely meant to be upper-class, Sidney is very much a *nouveau riche* businessman, as his occasional lapses in language and temper suggest). And when Stanley eventually joins Missiles, he soon encounters their equivalents among the ranks of the workers.

The narrator interjects once again to tell us, with more than a hint of irony, that the British worker has responded to the coming of the 'new age with a 'new sense of the dignity of labour to match his age-old traditions of brotherhood and comradeship'. The irony is compounded by the image of the workforce ambling lazily towards the factory gates until the hooter goes for the start of work, when there is a sudden mad scramble to clock on in sufficient time so as not to lose any pay. Thereafter we are treated to a rich array of practices as restrictive, as devious and as sharp as it is possible to imagine.

The men are reluctant to start work; they skive when they can seize the opportunity; and they down tools at the slightest provocation. Nobody is laid off, and those that are 'what is known as redundant' are kept on in fictitious jobs and spend all their time playing cards. Nobody works harder than is really necessary, and a strict demarcation of jobs is observed. 'They're an absolute shower, a positive shower,' says the personnel manager, Major Hitchcock (Terry-Thomas), who knows of men 'who can break out into a muck sweat merely by standing still'. But his jaundiced views are amply vindicated when workers talk of not having had 'a stoppage for ages, not since the week before last'.

Not surprisingly, Stanley, with his eagerness and enthusiasm, does not fit easily into this set-up. He is dubbed a 'creep' and is given a hostile reception by the workers, who readily and instantly appreciate that he is not one of them and suspect his motives. However, he succeeds in establishing a relationship of sorts with them, especially after he agrees to join the union – 'It's not compulsory, only you've got to join, see.' He is befriended, in particular, by Fred Kite (Peter Sellers), who is the chief shop steward on the works committee, and he takes lodgings at Kite's house after he has taken a fancy to Kite's daughter, Cynthia (Liz Fraser).

Kite is meant to epitomize the archetypal 'bolshy' shop steward and is brilliantly drawn by Sellers, who rightly won the British Film Academy's award as best actor of 1959 for his performance. He has a short cropped haircut and a purposeful stride. He delights in long, convoluted sentences, which sound good and appear to go down well with the workers but are always slightly wrong ('reverberate to the detriment of the workers', 'barefaced provocative of the workers'). He has intellectual pretensions and boasts to Stanley of having gone to Oxford himself, though it quickly transpires that it was only for a short summer school. 'Very nice tea and preserves they give you,' he says, with just the right air of inverted condescension. Kite's library at home is suitably filled with the works of Lenin, books on Lenin and books with titles such as *Decline of the Privileged Classes*. He dreams of going to Russia someday to enjoy 'all them cornfields and bally in the evening'. Yet despite his talk of the equality of man, he is a racist and fears that the 'blacks' might take over his men's jobs.

For all the power he wields at the factory and for all the influence he initially exerts over Stanley, Fred Kite is by no means the master in his home. That is largely the domain of Mrs Kite (Irene Handl), and she runs it most effectively and respectably. Her naturally conservative inclinations are displayed when she slips easily – and, of course, somewhat deferentially – into a friendly chat with Lady Dorothy when the latter arrives unexpectedly. Mrs Kite shows her into the 'front room' and engages in cosy conversation on the subject of good manners, respect and the like. But without her Fred is lost and his male incompetence in practical matters is revealed after she has temporarily deserted him to pursue her own 'strike'. Harmony is restored only at the film's end, when Fred gains in confidence and reasserts his dominance over recalcitrant wife and fun-loving daughter alike.

In the event, though, the relationship between Stanley and Kite is short-lived. Stanley is unwittingly timed working harder than the other men would like; new schedules are introduced; and Kite calls a strike. At first Stanley is merely 'sent to Coventry', but when he insists, at his Aunt's prompting ('Officers don't mutiny,' she says), upon going into work and breaks the picket line, he becomes a 'blackleg' and is totally ostracized. He wins a considerable amount of press and public sympathy, much to Kite's chagrin and his uncle's delight. But his uncle Bertie is also alienated when a sympathy strike closes down Sidney's factory in turn, and their carefully laid plans are scuppered. The strike spreads throughout the country; millions come out; but all that the Minister of Labour can say is, 'I shall act . . . but I shall not interfere', and all that the Trades Union Congress can say is, 'We are not prepared either to endorse the strike officially, nor to condemn it.'

Prevarication rules on those fronts, and it is left to the bosses and the workers to find a solution to the industrial crisis with, as the narrator wryly puts it, 'the traditional respect of the British for the individual, allied to a rare genius for compromise and the unorthodox approach'. The resulting compromise in this instance, however, is a sour one. Bertie, Sidney, Hitchcock and Kite connive to get rid of Stanley. With a bit of luck, not to mention Stanley's inherent naivety and gullibility and the force of the law in the shape of a magistrate (Raymond Huntley) who roundly condemns him and binds him over to keep the peace, Stanley is accused of 'mental instability' and 'ill health brought on by overwork'. The overwork is put down to the new schedules – that was Kite's bright idea – and they will be withdrawn. The strike will end and 'industrial peace' will be restored. Stanley, for his part, is suitably disillusioned, and he retires to join his father in the untroubled retreat of the Sunnyglades nudist camp.

The film finishes on the same pessimistic, if comic, note on which it starts. But it achieves its desired effect, sometimes with broad and exaggerated strokes, always with considerable humour. Visually it is not a particularly exciting film, though that failing does not ultimately detract from its other qualities. The Boultings depended, in the main, upon the benefits to be gained from a sound script, well versed in the nuances and subtleties of British life, and character acting of the sort for which the British cinema is, and always has been, renowned. And there they scored an undoubted success.

The film's triumph was more than reflected by its box-office returns. It was the biggest money-maker in Britain in 1959, ahead of America's *The Big Country,* a lavish western with a large all-star cast, ahead of more traditional British fare, *Carry on Nurse,* and way ahead of the critically acclaimed *Room at the Top.* A British Lion spokesman believed that 'word-of-mouth recommendation' largely turned it into a hit, since the film had not been given an unusual advertising budget, and the only places where it did not go down well was 'in a few cinemas in the Welsh mining districts'.[25] It was still playing to capacity audiences at London's Studio One cinema after seventeen weeks, and more than 2 million people saw it in that time.[26] The film also, incidentally, took more money on its New York run at the Guild Theatre than any film ever shown at that cinema before, and by its fifteenth week was taking an average of about £4,000 a week.[27]

It was clearly popular, but among British critics, at least, it elicited a divided response. The 'quality' press proved to be more than a little bit snooty about it, and damned it in the main, except for honourable mentions of Peter Sellers's performance, while the 'popular' press revelled in it and found it very much to its liking. *The Times,* for instance, found 'its barbs, very fairly divided between Capital and Labour'. It was all right 'for an evening's light entertainment', *The Times* continued, but 'For satire worthy of the name, if it exists at all today, we shall have to look elsewhere.'[28] C. A. Lejeune in the *Observer* thought that it seemed 'bound to be a triumphant popular success' and felt compelled to add: 'I should be the last one to deny that it has the common touch.' But obviously that 'common touch' was really not to her liking – 'A number of the jokes are fairly blue' and 'The tasteless opening in the nudist camp has no real relevance to the film at all.'[29] (In fact, the opening and closing nudist camp scenes caused the film to be threatened with a ban in Eire if the Boultings proved unwilling to cut them out. They chose not to do so.)[30]

David Robinson of the *Financial Times* also thought that the film 'ingeniously echoed the popular audience's narrowest and meanest fears and prejudices'. 'All is defeatist and destructive,' he concluded, 'And the worst of it is that it is rather well done.'[31] Isabel Quigly in the *Spectator* agreed that there was no 'better target for satire at this very moment than our industrial strikes' but found herself totally 'unamused' and thought the film failed because it had 'no central standard from which to judge anything, no central idea or point of view'.[32] Again, the *Manchester Guardian* harped upon the 'topical and sensitive theme' which was 'not so far from the reality as told in the daily news of strikes'. But, virtually alone among the 'quality' press, it decided finally, 'A remarkable film as to its topic and its tone, it has also been made with a wholly satisfactory sense of form.'[33] And Dilys Powell, in the *Sunday Times,* at least considered it 'uproariously funny' and was grateful to the Boultings for 'their nerve in daring to joke about that sacred institution, trade unionism'.[34]

The 'popular' press loved the film, of course, and its feelings towards it are perhaps best summarized by the comments made in the *Sunday Express,* under the headline 'Are we really as mad as this?' which applauded 'this brilliantly made, gloriously funny, magnificently acted film'.[35] And, again not surprisingly, the left-wing press was suitably outraged. The film was 'All *Right* Jack and No *Left,'* said Nell Vyse in the *Daily Worker,* adding that it painted too black a picture of the workers,[36] while Derek Hill of *Tribune* found himself in a real dilemma: 'Peter Sellers's performance is as brilliant as it is contemptible,' he wrote, and 'The film – I hate to admit – is very well made and often extremely funny. I loathed myself for laughing at it.'[37] So, to put the record straight, one week later *Tribune* published a selection of letters which condemned it in no such uncertain terms. Indeed, left-wing outrage at the film continued for many years thereafter. And in April 1979 the *Evening Standard* reported that the film had been dropped from its proposed slot in London Weekend Television's Easter Sunday schedule after a Labour MP had complained about it, on the eve of a by-election, to Transport House, which had complained in turn to the Independent Broadcasting Authority.

Still, as the same article went on to recount, some people had found the film to be of considerable merit, for when the Prime Minister, Harold Macmillan, went to Balmoral in September 1959 to ask for the dissolution of Parliament, the film that the Queen apparently chose for her house guests was none other than *I'm All Right Jack*.[38] Doubtless it entertained them as much as it entertained a good many people elsewhere in the country at the time. Certainly, the country agreed that it had 'never had it so good'. In 1970, furthermore, the film was put to informational and instructional use as an 'object lesson in reality' when it was included, ironically, on the curriculum of management training courses being run in Britain by Unilever.[39]

For anybody who cared to look and listen, then, *I'm All Right Jack* amply demonstrated that it was relevant enough.

Notes

1. Neville March Hunnings, *Film Censors and the Law*, London, 1967, pp. 408–9.

2. Quoted in Jeffrey Richards, 'The British Board of Film Censors and Content Control in the 1930s: Images of Britain', *Historical Journal of Film, Radio and Television*, 1, October 1981, p. 112.

3. *British Board of Film Censors Scenario Reports*, 1933, p. 209 (bound volume; BFI Library, London).

4. This film is discussed further in Tony Aldgate, 'Comedy, Class and Containment', in James Curran and Vincent Porter (eds.), *British Cinema History*, London, 1983.

5. *BBFC Scenario Reports*, 1934, p. 364.

6. Arthur Marwick, 'Print, Pictures and Sound: the Second World War and the British Experience', *Daedalus*, Fall 1982, p. 147. See also James C. Robertson, 'British Film Censorship Goes to War', *Historical Journal of Film, Radio and Television*, 2, March 1982, pp. 49–64.

7. Keith Jeffery and Peter Hennessy, *States of Emergency, British Governments and Strikebreaking since 1919*, London, 1983, p. 145.

8. See also Richards, 'The British Board of Film Censors', pp. 111–12, and Stephen Constantine, *'Love on the Dole* and its Reception in the 1930s', *Literature and History*, 8, Autumn 1982. pp. 244–5.

9. Marwick, 'Print, Pictures and Sound', pp. 147–8.

10. In *Kinematograph Weekly*, 11 January 1945, p. 163.

11. Reprinted in Edgar Anstey (ed.), *Shots in the Dark*, London, 1951, pp. 159–160.

12. ibid., pp. 160–2.

13. Quoted in the *Guardian*, 2 January 1981, on the occasion of the release of the appropriate papers from 1950 to the PRO.

14. See Jeffery and Hennessy, *States of Emergency*, pp. 172, 191, 200.

15. See Raymond Durgnat, *A Mirror for England*, London, 1970, pp. 70–1 and 234–5. Interestingly, Jeffery and Hennessy, *States of Emergency*, p. 217, quote Lord Citrine's fears of August 1950 that 'the Russians regarded our Power Stations as the nerve centre of British industry, and that they had made special efforts to get influence among workers in Power Stations'.

16. Charles Barr, *Ealing Studios*, London, 1977, p. 137.

17. Arthur Marwick, *British Society since 1945*, Harmondsworth, 1982, p. 163.

18. Alan Hackney's book *Private's Progress* came out in 1954 and was reprinted in paperback in 1957. *Private Life* was published in 1958 and republished under the film's title of *I'm All Right Jack* in 1972 (both by Gollancz). In the meantime Hackney's

characters of Stanley Windrush and Fred Kite had appeared also in *Keep Religion Out of This* (1963) and were to reappear in *Whatever Turns You On, Jack* (1972).

19. Durgnat, *A Mirror for England,* p. 235.

20. See *Sunday Times,* 16 August 1959.

21. Marwick, *British Society,* p. 165.

22. Jeffery and Hennessy, *States of Emergency,* pp. 145–6.

23. ibid., p. 189.

24. Ironically, Al Saxon scored his first pop chart hit in the month that the film opened, August 1959, with 'Only Sixteen'. It was, almost inevitably, a poor cover version of an excellent American record and was in fact the second such cover version, the other one being by Craig Douglas. Al Saxon's record did not do particularly well, reaching number 17 in the charts.

25. *News Chronicle,* 11 December 1959.

26. *Star,* 11 December 1959.

27. *Daily Telegraph,* 15 August 1960.

28. *The Times,* 17 August 1959.

29. *Observer,* 16 August 1959.

30. *Daily Telegraph,* 31 October 1959.

31. *Financial Times,* 17 August 1959.

32. *Spectator,* 21 August 1959.

33. *Manchester Guardian,* 15 August 1959.

34. *Sunday Times,* 16 August 1959.

35. *Sunday Express,* 16 August 1959.

36. *Daily Worker,* 15 August 1959.

37. *Tribune,* 21 August 1959.

38. *Evening Standard,* 17 April 1979.

39. *Daily Mirror,* 6 January 1970.

The Loneliness of the Long Distance Runner (1962)

11

New Waves, Old Ways and the Censors

The Loneliness of the Long Distance Runner

T hat widespread and profound changes were afoot in British cinema is an instantly discernible feature of the late 1950s and, as Stuart Laing notes, in particular:

> The period 1959–63 was marked by the appearance (and subse-
> quent sudden disappearance) of a 'New Wave' of social realist
> films which seemed to signal a renaissance of seriousness and
> contemporary relevance within British cinema. One immediately
> apparent paradox is that this was also precisely the period in which
> the collapse of cinemagoing in Britain as a mass leisure pursuit
> became confirmed as a long-term trend.

Going to the cinema, for a start, was no longer anything like the prevailing or essential social habit it had been during the 1930s and 1940s. The advent of television as an easily accessible mass medium from the mid-1950s quickly made substantial inroads on the size of film audiences and it increasingly supplanted cinema's role as the means of family entertainment par excellence. Many cinemas were soon closed and demolished or hastily converted to fulfil a brand new function as bingo halls. Cinemagoers, furthermore, were changing in composition and character. 'The overall decline in admissions had the effect of increasing the proportion of the audience in the young adult category', Laing continues. So much so that by the end of the decade, in fact, young adults between the ages of 16 and 24 constituted fully 44% of those frequenting the cinema regularly – once a week or more – as well as another 24% of those attending on an occasional basis – at least once a month.[1]

That there were concomitant changes in the traditional products of mainstream British cinema again goes without saying and most commentators agree they occurred in large measure around the turn of the sixties. 'It is certainly true to say that [the] characteristic themes treated in popular cinema underwent marked changes', argues Janet Thumim; while Jeffrey Richards maintains that 'The 1960s witnessed a revitalisation of British cinema and the emergence of a flourishing and diverse film culture after what was widely perceived to be the "doldrums era" of the 1950s'. The implied note of caution about the way in which cinema of the 1950s was previously perceived is important. For just as the notion of fifties British cinema as necessarily a 'doldrums era' is now undergoing a well merited albeit tardy revision so, too, that aspect of late 1950s and early 1960s British cinema which has hitherto attracted most attention when discussing the advances evidently made during the period – in debates, principally, surrounding the 'new wave' films – is once more, and for its own part, receiving renewed and closer scrutiny.

British new wave cinema has been variously interpreted since its heyday. Then contemporary critical opinion, for instance, found much to espouse in its auspicious mix of vivid social realist themes, readily identifiable characters and grimly naturalistic settings which were usually located in the north of England, well outside the confines of the traditional studio-based film-making process. Dilys Powell spoke for many critics at the time when her highly enthusiastic review of Jack Clayton's *Room at the Top* (1959), generally accepted as the first of the new wave cycle of films, maintained in her column for the *Sunday Times* that 'It gives one faith all over again in a renaissance of the British cinema'.[3] But it was precisely this idea which Raymond Durgnat questioned some years later in his 1970 book, *A Mirror for England*, where he saw scant substance in claims for either a renaissance or even much by way of a new wave:

> If we look at the development of the newer style in features, we
> find the trailblazer is Jack Clayton's *Room at the Top*, based on a

bestselling novel. It wasn't *Momma Don't Allow* that brought Tony Richardson into the directorial chair of *Look Back in Anger*; it was the fact that he had directed the play on the London stage. While the partisans of Free Cinema were directing stage plays and TV commercials, the new wave arose from response to the work of artists in other media. Far from originating in a new documentary approach, the impulse came from the plays of John Osborne, Keith Waterhouse and Willis Hall, Wolf Mankowitz and Shelagh Delaney, novels by John Braine, Alan Sillitoe, Stan Barstow and David Storey, and a new generation of actors, like Albert Finney, Rita Tushingham, Rachel Roberts, Tom Courtenay, Richard Harris and Ronald Fraser. The films are based on proven successes in other media, their production stimulated by the influence of new talents on commercial producers.[4]

Durgnat found the new wave films and their directors wanting in several respects. For one thing, though the likes of Tony Richardson, Karel Reisz and Lindsay Anderson had gained their first experiences in film production while making the 'Free Cinema' documentaries of the mid-1950s, Durgnat felt there was little sign of any lasting influence being carried over into their feature film work. Which was hardly surprising in his opinion given that they betrayed, if anything, their origins as essentially theatre directors. Far from finding much of novelty value in their new found role as feature film directors, moreover, Durgnat concluded that they had resorted to the 'orthodox commercial procedures' usually employed by the British film industry in general: namely, transposing successful stage or literary texts to the cinema screen. And for all that these comprised new vehicles based on the 'kitchen sink' dramas of the 'Angry Young Men' or novels by the 'Northern Realists', and their screen renditions cast from a younger generation of naturalistic actors, they were invariably chosen for filmic adaptation because they were already proven successes in other fields – tried, tested and true, in the time honoured fashion of traditional mainstream British cinema. For Durgnat, in short, the British new wave was hardly anything of the sort.

Roy Armes followed in similar vein though he expressed his dislike for the work of Anderson, Reisz and Richardson, in 1978, with even greater vehemence. While pinpointing their 'middle-class background' as a setback at the outset and drawing attention to the fact that they also enjoyed 'the public school-Oxbridge educational pattern conventional to this class (Anderson and Richardson both studied at Wadham College, Oxford, and Reisz at Emmanuel College, Cambridge)', furthermore, Armes's distinctly class-based reading inevitably criticised the film-makers because they did not 'create out of their own lived experience'. Thus, in Armes's opinion, their vision was pretty much rendered null and void from the start. They constituted no more than 'the university-educated bourgeois making "sympathetic" films about proletarian life, not analysing the ambiguities of their own privileged position', with the result that 'The self-analytical insight which would be needed for this latter alternative is precisely what is lacking from both Free Cinema and the early Woodfall films'. As judgments go, it was both damning and ideologically loaded albeit, perhaps, not unsymptomatic of its times.[5]

For Arthur Marwick, by contrast, there was a lot to admire in new wave cinema generally and, indeed, the films of Anderson, Clayton, Reisz and Richardson in particular. Writing on the subject first in 1984 (but soon followed by numerous further publications), he sought to examine the impact of the new wave in the context of the wider cultural changes affecting British society at large. In this regard, especially, he found the films to be representative of the 'cultural revolution' which he identified as taking root in Britain around 1959 and was to reach its peak in the 1960s, with 1967 proving perhaps the 'annus mirabilis' as far as liberalising legislation was concerned – when the Abortion Act, the National Health Service Act, and the Sexual Offences Act were all passed – thereby consolidating the gains for the 'permissive society' that had accrued during the 'swinging sixties'. 'The most potent evidence of intellectual and artistic renewal in Britain was to be found in the cinema', Marwick concluded as he traced its progress from 1959 in displaying three distinct tendencies: a perceptive social criticism and social satire; an authentic presentation of working-class lifestyles; and genuine innovation in breaking away from the purely naturalistic film. The significance of films like *Room at the Top, Saturday Night and Sunday Morning* and others in the new wave genre was that they 'showed that critical change was actually taking place during the particular few years in which they were made'; they were both 'new cultural artefacts born of change, and themselves productive of more rapid change'.[6]

Situating the new wave in its social and cultural context as well as appreciating the textual characteristics of its films were also the ostensible pursuits of John Hill's survey in 1986. But he began by taking issue with the critiques forthcoming from Durgnat and Armes, in particular: 'It has been a common enough criticism of the "new wave" films that, although about the working class, they nonetheless represent an outsider's view'. He continued: 'The importance of the point, however, is less the actual social background of the film-makers, none of whom ever lay claim to be just "one of the lads", than the way in which this "outsider's view" is inscribed in the films themselves, the way the "poetry", the "marks of the enunciation" themselves articulate a clear distance between observer and observed'. Identifying the 'poetry' evident in new wave films and isolating 'the marks of enunciation' manifested by new wave film-makers became, in effect, the hallmarks of Hill's research. But for all his dutiful nods in the direction of contextual study, which remained arguably no less perfunctory than that by Armes and Durgnat, Hill's work was undoubtedly strongest and richest in its textual analysis. Hence, and perhaps unsurprisingly, he attracted as much criticism as praise from subsequent commentators.[7]

Robert Murphy, for instance, maintained in 1992 that Hill's 'Marxist perspective' prompts him all too easily to dismiss the 'well-meaning liberalism' of new wave films as 'ideologically pernicious' and that his 'Marxist puritanism', furthermore, 'leads him into dangerously wide generalisations'. This was particularly evident, to Murphy's mind, in Hill's overarching tendency to condemn the new wave for what he considered was its 'misogynist attitude towards women'. What Hill misses, he argued, is the fact that the women portrayed in new wave films had 'a seriousness, an emotional weight, altogether lacking in the pathetically trivial roles women had to play in most 1950s British films'. Regarding new wave films generally, he continued, 'Time having exposed their ideological assumptions and prejudices, their fictions become less important than the reality of the attitudes they embody, turning them into cultural artefacts'. For Murphy finally, as for Marwick before him, 'it is the aura of social significance, the glimpse they offer into a past society, which makes them valuable'.[8]

Probably the most trenchant critique of new wave cinema, however, is also one of the most recent and it was advanced by Peter Wollen in an article published in 1993. Wollen laid three major charges at the door of British new wave cinema and to press home his arguments compared it (unfavourably) with its then contemporary French equivalent, the *nouvelle vague* cinema forthcoming from film-makers such as Francois Truffaut, Jean-Luc Godard, Claude Chabrol and Alain Resnais – most of whom had started life as critics on the influential *Cahiers du Cinema* magazine. If his first two criticisms were largely echoes of those made earlier by both Durgnat and Armes – that British new wave film-makers lacked a distinctive 'authorial' voice or vision (a matter better nuanced by Hill who conceded that they did, in point of fact); their cinema comprised merely adaptations of literary successes, anyway, and therefore subordinated film to novels or plays (as all previous commentators agreed) – his last complaint undoubtedly raised vital or salient issues about the nature and import of the British new wave:

> Third, both critics and the directors themselves explicitly justified the Angry Young Men films in terms of 'realism'. Their attitude reflected an old shibboleth and plaint of the British cinema establishment, both in production and reception, best summed up by Michael Balcon's programmatic preference for 'realism' over 'tinsel'. This system of value, though most strongly entrenched on the Left, ran all the way across the political spectrum. For the Right, as with the Left, the aesthetic preference was bound up with nationalism. 'Tinsel', of course, was identified with Hollywood escapism and, in contrast, realism evoked local pride and sense of community. It meant showing ourselves honestly to ourselves, rather than indulging in other people's alien and deceptive fantasies. British critics praised films they liked in terms of their realism and damned those they did not as escapist trash. The French New Wave, however, aimed to transcend this shallow antinomy. The third term that made this possible was, of course, 'modernism'. The films of Resnais and Godard, even when adaptations, placed themselves clearly in a modernist tradition, as did Truffaut's crucial *Jules et Jim* (1962). Resnais, to take the most obvious example, collaborated with writers like Robbe-Grillet and Duras. The *Cahiers* group followed the path blazed by the Nouveau Roman and recognised Jean Cocteau as their godfather. Yet in Britain film-makers fetishized the second-rate novels of regionalists, realists, and reactionaries.[9]

Though there are some aspects of Wollen's account that appear to be needlessly and unfairly judgemental – not least his scathing denunciation of the 'Northern realist' novelists or the 'Angry brigade' dramatists

– his substantive claim that the British new wave was a decidedly insular phenomenon and overly preoccupied with 'realism' (albeit not of the Griersonian documentarist variety) at the expense of different kinds of cinema, contains much of merit and substance. Such features do, indeed, define its essential characteristics and explain in large measure, as Wollen rightly notes, why it proved a considerable success with many film critics in its day. The critical consensus undoubtedly favoured 'realist' films in preference to films of 'fantasy', and 'realism' was equated with 'quality' in their eyes. But there were other key factors besides which must be taken into consideration when seeking to fully contextualise British cinema during the period 1959–63 and which also explain its evolution in that time. In particular, the British Board of Film Censors made its own distinctive contribution towards defining the parameters of the prevailing critical consensus. It, too, espoused 'realist' film-making as the preferred mode of expression, and the BBFC had a considerable impact upon both new wave directors and their methods of production.

Comparisons between British new wave cinema and its contemporary French equivalent in the *nouvelle vague,* furthermore, are neither new nor original. In retrospect, of course, Wollen draws such comparisons to highlight what he perceives as the British new wave's overall failure to engage sufficiently with 'modernist' cinema or to progress meaningfully in the manner that he felt was evident among French film makers. At the time, it appears, British film critics were more inclined to pinpoint the similarities between the two and noted the extent to which the former seemingly draw upon the latter for stylistic inspiration, though whether the results were considered wholly beneficial for the development of a national cinema clearly remained open to question. When reviewing *The Loneliness of the Long Distance Runner* in the *New Statesman,* for instance, John Coleman judged it a 'sometimes brilliant film' and praised 'its enterprising gleanings from the sort of cinema Truffaut seems to be after'. But still maintained that 'you can almost hear the clashing of the new waves, English and French, and it's their head-on confrontation that finally rocks the boat', as he continued:

> Camera, in fact, comments as intrusively as those crafty imperfects of Flaubert's, making one conscious of artifice when one ought to be taken by art, doing swimming things with trees as the runner plods on, going for loveliness when something else would suffice. And then there are the naughty 'French' gags loading the argument.

When Colin and his chum thieve from the bakery, they escape in a speeded-up Chaplinesque chase, disarming things that they are. Their gaiety when they pinch a car and Colin shoves on a Belmondo-type hat is caught in jump-cuts that might be a parody of Godard-*et-cie*.[10]

And the film critic for the *Manchester Guardian* also had reservations:

A British film nowadays, if it is to be taken seriously, must set its scene among the more or less rebellious young people of the industrial North or Midlands; it must be tough, realistic, icono-clastic (possibly nihilistic too) and thoroughly 'working-class' ... Mr.[Tony] Richardson, having already directed *Look Back in Anger* and *A Taste of Honey* must be regarded as a specialist in the genre. This rather slow-pulsed British counterpart to the French 'new wave' was a good thing when it started. And it is still a good thing if only because it means that our film-makers – traditionally so imitative of the ways of Hollywood – are making a sustained effort to keep in touch with the realities of modern Britain as they affect large areas of the country and large, previously 'submerged', sections of the population. The only worry is that the fashion, being no longer new, is losing the fine edge of its distinction and is beginning to turn to formulae of its own. And these, like any other formula, are likely to be tedious.[11]

Whether based upon judgments immediately forthcoming or made with the benefit of hindsight, in short, the balance of critical opinion is plainly that whatever the formal influences occasionally brought to bear, the new wave remained pre-eminently a realist cinema which was essentially preoccupied with domestic concerns, and, to the last, it was a distinctly British phenomenon. *The Loneliness of the Long Distance Runner* does, indeed, make the point well enough. If Tony Richardson's 1962 production for Woodfall Films differed somewhat from its new wave predecessors in employing a greater array of technical devices and an enhanced measure of artifice to draw attention to itself as a film in a self-conscious manner, its social realist trajectory was still paramount and firmly anchored in a British context.

Tony Richardson, for his part, openly professed admiration for 'foreign' film directors and acknowledged their formative influence upon his work for the cinema. But, interestingly, it was Vittorio De Sica and Luis Bunuel he claimed to favour most – men from a generation of film-makers before the French *nouvelle vague*. And, just as interesting, in the same breath as he extolled their virtues, he continued to express his principal cinematic purpose in terms which were inextricably linked with his origins in British theatre. 'It is absolutely vital to get into British films the same sort of impact and sense of life that, what you can loosely call the Angry Young Man cult, has had in the theatre and literary worlds', Richardson maintained: 'It is a desperate need'.[12] Moreover, during the course of his posthumously published auto-biographical 'memoir', *Long Distance Runner,* Tony Richardson elaborated what his 'aesthetic' objectives were, how much he shared with foreign film-makers, and, in addition, what he deliberately eschewed by way of extraneous stylistic influences.

It is evident there, for instance, that one of the major reasons why Richardson parted company eventually with the cinematographer, Oswald Morris, who had shot both *Look Back in Anger* (1959) and *The Entertainer* (1960), was because they differed increasingly over matters of style. Richardson had in fact wanted Walter Lassally, cameraman on his Free Cinema documentary, *Momma Don't Allow* (1956), from the outset of his venture into feature film making with *Look Back in Anger* but was persuaded by producer Harry Saltzman to opt for the more experienced Ossie Morris. And though Richardson did not regret the decision and was unstinting in his praise for Morris's work on both that film and its successor, *The Entertainer,* their differences in approach soon became obvious, as he recounted:

> *The Entertainer* was a key moment in my development, because all the ideas and convictions I was to work with afterwards were crystallized in its making. I began to sense how great a jump would be involved when my great mentor and friend Ossie Morris thought I was becoming too careless and irresponsible: I didn't insist on take after take; I didn't care about minor imperfections. I thought I was becoming free. Ossie, ever the technician, thought I was becoming spoilt and sloppy. From the Free Cinema manifesto, 'Perfection is not an aim' came back to me. Life was more important.[13]

Richardson's twofold conviction that 'Film is a totally realistic medium' and that 'Casting [is] the key to all film reality' – maxims surely borne, once again, of his theatrical grounding – doubtless militated against an ongoing and fruitful partnership with Morris. Not least when in subsequent discussions between the two men, Richardson found that there were 'too many art books consulted and too much aesthetics talked' by his erstwhile cinematographer with the result that 'we realised our philosophies were even further apart than before'. Thus, perhaps inevitably, Richardson turned increasingly towards his earlier cameraman, Walter Lassally, to do the precise job he wanted on both *A Taste of Honey* (1961) and *The Loneliness of the Long Distance Runner* (1962) – as well as, incidentally, the Oscar-winning *Tom Jones* (1963) where he had in fact considered, albeit fleetingly, re-engaging Morris.[14]

Lassally's particular skills were altogether more in tune with Richardson's liking and preference for realist films shot in what he construed as a realist fashion. And they were praised in terms which make it abundantly clear, moreover, that Richardson drew a clear line of divide between his kind of cinema and that of his French contemporaries. 'He was an important figure in England', Richardson said of Lassally, 'being the first of our lighting cameramen (as distinct, for example, from what was happening in France with the *nouvelle vague*) to be able to work in what was becoming known as the Free Cinema style – a minimum of equipment, real locations and a natural, unmade-up look'. When read in conjunction with further opinions scattered throughout his memoir – to the effect, for instance, that 'the substitution of director for writer was one of the excesses of the so-called auteur theory at its height' – it is clear that Richardson consciously espoused precisely those features of new wave cinema which later drew fierce criticism from commentators: namely, an emphasis upon realist techniques at the expense of modernist aesthetics; privileging the author of the original literary text instead of the auteur's filmic vision; and, in all, producing a national even if self-evidently insular cinema, regardless of what was going on in national cinemas elsewhere.[15]

Nor, indeed, was Richardson alone in his intentions for British cinema. The British Board of Film Censors was also intent upon fostering its own concept of a national cinema and had therefore looked with growing interest at new wave films for that very purpose. John Trevelyan's tenure as BBFC secretary from 1958 coincided fortuitously with the advent of the new wave and no sooner had he formally taken over the post, in July of that year, than he was presented with the completed film of *Room at the Top* for consideration and the script of *Look Back in Anger* for pre-production scrutiny. The 'angry brigade' had arrived at the censor's doorstep in earnest and from the outset he embarked upon a path of pragmatic and liberal compromise whereby, in effect, he settled an issue which had long proved the source of much concern in relations between the BBFC and the film industry at large – how best to promote British films of 'quality'.

The criteria evolved and applied by Trevelyan to *Room at the Top* substantially set the parameters in this respect and helped to determine the critical consensus that existed across the industry when judging 'quality' film thereafter. That this critical consensus defined 'quality' in terms of realist films and literary pedigree aided or abetted the cause of new wave cinema wonderfully, even if its film-makers were compelled to see their films landed with a 'X' certificate so as to avoid the threat of censorious cuts and excisions. But then investing the 'X' certificate with such 'quality' fare – 'serious' films on 'genuinely adult' themes, done with 'sincerity' – was exactly what Trevelyan wished to promote in order to pit them against the more likely or common 'X' rated materials – 'sensational', 'exploitative' and 'commercial' films of fantasy, made in 'poor taste'. And it helped Trevelyan enormously, of course, that his criteria of quality accorded quite neatly with the criteria increasingly advocated by mainstream film critics across the board.

It would be wrong, however, to paint too rosy or harmonious a picture of working relations between the new wave film-makers and the BBFC. Censorship was a negotiated process in which a considerable amount of give-and-take was exercised by all parties. Tony Richardson's Woodfall Films encountered continual problems with the censors and Alan Sillitoe's draft scripts, in particular, were the cause of many pre-production difficulties. In the case of their 1960 film, *Saturday Night and Sunday Morning,* negotiations had taken place on several occasions for the purpose of toning down the 'language' and use of the vernacular evident throughout, and discarding what the BBFC considered to be highly objectionable themes or incidents carried over from Sillitoe's original novel – not least the promise of a successful abortion scene which was definitely barred from the screen and turned out an unsuccessful abortion attempt in the finished film.[16]

The BBFC was greatly tested yet again with the arrival late in 1961 of Sillitoe's second script for Woodfall, a screen adaptation of the title story from his 1959 collection, *The Loneliness of the Long Distance Runner.* Though the collection of short stories had won the Hawthornden Prize in 1960, Sillitoe was already viewed by some BBFC examiners as a 'socially irresponsible' writer. In the script tendered for pre-production censorship scrutiny, moreover, his characterisation of the anarchic, anti-authoritarian Borstal boy, Colin Smith (Tom Courtenay), who deliberately throws a cross country race he could easily win, was judged little more than the portrayal of 'a good hero of the British Soviet, in fact'. After seeing his father die in agony and his mother blow the insurance money on luxuries and a new-found boyfriend, Colin is understandably disenchanted and disaffected. But Sillitoe's depiction of Smith's consequent lapse into a life of petty crime and his stubborn refusal at the last, once landed in Borstal, to 'play the game', capitalise on his obvious running skills or bring credit to his institution by beating the representatives of a public school, clearly did not meet with approval on the part of the BBFC's script scrutineers. And the matter of 'language', unsurprisingly, emerged once again as a key stumbling block in Sillitoe's efforts to transpose his story for the cinema. One script-reader, Audrey Field, commented in her report on Sillitoe's screenplay of 3 January 1962:

> I am very much disappointed in this script. I liked *Saturday Night* and, despite the hero's trying little ways, I liked him, because I felt he had the makings of becoming a sensible human being who would take people as he found them and not go on for ever taking refuge in a lot of claptrap like 'All Army officers and policeman are bad and all workers are good'. But this story is blatant and very trying Communist propaganda, and particularly worrying for us because the hero is a thief and yet is held up to the admiration of silly young thugs. If the leading citizens of Nottingham didn't like *Saturday Night* because they thought the hero was not a good representative of that city, I don't know what they will say about this epic. But basically I think we must leave this script alone (for 'X', which it must be because of the language quite apart from the moral tone) and hope that the common sense of the cinemagoing public will be equal to seeing some flaws in logic. When I say that 'basically it may have to be left alone' I am not, of course, referring to the language, which must be cleaned up in accordance with our well known rules in dealing with 'X' films.

Field felt, furthermore, that the 'socially irresponsible' elements in the script were noticeably evident with dialogue like 'We should be working for each other, not working against each other', which prompted the remark:

> This sort of high-souled talk is the reason why young people are liable to think that Colin is a Good Man. It is true party line stuff. What the objection is to an honest-to-goodness prize openly and honestly competed for and judged, I can never see myself. People are always competing, and the secret, unacknowledged competitions are far more bitter and deadly. (Particularly in Communist countries, where the loser commonly gets shot).

And the 'violently intemperate and wrong-headed social sentiments' contained in lines stating 'As long as you keep fighting bastards like the Governor, that's all that matters', also elicited wry comment at the expense of the writer and Board of Directors at Woodfall Film Productions: 'I don't think messrs. Sillitoe, Osborne, Richardson (or the other Englishmen with the funny-sounding names on the letter-heading) would feel so sure of their ground if Colin were a real thief of their own acquaintance who had taken away their lovely Jaguars or whatever'.[17]

But it was the 'language' used throughout Sillitoe's screenplay that worried the script-reader most of all. And it was the matter of 'language', moreover, which exercised Trevelyan when he wrote to Woodfall Productions on 9 January 1962 to express his principal reservations over the script. If it was mixed with a measure of genuine concern at the damage likely to be done to the film's commercial prospects in the potentially lucrative overseas market, it was crucial none the less:

> The main thing that worries us is that, like Alan Sillitoe's previous script for *Saturday Night and Sunday Morning*, there is an excess of what is sometimes called 'language'. Once again he produces the word 'bogger'. This word we still find unacceptable. There are two other expletives which we also find unacceptable; these are 'Christ' (or 'For Christ's sake') and 'sod'. There are also two other expressions which we must put into the same category: these are 'clapped out' and 'caltfart'. Apart from these the word 'bloody' or 'bleddy' is used extensively – actually 32 times according to the reader whom I asked to count them. 'Bastard' is used 11 times. 'Bleeder' and 'Bleeding' are used on a few occasions but we would not worry about these. I appreciate that Alan Sillitoe wants the dialogue to be the natural speech of the kind of people shown in this film

but I would suggest that there should be some reduction neverthe-less.

The question of language is likely to affect the category in which the film is placed. If there were too much 'language' used we would have to give the film an 'X' certificate. I appreciate that the film is being made essentially for the British market, but I imagine that the export market in a good many English speaking countries is not unimportant, and I know that in a good many English speaking countries language of this kind is automatically removed regardless of its effect on the film. However, this is your problem and not mine. We are prepared to accept a reasonable degree of 'language' but, as I have already pointed out, there are certain words and phrases that are still unacceptable to us.[18]

In the event, after negotiation, Woodfall relented over the key words found objectionable whilst retaining a measure of the more acceptable ones. Thus, *The Loneliness of the Long Distance Runner,* like *Saturday Night and Sunday Morning* before it, was granted an 'X' certificate at the last, on 3 August 1962. Where, previously, Sillitoe had offended because of both his chosen theme and language, here, though the theme was deemed less troublesome – Trevelyan, for his part, believed it 'presents no important censorship problems' – language was still the occasion for considerable concern, and largely dictated the certificate the film would receive. While the BBFC readily conceded that Sillitoe's use of the vernacular was 'naturalist' in intent, it was also considered highly 'dubious' and not what was expected in British films. 'Quality' cinema should not include too much by way of ordinary parlance and some words – 'bogger' especially – were definitely prohibited.

For all the advances made and concessions granted over the liberalising of film content during the 'cultural revolution' in British society of the 1960s, the cinematic vision of everyday life was still bounded or circumscribed by a newly evolving consensus which was determined, in effect, by the ongoing censorship process. And the BBFC made its own distinct contribution to the 'realism' forthcoming in new wave films and, indeed, the construction of a British national cinema during the 1960s, generally. To castigate British new wave cinema of the day for its failings and shortcomings on both these fronts, therefore, is perhaps the result (*pace* Peter Wollen) of failing to contextualise its situation adequately.

Moreover, those contemporary critics who felt that with *The Loneli-ness of the Long Distance Runner* the new wave had 'come near to running its course' or was in danger of becoming 'derivative' and 'predictable', that there had been 'enough stylistic borrowings from the French *nouvelle vague*' and that British cinema should now strike out in other directions to forge a stronger national cinema, had more in keeping with the new wave film-makers than they perhaps imagined. Tony Richardson certainly sensed the need to move on and with his next film, *Tom Jones* (1963), he produced an Oscar-winning success which not only pleased critics and audiences alike but also helped to secure an international reputation for British cinema.[19]

Notes

1. Stuart Laing, *Representations of Working-Class Life 1957–1964,* Basingstoke, 1986, pp 109–10. Laing is very useful on the broad changes in cinemagoing trends and the film industry at large but for more detail see the accounts, in particular, by Terence Kelly, *A Competitive Cinema,* London, 1966, and John Spraos, *The Decline of the Cinema. An Economist's Report,* London, 1962.

2. See Janet Thumim, 'The "popular", cash and culture in the postwar British cinema industry', *Screen,* vol. 32, no. 3, 1991, p. 249, and, Jeffrey Richards, 'New waves and old myths', in Bart Moore-Gilbert and John Seed, eds., *Cultural Revolution? The Challenge of the Arts in the 1960s,* London, 1992, p. 218.

3. *Sunday Times,* 25 January 1959, and reprinted in Christopher Cook, ed., *The Dilys Powell Film Reader,* Manchester, 1991, pp. 20–2.

4. Raymond Durgnat, *A Mirror for England: British Movies from Austerity to Affluence,* London, 1970, pp. 129.

5. Roy Armes, *A Critical History of British Cinema,* London, 1978, pp. 2–5.

6. See Arthur Marwick, '*Room at the Top, Saturday Night and Sunday Morning,* and the "Cultural Revolution" in Britain', *Journal of Contemporary History,* vol. 19, no. 1, 1984, p. 148; and, also, *Culture in Britain since 1945,* Oxford, 1991, as well as, *British Society since 1945,* Harmondsworth, 1995, 3rd edn.

7. John Hill, *Sex, Class and Realism: British Cinema 1956–1965,* London, 1986, pp. 132–3.

8. Robert Murphy, *Sixties British Cinema,* London, 1992, pp. 9, 31 and 57. Terry Lovell also mines greater riches than Hill from the new wave representation of women forthcoming in *A Taste of Honey,* especially, during her seminal article, 'Landscape and Stories in 1960s British Realism', *Screen,* vol. 31, no. 4, 1990, pp. 347–76.

9. Peter Wollen, 'The Last New Wave: Modernism in the British Films of the Thatcher Era', in Lester Friedman, ed., *British Cinema and Thatcherism. Fires were Started,* London, 1993, pp. 37–8.

10. *New Statesman,* 28 September 1962.

11. *Manchester Guardian,* 25 September 1962.

12. Tony Richardson, 'The Man Behind an Angry Young Man', *Films and Filming,* vol. 5, no. 5, February 1959, pp. 9 and 32.

13. Tony Richardson, *Long Distance Runner. A Memoir,* London, 1993, p. 109.

14.   Duncan Petrie's *The British Cinematographer,* London, 1996, is an excellent survey of cameramen throughout this period, and beyond, though it is ably supplemented by Walter Lassally's own account of his career, *Itinerant Cameraman,* London, 1987, and the occasional work from other cinematographers, such as Jack Cardiff, *Magic Hour. The Life of a Cameraman,* London, 1996, and Christopher Challis, *Are They Really So Awful?,* London, 1995.

15.   Richardson, *Long Distance Runner,* pp. 108, 120–1, and, 126–7.

16.   The matter is explored at length in Anthony Aldgate, *Censorship and the Permissive Society: British Cinema and Theatre, 1955–1965,* Oxford, 1995, pp. 89–98. My book draws extensively on the BBFC files for this and other new wave films which were kindly provided by the British Board of Film Classification. Grateful thanks go to James Ferman and his staff for making them available to me.

17.   BBFC file on *The Loneliness of the Long Distance Runner:* examiner's report, 3 January 1962.

18.   BBFC file: Trevelyan to Woodfall Film Productions, 9 January 1962. Once the film was completed and viewed by the BBFC president and secretary on 20 July 1962, Trevelyan worried somewhat about the depiction of the police. But a subsequent telephone conversation between Trevelyan and Richardson agreed that more dialogue would be dropped and the film's editor, Tony Gibbs, confirmed on 1 August 1962 that he had removed the line: 'If we get you down to the nick you will get a few bruises for your trouble'. After further discussion with the president, Trevelyan then passed the film with an 'X' certificate on 3 August 1962.

19.   The need for further change was neatly summarised by Penelope Houston when she stated that '*The Loneliness of the Long Distance Runner* makes what one assumes can only be conscious gestures in the direction of the *nouvelle vague,* with its bit of speeded-up action, its frozen final shot, its self-consciously "cinematic" emphases. . . . But the post-*Room at the Top* era has come near to running its course; and the directors who have emerged from it have to find their own way towards a more cinematic cinema, unaided by influences from across the Channel'. See *The Contemporary Cinema 1945–1963,* Harmondsworth, 1963, pp. 121 and 124. Similar sentiments were expressed by many critics in their newspaper reviews of the film, except for David Robinson who in *The Financial Times* for 28 September 1962 drew an interesting line of divide between the critics' expectations and what he perceived as continued support for new wave films on the part of cinemagoers who he felt were still willing to accept them: 'For years we begged for British films about real people and contemporary themes. Now that we have them (and as a result are re-establishing a reputation in the international cinema) it is alarming to detect – among critics, if not as yet in the audience – a growing resistance to such a film as *The Loneliness of the Long Distance Runner*'.

If. . . (1968)

12

The Revolt of the Young

If ...

The 1960s saw a full-scale, almost precipitate, retreat from the rigorous social controls imposed during the Victorian era by the forces of evangelical religion. In 1960 gambling was legalized, and this led to a proliferation of betting shops, bingo halls and gaming clubs. Capital punishment was abolished in 1965 and theatrical censorship in 1968. Abortion and homosexuality were legalized in 1967. Divorce was made easier by the 1969 Divorce Reform Act. At the same time there was a vast expansion of the welfare state, with massive slum-clearance programmes and the building of huge new housing estates, the extension of benefits and social services, the introduction of comprehensive education and the founding of a host of new universities and colleges. The campaign for women's rights was launched, leading to the Equal Pay Act (1970) and the Equal Opportunities Commission. Liberalization and egalitarianism were the keynotes of public policy. This spilled over into popular culture, which was dominated by the young working class and characterized by sexual permissiveness and the free use of drugs.[1]

Many felt, despite all this, that the old elites remained in charge, adapting to, and accommodating, social and cultural change. The public schools were their bastion, and as the public sector of education went steadily comprehensive, the voices raised against the private sector became more strident. Gone was the desire for cautious, evolutionary reform. Now the call was for the total abolition of those centres of privilege, power and class-consciousness. The opponents of the public school received potent ammunition from a film, Lindsay Anderson's *If* ... (1968).

Amusing and biting by turns, *If* ... brilliantly recreates the enclosed, all-male world of the public school. It lays bare the process by which the system produces an authoritarian elite to govern the country, deals with dissidents and induces unthinking conformism. The school is a rigidly ordered society with an unshakeable hierarchy, from 'scum' (fags) to 'whips' (prefects). Its exclusivity is reinforced by its arcane and self-perpetuating slang, in which we see a new boy being painstakingly instructed. He is made aware that it is not just content but style that counts here ('You do realize it's not just a matter of knowing the answers. It's how you say it'). Pride in belonging is fostered by compulsory games, with Matron entering into the supporters' bloodlust ('Fight, college, fight, fight, fight!') and with a celebratory 'House Thump' greeting the winning of the cup.

If ... opens with the start of term, recreating the turmoil and bustle of the return from the holidays and introducing the school through the eyes of a lost, bewildered and diminutive new boy, Jute. Thereafter the background of routine, ritual and discipline is meticulously recreated as the action is played out against an authentic background of chapel, dinner, medical inspection, dormitory inspection, cadet corps exercises and lights out. Significantly, given the traditional public school commitment to character-forming rather than academic attainment, lessons occupy only a small part of the film, and the boys are seen as unresponsive and apathetic during them. The film closes with Founder's Day, in which the time-honoured ceremonial is disrupted by the attack of the rebels.

The school is in effect run by the 'whips', cold, self-possessed, all-powerful figures, with distinctive dress (flowered waistcoats, canes) and privileges (fags, the right to beat). They revel in these privileges, constantly ordering silence or running in the corridor to remind everyone that they are in charge. They discourage initiative. 'It's not up to you to think,' house captain Rowntree tells his fag, Bobby Phillips. They deal with nonconformists summarily, inflicting cold showers and, when those fail, brutal floggings, performed ritually and with the entire house listening in tense silence. They either find outlets for their sexual urges in a light-hearted homosexuality, epitomized by the bantering discussion between Rowntree and the 'whips' about the attractions of various boys, or they sublimate them in sadistic authoritarianism, as Denson does. This elite is characterized by Mick Travis when he insolently tells Rowntree: 'The thing I hate about you, Rowntree, is the way you give Coca-Cola to your scum and your best teddy-bear to Oxfam and expect us to lick your frigid fingers for the rest of your frigid life.'

Rather less important in terms of running the school are the masters, whom the 'whips' control, as is tellingly illustrated when Denson on his night round virtually reprimands the new master, Mr Thomas, for being out late. The masters are almost all eccentrics, perverts or ineffectual nonentities. The history master (Graham Crowden) rides his bicycle through the corridors singing hymns at the top of his voice, opens all the windows and cheerfully confesses to having lost essays in the Mont Blanc Tunnel. The chaplain (Geoffrey Chater) twists the nipples of small boys in his maths class and pruriently asks for details of the 'dirty thoughts' confessed by Stephans. Housemaster Kemp (Arthur Lowe) and the new master Thomas (Ben Aris) are dominated by the 'whips'.

The headmaster (brilliantly played by Peter Jeffrey) is a bland, self-satisfied, platitudinous pseudo-liberal, a caricature of the liberal house tutor, Nigel Lorraine, in *The Guinea Pig* (1948). He strides round the school lecturing the sixth-formers on the modern world:

> College is a symbol of many things: scholarship, integrity in public office, high standards in the television and entertainment worlds, huge sacrifice in Britain's wars. Of course, some of our customs are silly; you could say they were middle-class. But a large part of the population is in the process of becoming middle-class, and many of the middle class's moral values are values that the country cannot do without. We must not expect to be thanked. Education in Britain is a nubile Cinderella, sparsely clad and much interfered with. Britain today is a power-house of ideas, experiments, imagination, on everything from pop music to pig breeding; from atom power stations to mini-skirts, and that's the challenge we've got to meet.

He takes the sixth form in the trendy subject of 'business management'. His is the voice of consensus, of change within continuity, that *The Guinea Pig* was endorsing, a standpoint *If* . . . decisively rejects.

The boys in the school fulfil several different roles. There are ambitious conformists like Stephans, who runs the dormitory where the three rebels sleep, sucks up to the 'whips', acts as if he were a 'whip' already, curries favour with the chaplain by confessing his 'dirty thoughts' and utters anti-Semitic remarks. There are blind opters-out like 'Peanuts', the scientist totally absorbed in his telescope and in looking out to the stars. When Mick hands him a bullet, he hands it back uncomprehendingly. There is the permanent outsider, Biles, persecuted and harassed and, in a chilling scene, hunted and hounded by the boys through the gym and finally tied, upside-down, with his head stuck down the lavatory. Finally, there are the three rebels, Mick Travis (Malcolm McDowell), Johnny Knightly (David Wood) and Wallace (Richard Warwick). Mick's nonconformity is established at the outset, when he returns to school in a broad-brimmed hat and muffled up in a long black scarf. In the privacy of his study he removes the scarf to reveal the moustache he has grown. He shaves it off but thereafter behaves with studied insolence to all in authority. He and his fellow rebels drink gin and smoke illegally, fantasize and dream of freedom ('When do we live?'). In one exhilarating sequence Mick and Johnny break bounds, go into town, steal a motorbike and race through the countryside. After all three have been beaten for their 'general attitude', they rebel, first turning their rifles on the cadet corps exercise and, in the explosive finale, bombing and machine-gunning the assembly of dignitaries, boys and parents at Founder's Day.

What the boys are rebelling against is essentially the repression and authoritarianism embodied by the 'whips' and endorsed by the headmaster. Sexual repression is represented by Denson's suppressed longing for Bobby Phillips, mirrored in a close shot of Denson's face as Bobby shaves him; the sequence of the dowdy and timorous Mrs Kemp wandering naked through the empty dormitories; the chaplain's enquiry into Stephans's 'dirty thoughts'. The rebels are sexual freedom incarnate. Mick encounters a waitress in a café; they romp together on the floor, imitating tigers, at first clothed and later naked. The Girl (Christine Noonan) joins the rebels in their final revolt, as does Bobby Phillips (Rupert Webster), Denson's fag, for he falls in love with Wallace, a process visually encapsulated in the beautifully conceived slow-motion sequence in which Bobby admiringly watches Wallace working out on the bars in the gym. Later Wallace and Bobby smoke a cigarette in the school armoury and are subsequently seen in bed together. Bobby is the fifth and last of the crusaders. Authoritarianism takes the form of the savage beating at the end of which Mick, broken and in tears, takes Rowntree's outstretched hand and says faintly: 'Thank you, Rowntree.' His acting out of the ritual confirms his submission. But the rebels fight back.

At Founder's Day, with parents, boys, staff and visiting VIPs assembled, General Denson, national hero and old boy, addresses the school in a speech that captures perfectly the public school ethos which the rebels have set themselves to oppose:

> You're lucky. Yes – a lot of men would give their eyeteeth to be sitting where you are sitting now. You are privileged. Now, for heaven's sake, don't get me wrong. There's nothing the matter with privilege as long as we're ready to pay for it. It's a very sad thing, but today it is fashionable to belittle tradition. The old order that made our nation a living force are for the most part scorned by modern psychiatrists, priests, pundits of all sorts. But what have they got to put in their place? Oh, politicians talk a lot about freedom. Well, freedom is the heritage of every Englishman who speaks with the tongue that Shakespeare spoke. But, you know, we won't stay free unless we are ready to fight. And you won't be any good as fighters unless you know something about discipline. The habit of obedience, how to give orders and how to take them. Never mind the sneers of the cynics. Let us be true to honour . . . duty . . . national pride. We still need loyalty. . . . We still need tradition. If we look around us at the world today, what do we see? We see bloodshed, confusion, decay. I know the world has changed a great deal in the past fifty years. But England, our England, doesn't change so easily. And back here in college today I feel, and it makes me jolly proud, that there is still a tradition here, which has not changed and by God it isn't going to change.

During the ceremony two old men in Crusader armour parade, reciting meaningless Latin formulae. But as the film makes clear, the rebels are the real crusaders, launching an attack on the entrenched forces of privilege and authority. The film's original title, indeed, was *Crusaders*. But as the two sides exchange fire, the headmaster steps out between them, urging a ceasefire and appealing to the rebels: 'Trust me.' The Girl shoots him through the head, and the battle continues. The choice of the Girl is significant. She is the only working-class character in the rebel band, and she is the only woman. She stands for female equality, unrepressed sexuality and youthful revolt. But, even more significantly, as the film ends the school forces, rallied by the bishop and the general, counter-attack, and Mick turns his gun on the audience.

It is a very personal film for its director, Lindsay Anderson. Not only was it filmed on location at his old school, Cheltenham College, but much of the detail was, as he has admitted, drawn from his own experience. 'I put a lot of myself into *If . . .* he said in 1969, 'It is largely autobiographical.'[2] The authors, David Sherwin and John Howlett, were also at public school (Tonbridge), and it is this first-hand experience that makes the texture of the life reconstructed on screen so convincing. But Anderson was not simply seeking to make a documentary study. He made his intentions clear in very detailed interviews both during and after shooting of the film:

> Probably all my work, even when it has been very realistic, has struggled for a poetic quality – for larger implications than the surface realities may suggest. I think the most important challenge is to get beyond pure naturalism into poetry. Some people call this fantasy, but these terms are dangerous, because words always mean different things to different people. I would call *If . . .* a realistic film – not completely naturalistic but trying to penetrate the reality of its particular world. I think that Brecht said that realism didn't show what things look like but how they really are.[3]

It is no coincidence that the film-makers whom he most admires are John Ford and Humphrey Jennings, who both aimed at a poetic truth and who both, like Anderson, were profoundly romantic.

The truth that he sought to portray through the life and structures of the school was the truth about society. He was deeply dismayed when critics saw it merely as an attack on the public schools. In his introduction to the published version of the screenplay he wrote:

> Essentially the public school milieu of the film provides material for a metaphor. Even the coincidence of its making and release with the worldwide phenomenon of student revolt was fortuitous. The basic tensions, between hierarchy and anarchy, independence and tradition, liberty and law, are always with us. That is why we scrupulously avoided contemporary references (on a journalistic level) which would date the picture; and why it is completely

unimportant whether its slang, its manners or its details or organization are true to the schools of this year or that. And this is why the film has been understood – recognized – by so many people, of so many ages and so many countries.[4]

Anderson, a former film critic, had been part of the 'free cinema' group, one of those energizing groups of artists that appeared in the late 1950s. Their object was to galvanize the cinema and to stimulate the production of films that were 'vital, illuminating, personal and refreshing'. Anderson's direction of documentaries (*Every Day Except Christmas, O Dreamland*), plays at the Royal Court Theatre (notably *The Long and the Short and the Tall* and *Serjeant Musgrave's Dance*) and a feature film (*This Sporting Life*, 1963) led to his being grouped with the 'new wave',[5] but he was always very much his own man ('No film can be too personal,' he wrote).[6] The critic John Russell Taylor, assessing his career in 1975, declared:

> Among the directors at present working in the British cinema, Lindsay Anderson is the only one, of any generation, who is truly an international figure, who is . . . undoubtedly and unarguably an *auteur.*[7]

If . . . can properly be seen, then, as a personal statement about the educational system, about Britain and about society. Anderson described *If . . .* as 'deeply anarchistic' and said:

> People persistently misunderstand the term anarchistic, and think it just means wildly chucking bombs about. But anarchy is a social and political philosophy which puts the highest possible value on responsibility. The film is not about responsibility against irresponsibility. It's about rival notions of responsibility and consequently well within a strong Puritan tradition.[8]

The evidence suggests that just as people misunderstand anarchy, according to Anderson, so also they misunderstood *If . . .,* a reaction that highlights the fact that audiences do not always take away from a film the message that the film-maker has intended to convey. Despite Anderson's explicit statements, many critics, particularly in the popular press, saw the film exclusively in terms of a critique of public schools. Felix Barker in the *Evening News* called it a 'savage attack on the public schools . . . witty, venomous, exaggerated but with a deadly underlying truth'.[9] Ernest Betts in the *People* saw it as a 'terrific swipe at the public school system'.[10] Madeleine Harmsworth in the *Sunday Mirror* regarded it as 'exploding a bomb under the English public school, blowing it to bits'.[11] Even Gavin Millar in *Sight and Sound* declared: 'No one has ever done such an effective hatchet job on the English public school.'[12]

Other critics, particularly those of the quality papers, saw beyond this and accepted Anderson's statement that he intended the school to be a metaphor. Patrick Gibbs in the *Daily Telegraph* wrote: 'Anderson uses, reasonably enough, satire on one aspect of the British educational system to attack the established order in general. It is an inventive, and well organized satire.'[13] Dilys Powell in the *Sunday Times* commented: '*If* . . . is not just about an imaginary public school. It is about the rigid ideas and the authoritarian society which Mr Anderson and his collaborators see rooted in the public school.'[14] John Russell Taylor in *The Times* called the film a 'rich, complex, obscure metaphor of the way we live now'.[15] Michael Walsh in the *Daily Express* called it a 'brilliant, merciless, indictment of the public school system and by inference of the Establishment'.[16] David Robinson in the *Financial Times* declared: 'the film offers a vivid metaphor for conflicts in contemporary society.'[17] Nina Hibbin in the *Morning Star* called it a 'devastating view . . . of the cruel traditions which go into the shaping of the ruling class'.[18]

Whatever the differences of opinion about its meaning, critics were almost totally united in praising the film's execution. Nina Hibbin in the *Morning Star* thought it the 'best and most significant film of the Sixties'.[19] Felix Barker in the *Evening News* called it 'superb'.[20] Ernest Betts in the *People* described it as 'brilliant and absorbing'.[21] Penelope Mortimer in the *Observer* proclaimed it a 'masterwork . . . a tremendous artistic success'.[22] Clive Hirschhorn in the *Sunday Express* declared it a 'masterpiece', as did Richard Roud in the *Guardian*.[23] Patrick Gibbs in the *Daily Telegraph* thought it 'superbly executed'.[24] Almost the only dissenting voice was that of Eric Rhode in the *Listener*. He called it the 'most hating film I know' and went on: 'You can't expect a spewing man to be articulate. . . . [His] films seemed to be working out personal grudges and resentments in terms of social conflict. . . . If the public schools had not existed, Anderson would have had to create something like them.'[25]

What is interesting about the critics' reaction to *If* . . . is that, by contrast with their response to *The Guinea Pig*, they did not on the whole engage with the issues on a personal level. Patrick Gibbs complained that the action looked like a parody of what went on around him at Oundle in the 1930s and did not present a contemporary view of the public school. But that was not Anderson's aim. Most people seem to have accepted Anderson's criticisms of the system at face value, indicating the success of several generations of literary conditioning.

Despite the film's critical success, it experienced considerable difficulty in obtaining a general release. It had been a long time gestating. It had originally been scripted under the title *Crusaders* by David Sherwin and John Howlett between 1958 and 1960, while they were at Oxford. Five years later Seth Holt expressed an interest in filming it, but when other commitments turned up to occupy his attention he drew Lindsay Anderson's notice to it. Anderson and Sherwin reworked the script in 1967, and Anderson took it to Memorial Enterprises, the company founded by actor Albert Finney and headed by Michael Medwin. They agreed to produce it, but they were totally unable to find a British backer. The American television company CBS, which had just formed a film division, accepted it, but it withdrew six weeks before shooting was due to start. Paramount stepped in just in time to save the project, and the film was shot and released in 1968.[26] Initially it was shown only at the Paramount Cinema, Lower Regent Street, London. After determined lobbying, supported by the fact that the film had taken £40,000 since it opened just before Christmas 1968, the ABC circuit agreed in January 1969 to give it a national release.[27]

The film marked yet another milestone in the progressive liberalization of film censorship. For although the censors removed a few shots in which male genitalia were in evidence, they permitted the full frontal view of a nude female for the first time, in the sequence of Mrs Kemp wandering through the dormitories. John Trevelyan, Secretary of the British Board of Film Censors, was quoted as saying: 'There is nothing erotic in the scene. In the context there's nothing offensive about it.'[28]

It was, however, not just the content of the film that must have given distributors pause for thought. Its form was extremely unusual. David Robinson called it the 'first English poetic feature film', by which he meant that it 'juxtaposes elements to produce impressions greater than the sum of these elements'.[29] John Russell Taylor called it an 'extra-ordinary film, a film that virtually defies ordinary verbal description, because it works as only the cinema can, on the indistinct border between fantasy which has the solidity of tangible experience and reality which seems as remote and elsewhere as a dream'.[30] Anderson himself said:

> Stylistically I don't really think *If* ... fits very closely into a contemporary picture of film-making, except in so far as developments in the last – what? – ten years have made it possible to work with much greater freedom in the cinema than before, and to be personal and not to be bound to the traditional and conventional ideas of narrative construction and narrative style. I think where it isn't contemporary is that its technique, I would say on the whole, is extremely sober. In fact this is both natural to me and the result of a quite conscious determination on my part. The more what we might call 'trendy', or eccentric, or showy technique has tended to become in the last few years, the more I have felt I wanted to try and make films with as much simplicity and as much directness as possible. . . . Qualities of rhythm and balance and composition inside a very straight-forward and sober technique are the problems that interest me most.[31]

A viewing of the film bears out this claim. Anderson avoids fancy camerawork, tracks on movement, uses close-ups for emphasis and keeps his camera still in medium shot when there is a lot of action going on in the frame. What is unusual is the blending of fantasy and reality, the switching from colour to black and white and back again and the division of the film into eight chapters, which follow the school through the term from the first day to Founder's Day. It thus creates an overall picture of school life, into which the story of the rebels is woven.

The changes from colour to black and white were justified by Anderson as a Brechtian device:

> *If* ... is not meant to be a film that excites or agitates but I hope that people understand it; this is why the division into chapters and, up to a certain point, the use of black and white and colour are what Brecht calls processes of distanciation which detach the spectator from his emotion.[32]

But there was a practical reason for it too:

> When Mirek [Ondricek] said that with our budget [for lamps] and our schedule he could not guarantee consistency of colour for the

chapel scenes in *If* . . . [I said] 'Well, let's shoot them in black and white.'[33]

In the light of this comment, it looks as if Anderson was making a Brechtian virtue out of a technical necessity. In fact, a number of interiors are in black and white, and Anderson said in his introduction to the screenplay:

> The important thing to realize is that there is no symbolism involved in the choice of sequences filmed in black and white, nothing expressionist or schematic.[34]

The problem with this is that many people have spent time trying to work out the justification for the black-and-white sequences. They have invariably ended up confused and frustrated.[35]

The division between fantasy and reality has posed another problem. Elizabeth Sussex sets the problem in perspective:

> The threshold between fantasy and reality in the film is then something that must vary according to how much reality the individual spectator can bear. And the film's supreme achievement is in enabling audiences to interpret it according to their own idea of what is real. Undoubtedly some people find a lot of fantasy in *If* . . . . For others, like Anderson himself, 'It's all real.'[36]

This is a sensible enough view. It could all be regarded as real, even the final rebellion. There had after all been the Great Marlborough Rebellion in 1851, when the boys, in protest against magisterial tyranny, starvation and beatings, arranged a great firework explosion for 5 November, a pyrotechnical precursor of *If* . . .:

> On the signal the school appeared to blow up. The court became ablaze with fireworks, and fireworks shot from every building. Mr Wilkinson, rushing out in a state of extreme agitation, had a bottle full of gunpowder exploded behind his back and rushed back. The other masters were equally powerless. Chaos reigned all night. The long corridors of B House echoed to ceaseless denotations. For two days the college reeked of gunpowder and smoke drifted through the smashed windows and broken doors. The authorities were paralysed.[37]

The rebellion was successful, and the cowed headmaster made immediate concessions.

However, there is one sequence in the film which disturbs this interpretation – the scene in which, after Mick has apparently bayoneted the chaplain, the headmaster produces him from a drawer in his office and gets the rebels to apologize to him. Up to that point none of the action has been intrinsically unlikely, but that sequence fatally dissipates the tension, compromising the finale. Anderson admitted of this scene: 'Harold Pinter got very upset about that moment. He thought it got very out of style. He may well be right.'[38] Of course, it could be yet another 'distanciation' device. If it is, it does as much to confuse viewers as the other devices.

Despite these problems, *If* ... remains a magnificent piece of film-making, savagely funny, gripping, richly textured and extremely well acted by a then unknown young cast backed up by some distinguished British character actors giving beautifully judged performances. However personal a film Anderson thought it, and whatever his own interpretation, it will probably be remembered – and was certainly interpreted at the time – as highlighting two preoccupations of the 1960s.[39]

First, it completely demolished the public school as an educational institution. The fact that public schools had changed considerably since Anderson's schooldays and that uniforms, fagging, beating, athleticism, compulsory chapel and the cadet corps had all declined in importance, and in some cases had even disappeared, was irrelevant. The bulk of Anderson's audience had never been to public school, and his cinematic version merely confirmed the picture that had emerged from literature, particularly in the inter-war period, of the public school as a source of arrogance, elitism, constraint, cruelty and conformism.

Second, it appealed dramatically to the self-image of the 'Swinging Sixties', an image that combined youth, sex and rebellion, individual self-expression as opposed to authority, tradition, hierarchy and age. The poster advertising the film appealed directly to this youthful audience. It featured a set of stills from the film grouped in the shape of a hand grenade. Superimposed on that were two pictures of Malcolm McDowell, one of him in school uniform carrying books and the other of him in leather jacket carrying a machine-gun, with the caption underneath: 'Which side will you be on?'[40]

In view of this, it is surely ingenuous of Anderson to claim:

Essentially the heroes of *If* ... are, without knowing it, old-fashioned boys. They are not anti-heroes, or drop-outs, or Marxist-Leninists or Maoists or readers of Marcuse. Their revolt is inevitable, not because of what they *think* but because of what they *are*. Mick plays a little at being an intellectual . . . but when he acts, it is instinctively because of his outraged dignity, his frustrated passion, his vital energy, his sense of fair play, if you like . . . In this sense Mick and Johnny and Wallace and Bobby Phillips and the Girl are traditionalists.[41]

For even if Anderson feels this, it is not a view that communicates itself to the majority of his audiences. He points to the fencing match in the gym when the boys cry things like 'England, awake!' and 'Death to tyrants!' as evidence of their essentially old-fashioned romanticism. But it is not this, nor the swearing of blood brotherhood with the oath 'Death to the oppressor', that catches the attention of the audience. Anderson makes the crusaders sound rather like Stalky and Co., a trio of public schoolboys who also broke bounds, smoked illegally, despised games, were beaten for misbehaving – and were created by Kipling, whose spirit the film seems to be mockingly evoking in its title, which it shares with Kipling's most famous poem. But the difference is that while Stalky and Co. were genuine patriots, believed that the headmaster was right to beat them and went off to serve the Empire, Mick and Co. are identified with Third World resistance to the imperial powers. Mick pins up a picture of a black freedom fighter on the wall and says admiringly, 'Fantastic.' He declares: 'Violence and revolution are the only pure acts.' He listens constantly to the *Sanctus* from the Congolese *Missa Luba,* with its throbbing, exciting, primitive rhythm, speaking of the rebellion, vitality and youth of an emerging continent. It is no coincidence that sales of the *Sanctus* rocketed after the film's release. This was the aspect of Mick that appealed, not his putative traditionalism.

Similarly, when Anderson says of his final sequence, 'Its violence is so plainly metaphorical' he is again misjudging its effect.[42] Audiences saw this as the message. The only way to deal with the public school system and the society that it supports is to sweep them both away. When the headmaster, the voice of compromise and consensus, is shot through the head, when the old lady in a flowered hat grabs a machine gun and opens up on the rebels, screaming 'Bastards! Bastards!', when Mick turns his machine gun on the cinema audience to fire directly into camera, it is indeed, as Anderson says 'exhilarating, funny, a bit shocking, magnificent', but so are all revolutions and this is surely the beginning of the revolution. Audiences who interpreted the film as a clarion call arousing them from their complacency saw Mick and his friends precisely as Anderson says they were not to be seen – 'as anti-heroes, dropouts, Marxist-Leninists.'

In retrospect, *If . . .* can be regarded as almost encapsulating the rise and fall of the 1960s. In his brilliant analysis of that decade, *The Neophiliacs,* Christopher Booker sees the 1960s as essentially a creation of fantasy, which eventually self-destructed. Booker divides the growth of this fantasy into five stages: anticipation, rising excitement, frustration, nightmare and death-wish, followed by the explosion into reality. *If . . .,* the title itself redolent of fantasy, follows exactly this course: the anticipation of rebellion, the breaking of bounds, the beating, the shooting up of the corps and, finally, the rebellion. But at the end of the film the Establishment is fighting back. As Anderson observed in 1969: 'It doesn't look to me as though Mick can win. The world rallies, as it always will, and brings its overwhelming fire-power to bear on the man who says "No."' In reality too the Establishment was fighting back. In 1970 the years of Labour Government came to an end with the re-election of the Conservatives. The years of prosperity drew to a close, and recession set in.

Like *If . . .,* the British film industry itself conformed to Booker's thesis. The social and cultural revolution of the late 1950s had seen the renaissance of British film-making in the so-called 'new wave'. A new and talented generation of film directors brought to the screen the frustrations, limitations and aspirations of the working-class young in films like *Room at the Top* (1959), *Saturday Night and Sunday Morning* (1960), *A Taste of Honey* (1961), *A Kind of Loving* (1962) and *The Loneliness of the Long Distance Runner* (1962). All these films were shot in black and white on genuine North Country locations; all had melancholy and dissonant jazz scores; and all featured a new breed of working-class anti-hero, played by a new breed of working-class actors like Albert Finney, Tom Courtenay and Alan Bates. But by 1964 the 'new wave' had spent itself. 'Swinging London' had been born, an increasingly frenzied saturnalia whose cult was the new and the now, a world of colour supplements, pirate radio, glamorous television commercials, dolly birds, discos and boutiques. With the backing of the Hollywood giants, British film-makers set out to capture the glitter and the glamour. Sober realism and earnest social comment gave way to fantasy, extravaganza and escapism; black-and-white photography and Northern locations to colour and the lure of the metropolis; Puritanical self-discipline to hedonistic sell-indulgence; plain, truthful settings to flamboyant, unrealistic decorativeness. Films became locked in a heady spiral of mounting extravagance, febrile excitement and faddish innovation. Seen from the depressed and sober vantage point of succeeding generations, these films seem akin to highly coloured ephemera from the last days of the Roman Empire, a madcap efflorescence preceding extinction.[43] If Tony Richardson was the key figure of the 'new wave', the celebrant of the 'Swinging London' style was Dick Lester. Lester's films, particularly *The Knack* and *Help*, were mercurial, modish mosaics, his style fragmented and breathtakingly fast-moving, an amalgam of influences from television commercials, cartoon strips and Goon Show surrealism. It was this style that Anderson resolutely eschewed.

Amidst all the fun and frenzy a few films looked honourably back to the 'new wave' and remained valiantly out of step with the mood of the times. Ken Loach's *Kes* (1969) notably kept the Orwellian flag flying amid the Byzantine excesses raging all around it. Anderson struck out on his own with *If* . . . . But the bubble of 'Swinging London burst when a clutch of grossly self-indulgent and hopelessly uncommercial films failed at the box office. The Hollywood companies lost heavily and in 1969 pulled out virtually all together. With the 1970s came the cinema's exposure to reality. London stopped swinging. The butterfly culture of the 1960s flew away. The cold, harsh light of reality broke in on the tinsel world. The British film industry collapsed, and the historians reached for their pens to chart its rise and fall.

Notes

1. On the 1960s, see Arthur Marwick, *British Society since 1945,* Harmondsworth, 1982; Christopher Booker, *The Neophiliacs,* London, 1969; Bernard Levin, *The Pendulum Years,* London, 1970.

2. Elizabeth Sussex, *Lindsay Anderson,* London, 1969. p. 68.

3. ibid., p. 12.

4. Lindsay Anderson and David Sherwin, *If . . .*, Lorrimer Modern Film Scripts. London, 1969, p. 9.

5. For a detailed discussion of Anderson's career see Sussex. *Lindsay Anderson.*

6. ibid., p. 31.

7. John Russell Taylor, *Directors and Directions,* London. 1975, p. 69.

8. Sussex, *Lindsay Anderson,* p. 89.

9. *Evening News,* 19 December 1968.

10. *People,* 22 December 1968.

11. *Sunday Mirror,* 22 December 1968.

12. *Sight and Sound,* Winter 1968–69, p. 42.

13. *Daily Telegraph,* 20 December 1968.

14. *Sunday Times,* 22 December 1968.

15. *The Times,* 20 December 1968.

16. *Daily Express,* 19 December 1968.

17. *Financial Times,* 20 December 1968.

18. *Morning Star,* 20 December 1968.

19. ibid., 15 March 1969.

20. *Evening News,* 19 December 1968.

21. *People,* 22 December 1968.

22. *Observer,* 22 December 1968.

23. *Sunday Express,* 22 December 1968; *Guardian,* 19 December 1968.

24. *Daily Telegraph,* 20 December 1968.

25. *Listener,* 26 December 1968.

26. For details, see Sussex, *Lindsay Anderson,* pp. 68–70.

27. *Guardian,* 17 January 1969.

28. *Daily Mail,* 18 December 1968.

29. *Financial Times,* 20 December 1968.

30. Taylor, *Directors and Directions,* p. 91.

31. Sussex, *Lindsay Anderson,* pp. 89–90.

32. ibid., p. 75.

33. Anderson and Sherwin, *If . . .* p. 10.

34. ibid.

35. I base this observation on discussions with students after showings of the film over several years.

36. Sussex, *Lindsay Anderson,* pp. 83–4.

37. Jonathan Gathorne-Hardy, *The Public School Phenomenon,* Harmondsworth, 1979, pp. 115–16.

38. Sussex, *Lindsay Anderson,* p. 86.

39. *If . . .* was the official British entry at the Cannes Film Festival in 1969.

40. The poster is reproduced in Lindsay Anderson's article '*If . . .*', in *The Movie,* 64, 1981, pp. 1276–7.

41. Anderson and Sherwin, *If . . .,* p. 12.

42. ibid.

43. The period is discussed in detail in Alexander Walker, *Hollywood, England,* London, 1974.

13

Remembrance of Times Past
Scandal

B y the time of the general release given to Michael Caton-Jones's film of *Scandal,* in spring 1989, Britain had experienced nearly ten years of Margaret Thatcher's term as Prime Minister, a period that was to end on 22 November 1990 when she resigned office following a leadership contest and John Major soon took charge of both their party and the government. Though her decade in power had done little if anything directly to ameliorate the parlous economic condition of the British film industry after a dramatic slump in production suffered during the 1970s, it is clear that culturally, at least, British cinema was as profoundly affected by Thatcherite policies as the rest of the country at large. If nothing else, as Sarah Street observes, 'Some film-makers were galvanised by their desire to provide cultural opposition to the Conservative Party's disturbing right-wing tendencies and to expose the harsh realities of life experienced by many under Thatcherism', and, 'Margaret Thatcher's attempt at charismatic leadership provided an obvious focus-point for opposition'. 'Although [a] political critique was not always as explicitly evident in mainstream films as in the defiantly oppositional art cinema of Derek Jarman', Street continues, nevertheless she – like others – finds much of ideological, thematic or stylistic substance in both the mainstream and art house cinemas as they evolved in Britain during the Thatcher years of the 1980s.[1]

Certain commentators have argued, in fact, that a cultural critique of sorts was evident in mainstream British films from the outset of Thatcher's premiership, and nowhere more so than in the gangster genre or underworld thriller. John Mackenzie's *The Long Good Friday*, for instance, which was based on Barrie Keeffe's screenplay and opened after censorship difficulties with its original production company on 26 February 1981, set the ball rolling on this front and was obviously intended as a thinly-veiled allegory of its increasingly Thatcherite era in its depiction of an East End criminal, Harold Shand (Bob Hoskins), who takes to mixing his nefarious underworld activities with crooked capitalist endeavours. The message came across loud and clear as far as most critics were concerned, not least in Alexander Walker's astute assessment of the film. He considered it 'an important "social" movie of the times' and commented:

> It had the distinction of being almost the only film at that date to have a Tory as a hero-figure, though this must immediately be quali-fied by stating that Bob Hoskins's character is an example of Toryism gone to bad and patriotism gone even further that way. . . . A property speculator who has fought and frightened his way up from Dockland; an implacable defender of private enterprise and the profit motive; even a good disciple of the EEC engaged in launching a crooked development scheme with aid from the Common Market, Hoskins is a monster because his hankering for the Conservative virtues is so wildly at variance with his practice of the terrorist ones. . . . It was a deeply subversive vision, implanting cynical truths in the social scene so as to turn it into a minefield that explodes in one's face. Helen Mirren, for example, is cast as a girl who once went to Benenden school with Princess Anne and now goes to bed with a public enemy, thus personifying the sexual slumming that matched the up-market trading of the turn of the decade.[2]

For the social historian, Arthur Marwick, moreover, Bob Hoskins's character of Harold Shand is 'a Thatcherite gone mad' while the film itself, he argues, 'captures the moment when collapsing consensus is being replaced by the bombastic claims of "enterprise culture"; it suggests that Britain is a banana republic'.[3] The corruption and sleaze evident in Mackenzie's The *Long Good Friday* found its echo a few years later, yet again, in Neil Jordan's *Mona Lisa* (1986) which also starred Bob Hoskins, albeit this time personifying an old world 'ex-con' who pits his wits against Michael Caine's exceptional characterisation of Mortwell, a new order of gangland boss intent on enriching his own burgeoning empire by pandering to the predominantly hedonist and avaricious society around him. Geoff Eley neatly summarises the contours of Hoskins's screen persona as well as the context for Jordan's film:

> As George, the old-style, working-class villain in *Mona Lisa,* like-able and moralistic, who emerges from prison to find that the world has changed, he is counterposed uncomprehendingly to the new Thatcherist sleaze of Mortwell, the gangland boss who services the demands of an amorally pleasure-seeking society. By contrast with some of the more radically experimental critiques of the new London, such as *Sid and Nancy* (Alex Cox, 1986) or above all *Sammy and Rosie Get Laid* (Stephen Frears, 1989), where the urban environment and its traditional class certainties are shown completely disordered, however, *Mona Lisa* is ultimately redeemed by precisely the old virtues – the loyalty, the stoicism, the rough-edged but comforting ironies, the resilience – of the lovable, working-class Londoner George, who despite everything the New World can throw at him is still left standing, secure on the ground of ordinary (male) friendship, within a relatively resistant everyday life.[4]

Nor, indeed, were *The Long Good Friday* and *Mona Lisa* the only examples of a distinct revival of interest among British film-makers in the gangster genre during the 1980s. There was, in all, a fair number of them. John Mackenzie, for one, followed up his big screen success with a film made for television presentation about the life of recently reformed Glasgow hoodlum, Jimmy Boyle, based upon the latter's book, *A Sense of Freedom* (1981). But the cycle of 'bio-pics' intended for cinema exhibition and also employing the device of well-known if notorious postwar criminal histories for their narratives included *McVicar* (Tom Clegg, 1981), partially scripted by former 'hardman' John McVicar himself, *Buster* (David Green, 1988) about the 'Great Train Robber', Buster Edwards, and *The Krays* (Peter Medak, 1990) which graphically depicted the Kray brothers' reign of terror over the East End of London in the 1950s and 1960s. Moreover, crucially, the underworld and its associated fringes or environs often served as meaningful backdrop to a variety of similarly 'retro'-inspired films which, as Geoff Eley succinctly puts it, 'focussed on the hypocrisies of British justice and upper-class sexual profligacy'.[5]

Although Michael Radford's *White Mischief* (1987) was set in 1940 with its tale of sexually promiscuous and decadent aristocrats in Kenya's 'Happy Valley' leading to the murder of Josslyn Hay, 22nd Earl of Errol, the remainder were firmly anchored in the 1950s or 1960s. Mike Newell's *Dance with a Stranger* (1985), scripted by Shelagh Delaney, centred on Ruth Ellis, the last woman to be hanged in Britain in 1955 for the murder of her upper class lover. *Personal Services* (1987, Terry Jones) pilloried the British legal system and judiciary in its comic court scenes which constituted the climax of a fictionalised account of the experiences of Streatham madam, Cynthia Payne. *Scandal* (Michael Caton-Jones, 1989) dealt with the much publicised 1963 Profumo affair and consequent high profile trial of Stephen Ward. *Let Him Have It* (Peter Medak, 1992) spotlighted the grave miscarriage of justice done to Derek Bentley who was hanged on 28 January 1953 for his role in the murder of a policeman.

With the exception of *White Mischief,* furthermore, these films consciously espoused a cause and sought to exculpate, in part, previously vilified or guilty parties – not least in the case of *Let Him Have It* where the end titles served to comment that public outrage at Bentley's fate had helped towards the eventual abolition of capital punishment in Britain, in 1964, as well as to draw attention to Iris Bentley's long-standing attempt to clear her dead brother's name. Her cause was helped further when, subsequently, video copies of the film for sale in High Street outlets also included in their packaging postcards inviting viewers to support the ongoing campaign for Bentley's retrospective pardon with the promise that 'Every signature counts and will be passed on to the Home Secretary'. By such simple 'crusading' means, the film makers hoped to add their voice to those seeking to persuade the then Conservative Home Secretary that justice of a sort, no matter how rough or tardy, might still be done.[6]

The twin principal focus evident in some retro films upon exposing the hypocrisies of British justice and upper-class sexual profligacy found its most obvious and telling targets, how ever, in Michael Caton-Jones's *Scandal.* And here, especially, it was surely no coincidence that the subject chosen for cinematic treatment surfaced as and when it did. Although the events which led to John Profumo's resignation in 1963 made for 'an exciting, anti-Establishment story', as one writer states, they were not at all welcome to the Conservative Government of the day led by Harold Macmillan in which he was Secretary of State for War. 'Jack' Profumo's disgrace in lying to the House of Commons over his relations with Christine Keeler, followed fast by Stephen Ward's trial for living off immoral earnings, which precipitated his eventual suicide on the eve of a guilty verdict, did much to ruin the reputation of the individuals concerned and the government alike. Inevitably, given the original lurid press revelations about the affair and its continuing connotations with the idea of corrupt Conservatism, such issues were no more welcome as a case for revived interest or scrutiny in certain quarters during the late 1980s. It was also no surprise, perhaps, that contemporary commentators on the 1989 film *Scandal* soon fell into two opposing camps – advocates of the argument that it held 'a lesson for today'; and those who thought it 'sad and bad' that the film should give the matter new found attention.[7]

Scandal experienced problems right from the outset, in fact, when its prospective producer, Joe Boyd, and the Australian scriptwriter, Michael Thomas, sought to interest the BBC in a three-part television mini-series of Thomas's treatment with each part running to an expected 90 minutes. Although funding was found for two of the scripts, 'The BBC's support did not last long', Angus Finney comments, when 'it turned out that internal BBC memos had been issued banning the production of any documentary or drama concerning the Profumo affair'. A similar rejection from Channel 4 on 'the grounds of alleged bad taste' did not bode well for the likelihood of future production even if in the meantime the dynamic young company, Palace Pictures, had come on board as joint partners investing nearly £200,000 in the project by 1985. Approaches to Robert Maxwell resulted in the advance of a further £184,319 towards development costs but since the television mini-series option was obviously 'going nowhere', as Finney recounts, Palace Pictures turned increasingly and with greater enthusiasm towards the idea of making a feature film. It might, at least, obviate some of the inherent problems surrounding the contentious subject matter as a television vehicle. But despite the fact that Scottish-born, National Film School graduate, Michael Caton-Jones, was engaged as director and the film was budgetted at £3.2 million, financing was yet to be found.[8]

The first tangible sign of substantial, financial support surfaced when Stephen Woolley and Nik Powell of Palace Pictures circulated potential partners in the United States with their production plans for the coming year of 1987–88 and, concurrently, they started a cleverly-timed campaign of hyping the promised *Scandal,* in particular, to those areas of the British press where it would undoubtedly have most impact. Baz Bamigboye, 'Chief Showbusiness Writer' on the *Daily Mail,* for instance, featured early gossip on casting of the more notorious personages in the newspaper for 17 October 1987 at precisely the time when the American Cinecom company was beginning to bite. Given that the report claimed the film would highlight 'the sex drama that shook the world' and 'Britain's most sensational postwar scandal that brought down a government and rocked high society in 1963', as well as 'two of our hottest young actresses starring as Mandy Rice-Davies and Christine Keeler', it was obvious if doubtless effective enough by way of exaggerated and salacious fare.

Though the much touted and then voguish Emily Lloyd, 'who has already taken America by storm with her debut picture *Wish You Were Here*', did not finally materialise in the role of Rice-Davies, Joanne Whalley was certainly a definite contender for the part of Christine Keeler (which she eventually secured). After noting also that John Hurt had been cast to play Stephen Ward and that Palace Pictures were 'working behind a great veil of secrecy', in view of prior attempts 'to prevent the movie from being made', Bamigboye's column proceeded to pose 'the big question' – 'Who will portray former War Minister John Profumo?' Citing the veteran Donald Pleasence and the up-and-coming RSC actor David Suchet as the current favourites, Bamigboye concluded predictably with a brief outline of the affair and tipped that filming will 'start sometime next year'.[9]

Before it did so, however, Cinecom were supplanted as partners in the project after a last minute if hotly contested deal was closed in New York between Powell of Palace Pictures and Harvey Weinstein at Miramax who guaranteed an instant Letter of Credit – a banker's letter ensuring money would be paid on completion of the film and a sticking point in negotiations with Cinecom – and $2.35 million for North American rights. By May 1988 and the occasion of the Cannes Film Festival, moreover, both parties were able to announce that Ian McKellen had landed the part of Profumo. The American actress Bridget Fonda, who had read and liked the script, was also present at Cannes. She was whisked by plane from Nice to London for a meeting with Caton-Jones and recruited for the task of portraying Mandy Rice-Davies on film. Everything was in place finally and, at long last, shooting could commence at the beginning of June 1988. No sooner had production started than the pressure from those who deemed the matter altogether unwarranted, intrusive, objectionable or regrettable, if not down-right reprehensible, increased in force and number. Exponents of the 'sad and bad' brigade were quickly and vocally to the fore with charges that the whole project smacked, in effect, of 'poor taste' and 'sensationalism'.

William Rees-Mogg was first off the mark in the pages of *The Independent* for 7 July 1988 where he condemned the prospect of reviving interest in the affair and stated that 'Obviously such a film is bound to defame many people, some of them still alive'. 'It cannot tell the story without doing so', he maintained, as he continued to argue that 'it is no man's right to renew the agony of offences, years after they have been expiated'. Clearly inspired by Profumo's praiseworthy efforts down the years since 1964 to immerse himself in work done as a volunteer at Toynbee Hall in the East End of London, for which he was awarded the CBE in 1975, Rees-Mogg was soon joined by the Bishop of Stepney, Jim Thompson, who believed that Profumo should not be made 'to face the cause of his shame all over again'. Thompson claims to have learned about the film more by chance than anything else when he happened upon the production crew as they set up a location shoot in a London house nearby his own. But he determined to act quickly thereafter by calling upon John Hurt and Ian McKellen to pull out and by writing to the press to express his conviction that a 'basic injustice' would be done by the film.[10]

None of these moves noticeably prevented the successful comple-tion of filming at the end of summer 1988. But they did serve to remind Palace Pictures, if such were needed, that potential problems and pitfalls aplenty still inevitably awaited the public release and exhibi-tion of *Scandal*. And it was really only with the onset of special screen-ings, held for prominent selected critics in November 1988, that they were able to judge the strength of likely feeling in their film's favour. Alexander Walker praised it immediately and proved an arch advocate of the argument that the film contained 'a message for the Eighties' and constituted a 'morality play for today'. His comments alluded neatly if ironically, moreover, to a crudely revisionist construction of the 'permissive society' or 'the swinging sixties' which was set in train by no less than Margaret Thatcher, herself, when stating early in her premiership that 'We are reaping what was sown in the sixties' and that 'The fashionable theories and permissive claptrap set the scene for a society in which the old virtues of discipline and restraint were denigrated'. As Walker drily noted, such jaundiced observations might better be laid at the door of the last years of 'wasted' Tory rule leading up to 1963:

> ... In Britain, the film will certainly divide and disturb. But I am convinced that no worse ill will befall Mr. Profumo by the way he is depicted in it, and much good may result if today's generation can take the measure of the permissiveness of an era that is now being blamed for all our present ills. The film shows much of the blame lies with the older generation of the 1960s, not the young people.
>
> If the affair itself didn't bring down the Harold Macmillan government, it certainly assisted the final collapse of an administration already exhausted by scandal. The moral temper of the early 1960s was summed up by Judge Gerald Sparrow in a phrase as applicable to the late 1980s: 'Ten years of Tory rule had made a god of materialism'.[11]

Despite Alexander Walker's bold and well-reasoned support of the film's cause, however, the forces militating against its public progress were noticeably gathering steam and marshalled to most vocal effect in the weeks immediately preceding the gala screening and world premiere held at The Odeon Leicester Square, in aid of the Terence Higgins Trust, on 2 March 1989. 'Already the Establishment is on the attack', Baz Bamigboye warned in the *Daily Mail* at the end of January, and 'Every sequence of *Scandal* will be monitored by watchers ready to invoke legal sanctions'. He reported upon the Bishop of Stepney's attempts at intervention through Ian McKellen and John Hurt, while the *Daily Telegraph Weekend Magazine* proceeded to carry the article by Thompson arguing that the film would only cause needless hurt and harm. 'Will this torture of Profumo never end?', Lynda Lee-Potter echoed in her column for *Daily Mail* where she went on to suggest that 'there is something very wrong with the British legal system' which condoned the invasion of Profumo's privacy, before she concluded: 'He made amends only to find that Britain continues to deny him any kind of acquittal'.[12]

Perhaps predictably, such pleas were greeted with obvious disdain and retaliatory responses from iconoclasts like Julie Burchill in the *Mail on Sunday* or Richard Ingrams in *The Observer*. 'Should the public forgive and forget'?', asked Burchill who had scant time for the 'FOPs (Friends of Profumo)'. 'I think not', she replied: 'Men like Profumo are born not just with a silver spoon in their mouths but with a spun-silver safety net dangling below their cradles'. Christine Keeler was the heroine of the piece as far as Julie Burchill was concerned: 'Girls such as Christine Keeler are unwittingly walking, talking, divining rods of judgment and we should thank them, not scorn them, for alerting us'. Ingrams was equally unsparing and just as unstinting in favour of the argument that there should be a profound rethink over precisely who suffered most from the affair. 'It tends to be forgotten that the real victim of the scandal was not Profumo but Dr. Stephen Ward . . . [who] . . . eventually became a scapegoat, was put on trial on flimsy charges and committed suicide', he commented, and 'Ironically, in view of the Establishment's current campaign to defend Profumo, none of Ward's posh friends did anything at all to support him'. 'If the film brings home to certain people how quickly an apparently well-entrenched and long-serving Tory Prime Minister can be subverted by smugness and scandal', Ingrams added as he joined advocates of the film's message for today, 'then it may well serve a useful purpose'. *The Guardian* followed suit over the next week or two with, first, an interview by John Cunningham with Christine Keeler in which she promoted her latest book (the fourth), published to tie-in with the occasion of the film's release and also bearing the same title; and, then, a long article by Logan Gourlay, former *Daily Express* columnist at the time of the affair, in which he compared the film with the original events and ended, once again, by taking a decidedly pro-Ward stance based on additional evidence forthcoming in recent books about the court trial.[13]

The battle lines between the warring parties were well and truly set, in effect, long before the moment of actual release for *Scandal* and the appearance of the film itself at the outset of March 1989 served merely to widen the divide further. Among the critics, of course, Alexander Walker continued to praise it and to champion the cause of its demonstrable relevance for the context in which it was produced and exhibited:

Scandal is intriguing and instructive for the bizarrely close parallel it draws between 1963 and 1989. Both eras had a Tory government fast losing popularity and showing the strain of long office.

The Sixties had the 'never had it so good' slogan of political complacency, the Eighties the 'you can have it all' incitement to material success. They had spies like Philby and Vassall; we have the Spycatcher ruction. They had Profumo's fall from grace; we have Cecil Parkinson's. Mrs Thatcher may, with hindsight, find this all to be more ominous than Mr Macmillan did in his time . . . *Scandal* won't take anyone's breath away nowadays. But it will take many of us revealingly back to the way we were and, for all purposes of political and moral expediency, the way we still are.

He was not alone. Most of the critics found much to applaud and even the *Daily Telegraph* critic felt compelled to highlight its new found contemporary significance. Director Michael Caton-Jones 'has cunningly understated the sensationalism of the story', Victoria Mather commented, and instead 'builds up his emphasis on the hypocrisy of British society at all levels: the politicians, the aristocracy, the police and the newspapers'. 'Had *Scandal* been made in the Seventies it might merely have inspired some "so-what?" shrugs', she argued, but 'Released amid the new puritanism of the late Eighties one has the uncomfortable feeling that if similar events occurred today the ruling classes would react in exactly the same way'. While Derek Malcolm of *The Guardian* also found it 'a lesson in hypocrisy and scandalous duplicity that manages to suggest that what happened a quarter of a century ago is still totally relevant now'.[14]

The Independent, however, hit upon the novel idea of inviting Richard Du Cann QC for his comments on the film's accuracy to supplement their own critic's column of review. If their critic was quite taken by it, Du Cann clearly was not. Having been a junior barrister at the time of Stephen Ward's trial in the chambers of the man who defended him, James Burge, Du Cann was understandably much more inclined to view the film as something of a wasted opportunity to provide 'insight into the legal quicksands of shifting moral attitudes'. Although he wisely acknowledged that *Scandal* 'does not claim to be a documentary' and 'We must assume that every level of licence can therefore be taken', he found its representation of the courtroom proceedings, in particular, not least a (wholly invented) outburst from Ward while in the dock, to be 'pure – no impure – and total invention'. It was a 'dramatic invention' to be sure, as Du Cann well recognised, 'But why distort the truth when the truth is more available and much more telling'. To Du Cann's mind, in short, there were matters which should have been better pursued to shed light on what certain key legal figures agreed was the 'historic injustice' done to Stephen Ward over his conviction, that the film-makers signally failed to address.[15]

For Du Cann, then, *Scandal* fell quite definitely into the category of the 'sad and bad' as *The Independent* commented in an editorial given over to the film, a day later, under the title of 'The line between fact and fiction'. Though sharing Du Cann's reservations, in part, *The Independent* leader plainly felt the film served a purpose. Two questions were raised by it: do documentary dramas produce unacceptable distortions of recent history? And is it fair that survivors of such episodes should be represented on screen in a way which may traduce their character and distort the record? The answer to the first question, according to *The Independent,* lay in some understanding – however brief or cursory – of the relationship between 'film' and 'history' within the contemporary context:

> All history is necessarily selective, prejudiced and subject to revision. Since film is not only a powerfully immediate medium but habitually deals with both actuality and fiction it is important that audiences should know whether they are watching fact or fiction, or a blend. Any film which portrays recent history should avoid, if only by an initial disclaimer, giving the impression of being an objective version of the known facts. . . . If the film had been made instead as a six-part television series, as originally intended, there would have been more time to explain the background and to give a more subtle interpretation of events. But such is the weight of censure now focusing on small-screen documentary drama that no backing could be found for such a project. It would be an irony of Mrs. Thatcher's Britain if such pressures made big-screen feature films the only safe refuge for the handling of controversial material – as in the Soviet Union and Eastern Europe.

The answer to the second lay in the nature of events depicted and their repercussions:

> The argument that those caught up in historical events should be spared dramatisation, with all its attendant distortions, arouses sympathy but is ultimately untenable. . . . We may sympathise or not with Mr. Profumo for having his past raked up again. We may deplore the element of hypocrisy in the film-makers' prurient

re-enactment of scandalous events – doubly ironic since the film itself poses as a critique of establishment hypocrisy. But any Conservative minister who enjoys himself with beautiful girls and then lies to Parliament about it is likely to go on paying the price up to and including his obituaries. His only comfort will be that since history is an endless process of adjustment and correction, there is always room for revisionist interpretation, and the ultimate hope of oblivion.[16]

Others remained firmly unconvinced, however, of the worth or value in filmically representing the past especially when, to their mind, it harped upon bygone events which contrasted noticeably with the state of affairs in the 'glorious' present. Thus, Paul Johnson reiterated the revisionist Thatcherite refrain that 'The Sixties were indeed a low, dishonest decade – a decade of illusions'. 'We paid for the follies of the Sixties in the painful decade which followed', he argued in the *Daily Mail*: 'Then came Thatcherism which has made Britain a saner and more sensible place – and I think a more honest one too. It has been a case, in the 1980s, of national self-redemption'. Johnson continued in the same vein:

Hence a film about that fascinating but ultimately unimportant episode of 1963 would have been more in tune with the spirit of today if it had concentrated on its one ennobling feature, the survival and recovery of Jack Profumo himself. . . . Jack Profumo transformed himself from a fallen minister into a shining example of quiet, self-effacing public service. It took a long time and it required courage, humility and perseverance on a heroic scale. The story of how he did it, and of the loyalty of his wife Valerie Hobson is a noble one.

Here indeed was the material for a truly notable film, for the great and age-old theme of redemption through suffering is one to which the public responds generously. But it is probably outside the sex-blinkered vision of our showbiz industry which is still, to a large and depressing extent, stuck in the cultural grooves of the Sixties. The rest of us, however, have moved on, and not only in Britain. The stress today is increasingly on high standards of public behaviour.[17]

Not to be outdone in the Thatcherite triumphalist stakes, the *Sunday Telegraph* dutifully trotted out a column by Anthony Hartley, the next day, in which he proceeded to take issue principally with the idea 'as told in the orthodox version for liberal intellectuals' whereby Stephen Ward was the 'scapegoat' of the affair. Hartley would have none of it and, like Paul Johnson before him, jumped on the Thatcher bandwagon in following her line that society's ills, then and thereafter, should be blamed on the 'permissiveness' and 'illusions' fostered during the 1960s:

> In the Sixties this interpretation of the Profumo case appealed to the prevailing taste for sending up the Establishment, individuals and institutions, and this has hardly lost its attraction.... So the legend of Stephen Ward was up and running, and it still runs today, to the satisfaction of consumers and narrators. It bears little resemblance to historical truth or even probability. The victimisation of Ward would seem to have required the collaboration of the Cabinet and the Commissioner of Police, the Head of the Security Service, and Lord Denning in a quite elaborate deception.
>
> Conspiracy theories are always a misleading approach to history, and this one is no exception. A more likely explanation is that Ward was guilty, but that, without the Profumo case, he and his cast of girls ... would not have swum up into anyone's notice. This is a boring conclusion, however. The probability is that the legendary Stephen Ward will remain with us, a meaningless, surviving symbol of one of the most depressing and self-deluding decades in British history.[18]

Short of criticising *Scandal* for 'the distress it is bound to cause the Profumo family', yet again, Hartley had little more to say in that regard. For Hartley, as for others, the film had become the catalyst for an ideologically-charged diatribe against the 1960s and the excuse for revisionist mythologising of a high order. The fact that the film might prove 'popular' had not escaped attention, however, and it was this which also doubtless prompted Tory antagonism towards *Scandal*. It was perceived as much a threat for what it revealed of the times in which it was produced and exhibited, in short, as for its representation of contentious historical events on the cinema screen.

Notes

1. Sarah Street, *British National Cinema*, London, 1997, p. 102. See, also, Lester Friedman, ed., *British Cinema and Thatcherism. Fires were Started*, London, 1993, and, especially, the essays by Thomas Elsaesser on 'Images for Sale: The "New" British

Cinema', Mary Desjardins on 'Free from the Apron Strings: Representations of Mothers in the Maternal British State', and Michael Walsh, 'Allegories of Thatcherism: The Films of Peter Greenaway'. Andrew Higson's essay in the same volume, 'Re-presenting the National Past: Nostalgia and Pastiche in the Heritage Film', can be usefully read in conjunction with a further piece on 'The Heritage Film and British Cinema' as reprinted in his edited collection, *Dissolving Views. Key Writings on British Cinema,* London, 1996. But in both cases, disappointingly, he cites films like *Scandal* as examples of just 'another group of contemporary British costume dramas' which, albeit 'dealing with the more recent past' and 'offering a rather different range of narrative pleasures and identifications', still appealed largely because 'their representation of the past remains in a conservationist mode such that even the *mise-en-scène* of ordinariness delights the eye, and invites the collector's curiosity'. This seems greatly to underestimate their worth and value to the historian.

2. Alexander Walker, *National Heroes. British Cinema in the Seventies and Eighties,* London, 1986, p. 252.

3. Arthur Marwick, *Culture in Britain since 1945,* Oxford, 1991, p. 150.

4. Geoff Eley, 'The Family is a Dangerous Place: Memory, Gender, and the Image of the Working Class', in Robert A. Rosenstone, ed., *Revisioning History. Film and the Construction of a New Past,* Princeton, New Jersey, 1995, pp. 234. Eley is principally concerned with analysis of Terence Davies's *Distant Voices, Still Lives* (1988) and situating the film within the context of earlier British filmic representations of the working class, which he does exceedingly well. But Eley's piece is also replete with interesting ideas or insights on British cinema of the postwar period generally, not least in regard to the 'new wave', as he proceeds fruitfully to elaborate on a key perceptive and telling observation that 'it is perhaps not surprising at this moment to find British film-makers revisiting the period between the Second World War and the sixties directly, treating it as a rich source of material'.

5. ibid., p. 25.

6. In 1992, Kenneth Clarke, then Home Secretary, turned down a pardon although he said that Bentley should not have been hanged. In July 1993, the new Home Secretary, Michael Howard, formally granted a limited pardon stating that the decision to hang Bentley was 'clearly wrong' but that a full pardon would be inappropriate. His action followed an unprecedented earlier High Court ruling that Bentley should have been reprieved. In 1995, Iris Bentley was given permission by the new Labour-controlled Croydon council to place a headstone on her brother's grave engraved with the words 'A Victim of British Justice'. Previously, the Conservative-controlled local council had refused to allow the Bentley family to put the words it wanted on the headstone. At the time of writing (spring 1998), Bentley's case was one of eleven referred back to the Court of Appeal by the Criminal Cases Review Commission as meriting fresh analysis for an alleged miscarriage of justice.

7. See Angus Finney, *The Egos Have Landed. The Rise and Fall of Palace Pictures,* London, 1996, p. 48, where he also quotes a crude if pertinent comment to the effect that the story 'had it all – tarts, titles, tits'. Finney provides much well-researched and valuable background material on the production history of *Scandal,* in particular, and Palace Pictures at large. Precise details about the affair itself and its repercussions are pretty exhaustively outlined in the near contemporary accounts by Wayland Young, *The Profumo Affair. Aspects of Conservatism,* Harmondsworth, Middlesex, 1963, and Ludovic Kennedy, *The Trial of Stephen Ward,* London, 1964, as well as the later more fulsome accounts by Brian Masters in *The Swinging Sixties,* London, 1985, and, especially,

Phillip Knightley and Caroline Kennedy, *An Affair of State: The Profumo Case and the Framing of Stephen Ward,* London, 1987.

8. As outlined in Finney, *The Egos Have Landed,* ppt14–54, and the microfiche for *Scandal* held at the British Film Institute Library, London.

9. Baz Bamigboye, 'Profumo Scandal', *Daily Mail,* 17 October 1987.

10. *The Independent,* 7 July 1988, and the *Daily Telegraph Weekend Magazine,* 4 February 1989, containing the Bishop of Stepney's piece, 'Hasn't John Profumo suffered enough?', where he expands retrospectively upon the reasons for his interest in the film and outlines his subsequent reaction during its course of production.

11. Alexander Walker, 'Profumo: morality play for today', *Evening Standard,* 5 December 1988. Mrs. Thatcher's comments were first made in March 1982 and are examined – in the context of other subsequent jaundiced and revisionist constructions of the 1960s – during the course of my book, *Censorship and the Permissive Society: British Cinema and Theatre 1955–1965,* Oxford, 1995, pp. 1–12.

12. See, respectively, *Daily Mail,* 27 January 1989; *Daily Telegraph Weekend Magazine,* 4 February 1989; and *Daily Mail,* 8 February 1989.

13. *Mail on Sunday,* 12 February 1989; *The Observer,* 12 February 1989; *The Guardian,* 14 February 1989; and *The Guardian Weekend Magazine,* 25 February 1989.

14. *Evening Standard, Daily Telegraph,* and *The Guardian,* all for 2 March 1989.

15. *The Independent,* 2 March 1989.

16. *The Independent,* 3 March 1989. This edition also contained an interesting and informative article by Sheila Johnston on the marketing and hype surrounding the film.

17. Paul Johnson, 'The real *Scandal*', *Daily Mail,* 4 March 1989.

18. Anthony Hartley, 'Scandal of Stephen Ward as scapegoat', *Sunday Telegraph,* 5 March 1989. *Scandal* did, in fact, turn out a popular success in box office terms by earning £3,705,065 gross in Britain and $8,800,000 in the United States (according to British Screen/Screen International sources) – making it one of the best British films in the UK and North American markets ever until it was superseded by subsequent hits such as *The Crying Game, Four Weddings and a Funeral,* and *The Full Monty.*

14

Resources
Selected Guide to Further Reading

Given the size of the subject and the lines of methodological divide that have emerged in the field (as elaborated in the first chapter of this volume), it is hardly surprising that no one book serves to fully cover the rich diversity of topics or wide variety of approaches which constitute the study of British cinema history. Thus, to better understand the precise points at issue in dealing with mainstream British cinema down the years, it is probably useful to adopt a chronological approach to its historiography. However arbitrary it may sometimes appear to divide a broad expanse of time into shorter discrete periods, this at least offers a twofold advantage in allowing for detailed comparison between differing methodologies and interpretations as applied to specific filmic examples, while also retaining a broad overview of contrasting reactions to the major sea changes affecting British cinema generally (not to mention social changes at large).

For the 1930s, these difference are most evident when comparing, on the one hand, the work by Anthony Aldgate and Jeffrey Richards in *Best of British* (1983, revised edition 1999, chapters 2 and 3), Anthony Aldgate, 'Comedy, class and containment' in *British Cinema History* (edited by James Curran and Vincent Porter, 1983), and Jeffrey Richards, *The Age of the Dream Palace* (1984), with, on the other hand, Marcia Landy's *British Genres* (1991) or Andrew Higson's *Waving the Flag* (1995).

The contrasts between, say, the emphasis laid by the former on appreciating the exact nature of the relationship between cinema and society as a prelude to interpreting the historical contours of the period, and the way in which the latter draw on the developments in textual analysis to promote alternative readings of key films (as well as different historical readings), are well highlighted in these writings. The received notions about what constituted 'popular' British films or genres during the 1930s, and their relative importance in regard to the perennial and ubiquitous presence of American films shown in British cinemas, moreover, are carefully scrutinised by all the contributors to *The Unknown 1930s: An alternative history of the British cinema, 1929–1939* (Jeffrey Richards, ed., 1998). Crucially, it revises many of the judgments or insights previously forthcoming in such standard accounts of mainstream cinema as Rachael Low's *Film Making in 1930s Britain* (1985).

By the same token, for the Second World War and the years 1939–1945, in particular, Anthony Aldgate and Jeffrey Richards, *Britain Can Take It* (1986, revised edition 1994), allied to Philip Taylor's edited collection of essays, *Britain and the Cinema in the Second World War* (1988), are best read along with Geoff Hurd's booklet, *National Fictions* (1984), as well as Landy and Higson, once more, to grasp the essentials of the debate over the wartime consensus in British society and its manifestation in films of the period. The historians, for their part, are as interested in the work of the Ministry of Information when utilising films to national advantage through propaganda as they are in analysis of the films themselves. The emphasis is as much on understanding the context, in short, as film texts. And this is nowhere more evident, yet again, than in the recent excellent contribution to the film historian's perspective on the subject, James Chapman's *The British at War* (1998). In addition, two worthwhile books shed vital light on the representation of women's roles in wartime Britain – Antonia Lant, *Blackout* (1991), Christine Gledhill and Gillian Swanson (eds.), *Nationalising Femininity* (1996). While *Mass-Observation at the Movies* (1987), edited by Jeffrey Richards and Dorothy Sheridan, is replete with primary source documentation on the cinemagoers' response to British long and short films of the day.

Although the period 1945 to 1955 has not been especially well covered hitherto, it is now at last attracting the sustained attention it deserves. Raymond Durgnat's *A Mirror for England* (1970) was a lone if fascinating and idiosyncratic incursion into the field until joined by Charles Barr's study of *Ealing Studios* (1977, revised edition 1993), as well as Aldgate and Richards (*Best of British*, chaps. 6–9). Robert Murphy's *Realism and Tinsel* (1989) and Charles Drazin's *The Finest Years* (1998) add substantially to the coverage but a lot can be gleaned in passing from Landy. Sue Harper's *Picturing the Past* (1994) also deals with the postwar years up to 1950 as part of an invaluable survey on 'the rise and fall of the British costume film' (which includes the 1930s). It is better by far than Pam Cook's lightweight and insubstantial attempt at the same project for *Fashioning the Nation* (1996).

If the 1950s have been too casually dismissed thus far as 'the doldrums era' (though much is promised for publication in the near future which should revise that judgment), then by contrast the late 1950s and early 1960s offer exceedingly rich ground and have been heavily mined already, not least in regard to the 'realist' import of British 'new wave' cinema, the films of Tony Richardson, Karel Reisz, Lindsay Anderson, John Schlesinger and their like. The key books are John Hill, *Sex, Class and Realism* (1986), Robert Murphy, *Sixties British Cinema* (1992), Arthur Marwick, *Culture in Britain Since 1945* (1991) and Alexander Walker, *Hollywood, England* (1974). Two essays are especially full of ideas on the topic – Jeffrey Richards's 'New waves and old myths' (in Bart Moore-Gilbert and John Seed, eds., *Cultural Revolution?*, 1992) and Terry Lovell's 'Landscapes and Stories in 1960s British Realism' (for Andrew Higson, ed., *Dissolving Views*, 1996) But more is found on the reception afforded the 'new wave' by the British Board of Film Censors, in particular, and its creative intervention in the film-making process during the 'cultural revolution' of the late 1950s which lead to the 'swinging sixties', in Anthony Aldgate, *Censorship and the Permissive Society* (1995).

For the 1970s, again somewhat devoid of extensive or substantial coverage, the best overview is provided by Andrew Higson, 'A diversity of film practices' (in Bart Moore-Gilbert, ed., *The Arts in the 1970s: Cultural Closure?*, 1994), who is responsible for some of the most interesting work on the emergence of 'The Heritage Film and British Cinema' (also in *Dissolving Views*). The journalistic accounts by Alexander Walker and John Walker – respectively, *National Heroes* and *The Once and Future Film* (both 1985) – traverse the 1970s and the 1980s. But several books better introduce the salient contours of debate surrounding British cinema's progress (or otherwise) during the 1980s: Duncan J.

Petrie, *Creativity and Constraint in the British Film Industry* (1991), Lester Friedman (ed.), *British Cinema and Thatcherism* (1993), and Wheeler Winston Dixon (ed.), *Reviewing British Cinema* (1994), though Geoff Eley's seminal essay, 'The family is a dangerous place', for *Revisioning History* (edited by Robert Rosenstone, 1995) stands out as the most valuable contribution on the 1980s and many other fronts.

Charles Barr's *All Our Yesterdays* (1986) coupled with James Curran and Vincent Porter, *British Cinema History* (1983), are essential edited collections of essays compiling the fruits of much research forthcoming in the years up to their respective dates of publication and include contributions by a wide variety of scholars (from the realms of film studies and history alike). And they have been added unto lately by Robert Murphy's exemplary edited anthology, *The British Cinema Book* (1997). Perhaps predictably, there have been few solo-authored single volume studies of note which successfully attempted to chart the full course of British cinema's evolution. Roy Armes, *A Critical History of British Cinema* (1978), offered some intriguing insights in its day but James Park's *The Lights that Failed* (1990) proved only fitfully interesting. This situation has changed considerably, however, since the advent of Sarah Street's *British National Cinema* (1997) which shows just what can be achieved by way of a concerted chronological and thematic approach to the subject.

But for discrete or specialist coverage of individual topics in British cinema history, see the following: 'film as evidence' – John Grenville, *Film as History* (1971), Arthur Marwick, *War and Social Change* (1974), Paul Smith (ed.), *The Historian and Film* (1976), Anthony Aldgate, *Cinema and History* (1979), K. R. M. Short (ed.), *Feature Films as History* (1981); 'class' – Arthur Marwick, *Images of Class* (1981), Peter Stead, *Film and the Working Class* (1989), Stuart Laing, *Representations of Working Class Life* (1986); 'films of empire' – Jeffrey Richards, *Visions of Yesterday* (1973); 'oral testimony' – Brian McFarlane, *An Autobiography of British Cinema* (1997); 'children's cinema' – Terry Staples's *All Pals Together* (1997); 'avant-garde' – Michael O'Pray (ed.), *The British Avant-Garde Film* (1996); and the 'sex film' – David McGillivray's *Doing Rude Things* (1992).

On censorship, two key books by James C. Robertson, *The British Board of Film Censors* (1985) and *The Hidden Cinema* (1989), contrast noticeably with Tom Dewe Mathews's muddled and misguided *Censored* (1994). While for the cinematic representation of Scotland, Wales and

Ireland, far and away the best accounts are Colin McArthur (ed.), *Scotch Reels* (1982), Eddie Dick (ed.), *From Limelight to Satellite* (1990), David Berry's *Wales and the Cinema* (1995), and the jointly authored *Cinema and Ireland* (1988) by Kevin Rockett, Luke Gibbons and John Hill. The question of national identity is explored at length, moreover, in Jeffrey Richards, *Films and British National Identity* (1997).

Surprisingly, there is really only one attempt at charting relations between government and the British film industry but it is a notable account: Margaret Dickinson and Sarah Street, *Cinema and State* (1985). Whereas auteur studies which seek to rethink, retrieve or rehabilitate previously neglected or denigrated bodies of film work, both genres and directors' oeuvres, have proliferated. They include: *Powell, Pressburger and Others* (1978) and *Arrows of Desire* (1985), both from Ian Christie; David Pirie's *A Heritage of Horror* (1973) and Peter Hutchings's *Hammer and Beyond* (1993); two essay collections from the editorial team of Alan Burton, Tim O'Sullivan and Paul Wells on Basil Dearden and the Boulting brothers, respectively, *Liberal Directions* (1997) and *The Family Way* (1999); George McKnight (ed.) on the films of Ken Loach, *Agent of Challenge and Defiance* (1997); Jeffrey Richards, *Thorold Dickinson* (1986); Tom Ryall, *Alfred Hitchcock and the British Cinema* (1986); Jonathan Hacker and David Price, *Take 10 Contemporary Film Directors* (1991). *Lindsay Anderson* is the title of two books about the 'maverick' director par excellence by Elizabeth Sussex (1969) and Erik Hedling (1998).

Studio output has not escaped attention either as is evident from: Pam Cook (ed.), *Gainsborough Pictures* (1997); Patricia Warren's *Elstree* (1983) and *British Film Studios* (1995); George Perry's *Movies from the Mansion. A History of Pinewood Studios*; and Derek Threadgall's *Shepperton Studios* (1994). While Geoffrey Macnab tackles *J. Arthur Rank and the British Film Industry* (1993), Stephen Bourne broaches the depiction of lesbians and gays in British cinema for *Brief Encounters* (1996) and the role of Black actors in this country for *Black in the British Frame* (1998). Angus Finney's *The Egos Have Landed* (1996) and *My Indecision is Final* (1990) by Jake Eberts and Terry Ilott cover the rise and fall, in turn, of Palace Pictures and Goldcrest Films.

Among individual films which have been the subject of detailed analysis are the following: Richard Dyer, *Brief Encounter* (1993); Christopher Frayling, *Things to Come* (1995); Penelope Houston, *Went the Day Well?* (1992); A. L. Kennedy, *The Life and Death of Colonel Blimp*

(1997); Tom Ryall, *Blackmail* (1993); Mark Sanderson, *Don't Look Now* (1996); and Dai Vaughan, *Odd Man Out* (1995). To see what the critics made of these and many other films, in their day, one need look no further than the various compendium collections of critics' reviews including: Anthony Lejeune (ed.), *The C. A. Lejeune Film Reader* (1991); Christopher Cook (ed.), *The Dilys Powell Film Reader* (1991); and David Parkinson (ed.), *Mornings in the Dark. The Graham Greene Film Reader* (1993).

But on the production, distribution and exhibition fronts, which have been greatly overlooked despite the plethora of publications on British cinema in recent years, Duncan Petrie admirably reinforces many a cameraman's reputation when noting their crucial contributions in *The British Cinematographer* (1996) and, by the same token, Allen Eyles continues his painstaking if praiseworthy investigations on the importance of the major cinema circuits in *ABC: The First Name in Entertainment* (1993) and *Gaumont British Cinemas* (1996); invaluable work that was greatly complemented by his joint effort with Margaret O'Brien, *Enter the Dream-House* (1993). Last but not least, mention should be made of two particularly useful journal publications which serve to disseminate much ongoing research into British cinema: the *Journal of Popular British Cinema* (UK) and the *Historical Journal of Film, Radio and Television* (US).

In short, the researches of numerous film scholars during the last thirty years – whether empiricists or theorists, textualists or contextualists – have contributed substantially to our knowledge and understanding of British cinema. Though some facets and areas still remain to he charted, for sure, there is no denying that the downbeat message at the heart of Alan Lovell's paper about the state or condition of British cinema history given at a BFI seminar in 1969 – that it constituted 'the unknown cinema', in effect, and that meaningful steps should be taken to remedy this lamentable situation – can now, thankfully, be pretty much laid to rest.

Films on video

The right and proper place to watch films is in a cinema. That goes without saying. But you won't find many bygone British films being shown in cinemas nowadays. The multiplex chains are geared almost exclusively towards the latest releases as, indeed, are what remain of the old ABC and Rank circuits. Well-meaning tokenism prompts the odd 'director's chair' celebratory event here and there. But these showings are still generally reserved for contemporary 'art house' films. The demise of repertory cinemas means, moreover, that apart from surviving venues such as The Phoenix in Oxford, Manchester's Cornerhouse or Edinburgh's Film House, there are few outlets for the exhibition of recognised 'classics' let alone the typical 'B' film, supporting features or even more obscure fare, There are occasional film festivals which sometimes include retrospective seasons dedicated to British films – notably in London, Edinburgh, Leeds, Cambridge and Birmingham – but not much else besides. The National Film Theatre (NFT) on the London South Bank, of course, regularly includes British films from the past in its ongoing programmes and when a major figure in the industry dies it usually inspires new-found analysis and heralds a selection of key films shown in tribute as after the death, in recent years, of directors like Tony Richardson and Lindsay Anderson.

But not everybody can get along to the NFT or to an urban arts complex. Many viewers will doubtless be in the habit of buying or hiring video cassettes, watching and recording off-air from television, or some permutation thereof. It's not ideal and probably won't please the purists, given especially the difficulties that inevitably ensue with tele-cine projection of scope films. The traditional practice of 'panning and scanning' for broadcast television purposes, which thereby renders 40% of the scope image invisible on the small screen, remains a profound problem for the technically-minded perfectionist. Though, in fairness, at least BBC 2 and Channel 4 have got considerably better in this regard of late and both are nowadays favourably inclined to broadcast scope feature films in 'letterbox' format just as, by the same token, the video distributors are more likely than ever to release widescreen versions as well as the academy format.

Since the arrival of cable and satellite broadcasting, furthermore, the BBC and ITV companies have been compelled to dig deeper than before into film libraries, collections and archives in order to fill their schedules and sustain their competitive output. The arrival of all-night broadcasting also means, quite simply, that viewers have been treated to a glut of British films from way back. There's a lot of dross on show, for certain, but a good many choice items besides. Broadcasters are still temperamentally inclined to force films into makeshift seasons, of course, whether of 'classic' fare, directors, actors, genres, themes or whatever. Thus, there's an abundance of the obvious, much publicised, high-profile series given over to Michael Caine, Peter Sellers, 'Ealing Comedy', 'War Films', and so on. In quieter moments, however, generally during the off-peak, early morning hours, there are many things to catch on your videocassette recorder, especially 'B' films and work from lesser-known directors.

And why not? It's the cheapest way and perfectly legal, too. The 1988 Copyright, Design and Patents Act – passed on 1 August 1989 – allows you to record any programme off air for replay at a more convenient time in the privacy of your home. Given that VCRs now also include a standard facility for recording and playback in Long Play mode, videotapes can therefore run to twice their designated length. Finally, if you take into account the fact that British films, save for recent releases, invariably retail in the lowest price range of the sell-through video market, it means that students or fans are able to acquire quickly and easily a representative collection of mainstream British films.

All but two of the dozen films highlighted in this volume have been made available on video and even these – *South Riding* and *Fame is the Spur* – have been frequently shown on television and are destined for imminent video distribution. Films come and go on video, it must be said, just like video companies themselves. But copyright is invariably owned by somebody somewhere intent on exploiting their commercial potential. So, they are either retained or sold on with the result that deletions are regularly re-released and decisions taken that films be issued anew on video, albeit often on new found video labels as well. Thus, for example, *Sanders of the River* is currently found among a crop of Alexander Korda's productions released by Carlton Video in 'The Korda Collection' comprising many of his best films from the 1930s including the transatlantic hit, *The Private Life of Henry VIII* (1933), the futuristic *Things to Come* (1936) and the Empire trilogy – *Elephant Boy* (1937), *The Drum* (1938) and *The Four Feathers* (1939) – along with his opening wartime propaganda piece, *The Lion Has Wings* (1939). While Victor Saville's work for thirties British cinema is well represented in the shape of *Evergreen* (1934), *The Iron Duke* and *First a Girl* (both 1935). Among other key directors of the period available on video are Alfred Hitchcock with *Murder* (1930), *The Skin Game* (1931), *Rich and Strange* and *Number 17* (both 1932), *The 39 Steps* (1935); Michael Powell – *Red Ensign* (1934)

The Edge of the World (1937), *The Spy in Black* (1939); Carol Reed – *The Stars Look Down* (1939); Walter Forde – *Forever England* (1935); Thorold Dickinson – *The Arsenal Stadium Mystery* (1939); Robert Stevenson – *Owd Bob* (1938); and Norman Walker with *Turn of the Tide* (1935).

To contrast with such obvious mainstream fare, however, there are numerous instances of so-called 'lowbrow' comedies of the day which, though critically despised, undoubtedly commanded huge popular appeal. If the likes of George Formby, Gracie Fields and The Crazy Gang are most often found on television (though video distribution is promised for all of them), several Will Hay films have been issued already such as the following: *Boys Will Be Boys* (1935), *Good Morning Boys* (1937), *Oh Mr. Porter* (1937), *Old Bones of the River* (1938), and *Ask a Policeman* (1939).

Both the wartime Powell and Pressburger films selected for consideration in this book – *A Canterbury Tale* and *The Life and Death of Colonel Blimp* – have been out on video for some time now as, indeed, have the majority of classic British propaganda efforts of the day including the Ealing productions by Alberto Cavalcanti of *Went the Day Well?* (1942) and Charles Frend's *San Demetrio London* (1943), in addition to Pat Jackson's *Western Approaches* (1944) which was made for the Crown Film Unit. World War II films are easily got, in effect, because they constitute a common component of terrestrial and satellite broadcast scheduling and few have escaped sustained critical attention. Given, also, that the Gainsborough melodramas have enjoyed an upsurge in critical scrutiny and acclaim of late they, too, have been regularly increasing in the numbers made available on video: e.g. *Love Story* and *Madonna of the Seven Moons* (both 1944), *The Seventh Veil* and *The Wicked Lady* (both 1945), *Caravan* (1946).

The postwar 1940s have been sparingly sampled hitherto, however, with market-led criteria traditionally dictating that distributors select the better known film genres or directors, and settle for those alone. Thus, there is much on release from David Lean – *Brief Encounter* (1945), *Great Expectations* (1946), *Oliver Twist* (1948) and *The Passionate Friends* (1949) – and the early Ealing comedies – *Hue and Cry* (1947), *Whisky Galore* (1948), *Passport to Pimlico*, *Kind Hearts and Coronets* (both 1949) – while Carol Reed's *The Third Man* (1949) seems to be endlessly recycled. Still, Powell and Pressburger continue to be admirably represented with *I Know Where I'm Going* (1945), *A Matter of Life and*

Death (1946), *Black Narcissus* (1947) and *The Red Shoes* (1948); as do the Boulting brothers with *Brighton Rock* (1947) and *The Guinea Pig* (with *Fame is the Spur* promised soon). Moreover, it appears that at long last the film libraries are being exploited afresh for further material from the later 1940s. In the process, viewers have been treated to the video release of a host of lesser known genre gems from the period, not least *Holiday Camp* (1947) and *Good Time Girl* (1948). Let's hope the trend continues.

For the 1950s and 1960s, by contrast, a great deal has already been forthcoming on video. Hence, the five examples explored in this book – *The Blue Lamp, The Ladykillers, I'm All Right Jack, The Loneliness of the Long Distance Runner* and *If . . .* – are easily obtained. Basil Dearden's progress after *The Blue Lamp* is best charted through watching his later efforts, *The League of Gentlemen* (1960) and *Victim* (1961). But for comparison with Alexander Mackendrick's film, numerous contemporary instances from the heyday of Ealing comedy readily abound – *The Lavender Hill Mob* (1951), *The Man in the White Suit* (1951), *The Titfield Thunderbolt* (1953) – as, also, do other notable British comedies of the time like *Genevieve* (1953).

The Boultings' harder satirical edge is well discerned on video in *Private's Progress* (1956), *Carlton-Browne of the FO* (1958) and *Heaven's Above* (1963), but more typical of their sixties vehicles, perhaps, are *The Family Way* (1966) and *Twisted Nerve* (1968). Video availability is no problem either for the many British 'new wave' products emanating from directors such as Tony Richardson, Karel Reisz and John Schlesinger. Jack Clayton's *Room at the Top* (1958) set the ball rolling on this front and is often recycled. But so, too, are *Look Back in Anger* (1959), *The Entertainer* and *Saturday Night and Sunday Morning* (both 1960), *A Taste of Honey* (1961), and *A Kind of Loving* (1962) with *The Loneliness of the Long Distance Runner* among them.

The new wave was fast followed by the vogue for 'swinging London', of course, and a variety of films-on-video illustrate the phenomenon with *Darling* (1965) and *Alfie* (1966) noticeably to the fore. But if the historical period pieces *Far From the Madding Crowd* (1967) and *The Charge of the Light Brigade* (1968) display the essentially 'realist' trajectory which still preoccupied the likes of Schlesinger and Richardson throughout the later 1960s, the same cannot be said for Lindsay Anderson who moved from *This Sporting Life* (1963) to *If . . .* of course, thereby proving that films of 'fantasy' still had an important part to play on the sixties British screen.

It is a point further borne out by Michael Powell's *Peeping Tom* (1960) at the outset of the decade, and Michael Reeves's *Witchfinder General* (1968) towards its end. While the work of Ken Loach (*Poor Cow*, 1967) demonstrates the modernising impulse in realist film-making which overtook the new wave realists, so too the work of Michael Reeves shows the revitalised impetus afforded the realms of the horror genre in the wake of Hammer's demise (which is readily charted since the Hammer horrors are extant in large measure). Sixties cinema is essential for exploring the continuing clash of realism and fantasy in British film culture and all the titles referenced above are on video to allow of just that.

For comparison with *Scandal*, finally, the films cited in the text will suffice for a start – *The Long Good Friday, McVicar, A Sense of Freedom* (all 1981), *Dance with a Stranger* (1985), *Mona Lisa* (1986), *White Mischief* and *Personal Services* (both 1987), *Buster* (1988), *The Krays* (1990) and *Let Him Have It* (1991). While *Villain* and *Get Carter* (both 1971) provide interesting and accessible examples from the 1970s on fruitfully comparable themes concerning underworld sleaze and civic corruption, as do *The Criminal, The Frightened City* and *Hell is a City* (all 1960) from an earlier era. And for a different slant on questions of cinema and national identity, by way of contrast, the 'heritage' films offer everything from *Chariots of Fire* (1981) to *Howard's End* (1992) and *The Remains of the Day* (1993).

But for British cinema in the period since 1970, generally, there is little of substance that has not been forthcoming on video at one point or another. All of which makes the film student's task that much easier. If the study of British cinema history is admirably equipped now in regard to book publications and other such printed materials, it is also especially well served by an abundance of filmic sources presented in video format.

Filmography

Sanders of the River (1935)

Production company: London Films
Distributors: United Artists
Director: Zoltan Korda
Producer: Alexander Korda
Screenplay: Lajos Biro and Jeffrey Dell (from the stories by Edgar Wallace)
Photographer: Georges Périnal
Editor: Charles Crichton
Art director: Vincent Korda
Music: Mischa Spoliansky
Cast: Leslie Banks (Commissioner Sanders), Paul Robeson (Bosambo), Nina Mae McKinney (Lilongo), Robert Cochran (Lt Tibbets), Martin Walker (Commissioner Ferguson), Richard Grey (Captain Hamilton), Tony Wane (King Mofalaba), Marquis de Portago (Farini), Eric Maturin (Smith), Allan Jeayes (Father O'Leary), Charles Carson (Governor)
Running time: 98 minutes

South Riding (1938)

Production company: Victor Saville Productions for London Films
Distributors: United Artists
Director–producer: Victor Saville
Screenplay: Ian Dalrymple and Donald Bull (from the novel by Winifred Holtby)

Photographer: Harry Stradling
Editor: Hugh Stewart
Art director: Lazare Meerson
Music: Richard Addinsell
Cast: Ralph Richardson (Robert Carne), Edna Best (Sarah Burton),
  Edmund Gwenn (Alfred Huggins), Ann Todd (Madge Carne), Glynis
  Johns (Midge Carne), John Clements (Joe Astell), Marie Lohr (Mrs
  Beddows), Milton Rosmer (Alderman Snaith), Joan Ellum (Lydia Holly),
  Herbert Lomas (Castle), Peggy Novak (Bessie Warbuckle), Gus
  McNaughton (Tadman), Lewis Casson (Lord Sedgmire), Felix Aylmer
  (Chairman of Council), Jean Cadell (Miss Dry), Edward Lexy (Mr
  Holly), Josephine Wilson (Mrs Holly), Skelton Knaggs (Reg Aythome)
Running time: 91 minutes

The Life and Death of Colonel Blimp (1943)

Production company: The Archers
Distributors: GFD
Director–producer–screenplay: Michael Powell and Emeric Pressburger
Photographer: Georges Périnal
Editor: John Seabourne
Production designer: Alfred Junge
Music: Allan Gray
Cast: Anton Walbrook (Theo Kretschmar-Schuldorff), Roger Livesey
  (Clive Candy), Deborah Kerr (Edith Hunter, Barbara Wynne, Angela
  'Johnny' Cannon), Ursula Jeans (Frau von Kalteneck), Roland Culver
  (Colonel Betteridge), Albert Lieven (Von Ritter), John Laurie
  (Murdoch), Robert Harris (Embassy Secretary), Arthur Wontner
  (Embassy counsellor), Felix Aylmer (Bishop), Harry Welchman (Major
  Davis), David Hutcheson (Captain 'Hoppy' Hopwell), James
  McKechnie (Captain 'Spud' Wilson), Reginald Tate (Captain Van
  Zijl), Neville Mapp ('Stuffy' Graves), David Ward (Kaunitz), Eric
  Maturin (Colonel Goodhead), Muriel Aked (Aunt Margaret),
  Valentine Dyall (Von Schonborn), Frith Banbury ('Babyface' Fitzroy),
  A. E. Matthews (President), Carl Jaffe (Von Reumann), Dennis
  Arundell (Orchestra leader)
Running time: 163 minutes

A Canterbury Tale (1944)

Production company: The Archers
Distributors: Eagle–Lion
Director–producer–screenplay: Michael Powell and Emeric Pressburger
Photgrapher: Erwin Hillier
Editor: John Seabourne
Production designer: Alfred Junge
Music: Allan Gray
Cast: Eric Portman (Thomas Colpeper), Sheila Sim (Alison Smith),
   Dennis Price (Sgt Peter Gibbs), Sgt John Sweet (Sgt Bob Johnson),
   Esmond Knight (Narrator, Seven Sisters soldier, Village idiot),
   Charles Hawtrey (Thomas Duckett), Hay Petrie (Woodcock),
   George Merritt (Ned Horton), Edward Rigby (Jim Horton),
   Freda Jackson (Prudence Honeywood), Betty Jardine (Fee Baker),
   Eliot Makeham (Organist), Harvey Golden (Sgt Roczinsky), Esma
   Cannon (Maid), John Slater (Len), Graham Moffatt (Stuffy),
   Anthony Holles (Sgt Bassett), Leonard Smith (Leslie), James
   Tamsitt (Terry), David Todd (David), Judith Furst (Dorothy
   Bird)
Running time: 124 minutes

Fame is the Spur (1947)

Production company: Two Cities Films
Distributors: GFD
Director: Roy Boulting
Producer: John Boulting
Screenplay: Nigel Balchin (from the novel by Howard Spring)
Photographer: Gunther Krampf
Editor: Richard Best
Art director: John Howell
Music: John Wooldridge
Cast: Michael Redgrave (Hamer Radshaw), Rosamund John (Ann
   Radshaw), Bernard Miles (Tom Hannaway), Hugh Burden (Arnold
   Ryerson), Carla Lehmann (Lettice, Lady Liskeard), Marjorie Fielding
   (Lizzie Lightowler), Sir Seymour Hicks (Lord Lostwithiel), David
   Tomlinson (Lord Liskeard), Anthony Wager (Hamer as a child), Brian

Weske (Arnold as a child), Gerald Fox (Tom as a child), Milton Rosmer (Magistrate), Wylie Watson (Pendleton)
Running time: 116 minutes

The Guinea Pig (1948)

Production company: Pilgrim Pictures
Distributors: Pathé
Director: Roy Boulting
Producer: John Boulting
Screenplay: Warren Chetham Strode, Bernard Miles and Roy Boulting (from the play by Warren Chetham Strode)
Photographer: Gilbert Taylor
Editor: Richard Best
Art Director: John Howell
Music: John Wooldridge
Cast: Richard Attenborough (Jack Read), Sheila Sim (Lynne Hartley), Bernard Miles (Mr Read), Cecil Trouncer (Lloyd Hartley), Robert Flemyng (Nigel Lorraine), Edith Sharpe (Mrs Hartley), Joan Hickson (Mrs Read), Tim Bateson (Ronald Tracey), Clive Baxter (Gregory), Basil Cunard (Buckton), John Forrest (Fitch), Maureen Glynne (Bessie), Brenda Hogan (Lorna Beckett), Herbert Lomas (Sir James Corfield), Anthony Newley (Miles Minor), Anthony Nicholls (Mr Stringer), Wally Patch (Uncle Percy), Hay Petrie (Peck), Oscar Quitak (David Tracey), Kynaston Reeves (Bishop), Peter Reynolds (Grimmett), Olive Sloane (Aunt Mabel), Anthony Wager (Bert), Percy Walsh (Alec Stevens), Norman Watson (Fanshaw)
Running time: 97 minutes

The Blue Lamp (1950)

Production company: Ealing Studios
Distributors: GFD
Director: Basil Dearden
Producer: Michael Reiph
Screenplay: T. E. B. Clarke (story by Ted Willis and Jan Read)
Photographer: Gordon Dines
Editor: Peter Tanner
Art director: Tom Morahan

Music: Ernest Irving

Cast: Jack Warner (PC George Dixon), James Hanley (PC Andy Mitchell), Robert Flemyng (Sgt Roberts), Bernard Lee (Inspector Cherry), Dirk Bogarde (Tom Riley), Patric Doonan (Spud), Peggy Evans (Diana Lewis), Frederick Piper (Mr Lewis), Betty Ann Davis (Mrs Lewis), Dora Bryan (Maisie), Norman Shelley (Jordan), Gladys Henson (Mrs Dixon), Bruce Seton (PC Campbell), Meredith Edwards (PC Hughes), Clive Morton (Sgt Brooks), William Mervyn (Chief Inspector Hammond), Campbell Singer (Station Sgt), Michael Golden (Mike Randall) Glyn Houston (barrow boy), Muriel Aked (Mrs Waterbourne), Renee Gadd (woman driver), Tessie O'Shea (herself)

Running time: 82 minutes

The Ladykillers (1955)

Production company: Ealing Studios
Distributors: Rank Film Distributors
Director: Alexander Mackendrick
Producer: Michael Balcon
Screenplay: William Rose
Photographer: Otto Helter
Editor: Jack Harris
Art director: Jim Morahan
Music: Tristram Cary

Cast: Katie Johnson (Mrs Louisa Wilberforce), Alec Guinness (Professor Marcus), Cecil Parker (Major Courtney), Herbert Lom (Louis), Peter Sellers (Harry), Danny Green ('One-Round'), Jack Warner (Superintendent), Philip Stainton (Police sergeant), Ewan Roberts (Police constable), Frankie Howerd (Barrow boy), Kenneth Connor (Taxi driver), Edie Martin (Lettice), Helen Burls (Hypatia), Evelyn Kerry (Amelia), Phoebe Hodgson (Fourth guest), Leonard Sharp (Pavement artist), Harold Goodwin (Parcels clerk), Stratford Johns (Security guard)

Running time: 97 minutes

I'm All Right Jack (1959)

Production company: Charter Films
Distributors: British Lion
Director: John Boulting

Producer: Roy Boulting

Screenplay: Frank Harvey and John Boulting with Alan Hackney (from the novel *Private Life* by Alan Hackney)

Photographer: Max Greene

Editor: Anthony Harvey

Art director: Bill Andrews

Music: Ken Hoare and Ron Goodwin

Cast: Ian Carmichael (Stanley Windrush), Terry Thomas (Major Hitchcock), Peter Sellers (Fred Kite), Richard Attenborough (Sidney de Vere Cox), Margaret Rutherford (Aunt Dolly), Dennis Price (Bertram Tracepurcel), Irene Handl (Mrs Kite), Miles Malleson (Mr Windrush), Victor Maddern (Knowles), Liz Fraser (Cynthia Kite), John Le Mesurier (Waters), Marne Maitland (Mr Mohammed), Kenneth Griffith (Dai), Raymond Huntley (Magistrate), Cardew Robinson (Shop steward), Terry Scott (Crawley), Esma Cannon (Spencer), Ronnie Stevens (Hooper), Basil Dignam (Minister of Labour), Frank Phillips (BBC announcer), Harry Locke (TUC official), John Comer (Shop steward), Wally Patch (Old worker), Muriel Young (Announcer), Malcolm Muggeridge (Himself)

Running time: 105 minutes

The Loneliness of the Long Distance Runner (1962)

Production company: Woodfall

Distributors: BLC–British Lion–Bryanston

Director–producer: Tony Richardson

Screenplay: Alan Sillitoe (from his short story)

Photographer: Walter Lassally

Editor: Antony Gibbs

Art director: Ted Marshall

Music: John Addison

Cast: Tom Courtenay (Colin Smith), Michael Redgrave (Governor), Avis Bunnage (Mrs Smith), James Bolam (Mike), Alec McCowen (Brown), Dervis Ward (Detective), Joe Robinson (Roach), Topsy Jane (Audrey), Julia Foster (Gladys), James Cairncross (Jones), Philip Martin (Stacey), Peter Madden (Mr Smith)

Running time: 104 minutes

If . . . (1968)

Production company: Memorial Enterprises Ltd
Distributors: Paramount Pictures
Director: Lindsay Anderson
Producers: Michael Medwin and Lindsay Anderson
Screenplay: David Sherwin and Lindsay Anderson (from an original script, *Crusaders,* by David Sherwin and John Howlett)
Photographer: Miroslav Ondricek
Editor: David Gladwell
Production designer: Jocelyn Herbert
Music: Marc Wilkinson
Cast: Malcolm McDowell (Mick Travis), David Wood (Johnny Knightly), Richard Warwick (Wallace), Christine Noonan (The Girl), Rupert Webster (Bobby Phillips), Robert Swann (Rowntree), Hugh Thomas (Denson), Michael Cadman (Fortinbras), Peter Sproule (Barnes), Peter Jeffrey (Headmaster), Anthony Nicholls (General Denson), Arthur Lowe (Mr Kemp), Mona Washbourne (Matron), Mary Macleod (Mrs Kemp), Geoffrey Chater (Chaplain), Ben Aris (John Thomas), Graham Crowden (History master), Charles Lloyd Pack (Classics master), John Garrie (Music master), Tommy Godfrey (School porter), Guy Ross (Stephans), Robin Askwith (Keating), Richard Everitt (Pussy Graves), Philip Bagenal ('Peanuts'), Nicholas Page (Cox), Robert Yetzes (Fisher), David Griffin (Willens), Graham Sharman (Van Eyssen), Richard Tombleson (Baird), Richard Davies (Machin), Brian Pettifer (Biles), Michael Newport (Brunning), Charles Sturridge (Markland), Sean Bury (Jute), Martin Beaumont (Hunter)
Running time: 111 minutes

Scandal (1989)

Production company: Palace Pictures in association with Miramax and British Screen
Distributors: Palace Pictures
Director: Michael Caton-Jones
Producer: Stephen Woolley
Screenplay: Michael Thomas
Photographer: Mike Molloy
Editor: Angus Newton
Production designer: Simon Holland

Costume designer: Jane Robinson

Original music: Carl Davis

Cast: John Hurt (Stephen Ward), Joanne Whalley-Kilmer (Christine Keeler), Ian McKellen (John Profumo), Bridget Fonda (Mandy Rice-Davies), Leslie Phillips (Lord Astor), Britt Ekland (Mariella Novotny), Daniel Massey (Mervyn Griffith-Jones), Roland Gift (Johnnie Edgecombe), Jean Alexander (Mrs Keeler), Alex Norton (Detective Inspector), Ronald Fraser (Mr Justice Marshall), Paul Brooke (Detective Sergeant), Jeroen Krabbe (Eugene Ivanov), Keith Allen (Kevin), Ken Campbell (Editor of Pictorial), Iain Cuthbertson (Lord Hailsham), Susannah Doyle (Jackie), Joanna Dunham (Lady Astor), Trevor Eve (Matinee Idol), Oliver Ford Davies (Mr Woods), Deborah Grant (Valerie Profumo), Valerie Griffiths (Landlady), Leon Herbert (Lucky Gordon), Terence Rigby (James Burge), Johnny Shannon (Peter Rachman), James Villiers (Conservative MP)

Running time: 115 minutes

Index